100 THINGS
BLUES FANS
SHOULD KNOW & DO
BEFORE THEY DIE

100 THINGS BLUES FANS SHOULD KNOW & DO BEFORE THEY DIE

Jeremy Rutherford

TRIUMPH
BOOKS

Library of Congress Cataloging-in-Publication Data available upon request.

This book is available in quantity at special discounts for your group or organization. For further information, contact:

Triumph Books LLC
814 North Franklin Street
Chicago, Illinois 60610
(312) 337-0747
www.triumphbooks.com

Printed in U.S.A.
ISBN: 978-1-62937-788-9
Design by Patricia Frey
Photos courtesy of AP Images unless otherwise indicated

To the best hat-trick that I ever could have hoped for in my life—my two beautiful children, Georgia and Eli, and my lovely wife, Sarah.

Contents

Foreword *by Brett Hull* xi

1 Stanley Cup Champions! 1

2 MacInnis' Slap Shot 8

3 Gassoff Dies Tragically 12

4 Picard Trips Orr 16

5 Greatest Blue in History 18

6 Redhead Scores Six Goals 23

7 Monday Night Miracle 27

8 Consummate Competitor 31

9 Ironman Streak Almost Never Started 35

10 The Arena 38

11 Sutter Wills Brothers and Blues 43

12 St. Louis Apollos 48

13 Inception of the Blues 52

14 Wick 56

15 The Roots of the Blues' Community Efforts 61

16 A Hull of an Era 64

17 Picard Takes Break in Enemy Territory 73

18 "Meat on the Burner" 76

19 Blues-Blackhawks Rivalry 81

20 Courtnall Calls His Shot 85

21 Original Captain 89

22 Patrick Gone Too Soon 93

23 Francis Revitalizes Franchise 96

24 Federko Proves to Be Fabulous 99

25 From "Problem" to Playoff MVP 104

26 Old Man 109

27 Mayhem in Philadelphia 114

28 Blues Help Create Broad Street Bullies 117

29 Bowman Was "Great, Great Coach" 121

30 Craig Berube to the Rescue 126

31 Here Comes Cheveldae 132

32 Gilmour Traded after Civil Suit 135

33 The Building Went Silent 138

34 Iron Mike 141

35 Stevens Awarded to New Jersey 144

36 Rebirth for Hall 150

37 "Saved My Life" 154

38 Demitra Dies in Plane Crash 158

39 Friends and Foes 162

40 Jackman Captures Calder 167

41 JD 170

42 "It's a Privilege" 174

43 Hockey Prankster 177

44 Shanahan for Pronger: Yes or No? 180

45 Bergevin Throws Puck into Own Net 183

46 Tales from the Training Room 186

47 Take a Ride on an Olympia 190

48 Russian Invasion 194

49 Golf Getaway 197

50 One-Hit Wonder 201

51 Go to OB Clark's after a Game.............................. 204

52 Pronger's Heart Stops.................................. 207

53 Perfect Attendance.................................... 210

54 Hometown Hero: Pat Maroon.......................... 213

55 Do I Look Nervous?................................... 218

56 St. Louis Scribe Publishes Plus-Minus Stat............. 223

57 Voice of the Blues..................................... 226

58 "It's a Real Barnburner"............................... 231

59 KMOX and the Blues.................................. 234

60 Oh Baby.. 239

61 A Coup for Coach Q................................... 242

62 Pleau Forced to Trade Pronger......................... 245

63 How Swede It Is!...................................... 248

64 Mental Case.. 251

65 Shorthanded Success.................................. 254

66 Stastny Suits Up for Blues............................. 256

67 Salomons... 260

68 Ralston Purina.. 264

69 Harry Ornest.. 268

70 Mike Shanahan....................................... 273

71 Kiel Center Partners.................................. 276

72 Bill and Nancy Laurie................................. 280

73 Dave Checketts and SCP Worldwide.................... 283

74 Tom Stillman... 285

75 Where Were the Blues on 9/11?........................ 288

76 Ulterior Motive....................................... 292

77 Staniowski Stands on Head 296

78 Danton's Murder-for-Hire Case 298

79 Business Role Model 302

80 Spanish Conquistador 305

81 MacTavish, the Last Helmetless Player 308

82 Liut Worth the Wait 312

83 The Other Lemieux 313

84 Goalie Shoots, He Scores 318

85 Harvey Finishes Hall of Fame Career with Blues 321

86 Hull Scores 86 324

87 Blues Get Bold 327

88 Towel Man Tradition 331

89 Attend Blues Alumni Fantasy Camp 333

90 Go Ask Susie 336

91 "We Had the Cup" 342

92 Visit the Hockey Hall of Fame 346

93 The Record Shop 349

94 Hull & Oates 354

95 Blues Light Lamp 11 Times 358

96 Yzerman Turns Out the Lights 361

97 Sacharuk Joins Exclusive Club 364

98 Hrkac Circus 367

99 Wayne's World 370

100 Play "Gloria"! 377

Acknowledgments 381

Sources 385

Foreword

I think I was only in my underwear and socks when a trainer in Calgary tapped me on the shoulder and said, "Hey, Coach wants to see you." I didn't know what the meeting would be about. Hell, I was a rookie—he was always calling me into his office. But on this particular day, Terry Crisp, then the head coach of the Flames, sat me down and said, "Son, we've made a trade."

I didn't know what to say, so what came out was, "Just tell me I'm going somewhere good."

Terry told me I had been traded to St. Louis. I didn't know if that was good or bad because I knew absolutely nothing about the place other than they had a hockey team named the Blues and they played at a barn a few miles outside of downtown. I didn't know about the players that wore the Blue Note, the fans that stood behind them, or even the great people who lived in their city.

But I learned real quick.

One of those good people, Susie Mathieu, picked me up from the airport. She showed me around town and took me to a hotel, which was on the southeast corner of Hampton and I-44, not far from the old Arena. It only took a few hours, a few days at most, before I felt right at home. I went to my first practice, and we played a game later that night and all the guys were great. Gino Cavallini, Tony Hrkac, Doug Gilmour, Bernie Federko, Greg Millen, and Greg Paslawski to name a few...everyone treated me great and welcomed me to the team with open arms.

You know the rest of the story—you witnessed most of it. Within the pages of this book, you'll read more about my playing days with the St. Louis Blues. But the bottom line is this—we had great teams here; and there were a few times we had the potential to be serious Stanley Cup contenders. I'm not happy we didn't win a championship while I was here because it would have been special for us as players and for the wonderful fans who supported us.

You see, we had a special bond with the people in the front office, and we shared that bond with the fans in the stands. We were a family.

With that being said, it was hard to leave town back in 1998. I had developed more lifelong friendships and memories than I could ever count. I won't deny that I had plenty of good experiences after I left (including one with Dallas that I shared with Ken Hitchcock in a Game 6 against the Sabres), but I never once forgot about St. Louis.

Recently, when Tom Stillman called and asked me to come back and work in the Blues' front office, I realized I couldn't pass up that opportunity. To be able to be part of the organization again and feel that energy in the arena and feel the passion that exists here—it's an unbelievable feeling.

This team is on the rise. It has great leadership in Doug Armstrong and Ken Hitchcock, and the players have been together for awhile and have proven they are a great team. Everyone should be excited about the future—I know I am.

If you know me, you know I've never been at a loss for words, but my attachment to this team and this town is hard to explain. There's a relationship here between the players, the franchise, and the city that simply can't be put into words.

I think that's what makes wearing the Blue Note so special.

—Brett Hull
February 26, 2014

1 Stanley Cup Champions!

On July 1, 2018, when Blues general manager Doug Armstrong welcomed newly acquired center Ryan O'Reilly with a phone call, O'Reilly told him, "Let's go win a Cup."

On February 25, 2019, when Armstrong was asked if he'd regret staying pat at the NHL trade deadline with a third-place club, he replied, "What happens if we win the Stanley Cup?"

On June 12, 2019, when coach Craig Berube addressed the Blues before Game 7 of the Stanley Cup final against Boston, he declared: "We're going to go home with the Cup here tonight."

For more than a half-century, whenever someone mentioned the Blues and the Cup in the same breath, it was always about the harsh reality of them never winning one. Whether it was coming up just short, mismanagement, or being snakebitten, referencing the 100-year-old trophy sounded shallow and hoisting it seemed like a dream.

Then in one breathless moment, just hours after Berube's passionate plea to his players, the begging, the waiting, the fantasizing… it was over. With a 4–1 win over the Bruins, everything from that tumultuous trade in 1991 to Steve Yzerman's double-overtime goal in 1996 to the Presidents' Trophy team falling in the first round of the 2000 postseason suddenly washed away.

The Blues were finally Stanley Cup champions!

As the first group of players who could claim that distinction heaved their gloves and sticks and hugged one another on the ice at TD Garden in Boston, their fans sprayed champagne and sobbed back in St. Louis. Along with the tears of joy, there were also tears of sadness shed because of generations who had passed, including some of the original Blues from 1967–68.

"I'm at a loss for words in my vocabulary tonight," said Bobby Plager, one of those early Blues, who is never at a loss for words.

In a surreal scene that Blues fans had viewed countless times on TV, but never with their own team, captain Alex Pietrangelo accepted the Stanley Cup from NHL commissioner Gary Bettman, thrust the trophy into the air, and then passed it on to a parade of teammates.

"It's pretty awesome," said veteran defenseman Jay Bouwmeester, who, after playing in his 1,259th NHL game, was the first player to take the Cup from Pietrangelo. "You do it for long enough and you always think, and you hope, that you have a chance. You didn't want to waste this opportunity. We have such a special group. This is what it's all about."

"It's indescribable," said veteran forward Alexander Steen, who took it from Bouwmeester. "You can't put it into words. It's an unbelievable group we have."

O'Reilly, who won the Conn Smythe Trophy as the NHL playoff MVP, is among the most modest to ever play for the Blues, but even he saw the significance in the immediate aftermath of the accomplishment.

"This group of guys, we're legends… we're legends now," O'Reilly said on the ice. "One of the boys said to me, 'We're heroes.' We just brought a Cup to the city…. It's so cool. It's such an amazing city. They stuck with us through thick and thin this whole year and we got 'em a Cup now."

"We are!" Pietrangelo added. "First Stanley Cup in St. Louis. Legendary."

It was an historic feat for the city, but it was also an extraordinary season by NHL standards, as the Blues capped off the league's only worst-to-first campaign.

Alex Pietrangelo skates with the Cup after the Blues' Game 7 Stanley Cup victory over the Bruins on June 12, 2019. (AP Photo/Charles Krupa)

On January 3, after the Blues had fired Mike Yeo and promoted Berube, the Blues were 15–18–4 (34 points) and dead last in the NHL standings. At that point, although they had four games in hand, they were 11 points behind Anaheim for the second wild-card in the Western Conference.

"That was a hard time," Blues forward Vladimir Tarasenko said. "There were articles about us at the start of the year saying we're done, it's a useless year, and there's no turning around. But I used to tell you, 'We've got a great team, and as soon as we come closer to each other and find out how we need to play, we will be fine.' Even that time when we were last in the league, we all believed we could change the situation. We just had to work hard and results will come."

The results did come, as the Blues went 30–10–5 in their remaining 45 regular-season games, clinching a playoff spot on March 30. That made them one of only seven teams in NHL history to qualify for the postseason after being at the bottom of the standings on New Year's Day. They joined the Minnesota North Stars (1976–77), Edmonton Oilers (1979–80), Toronto Maple Leafs (1982–83 and 1987–88), Los Angeles Kings (1987–88), and Ottawa Senators (1996–97).

Armstrong wasn't completely surprised by the turnaround, he said, because the Blues were now playing like the club that media and fans had envisioned in the preseason.

"I'm much more surprised where we were in the first three months—October, November, and December—than the last three months—January, February, and March," Armstrong said. "Not everybody in the world was wrong and now [the team] is proving you guys right that they are a good team.

"And as I've said for years, if you make the Stanley Cup tournament, you have a chance to win the Stanley Cup. I think we have as good a chance as anybody, but you've got to get the job done.

Anybody that plays us believes they have as good of a chance as we do, so that's the beauty of the tournament."

Miraculously, the Blues almost won the Central Division on the final day of the regular season, but finished third, drawing Winnipeg in the first round of the playoffs. They were seen as a dark horse to win the Cup, but perhaps a little underestimated because of the uncertainty surrounding how rookie goalie Jordan Binnington would respond to the postseason spotlight. The poster-boy for the team's second-half resurrection went 24–5–1 with a 1.89 goals-against average and a .927 save percentage through the end of the regular season, but the 25-year-old had never suited up for a Stanley Cup playoff game.

"This team is really strong and deep, and I'm just going to continue to work hard every day, and hopefully have a good playoff run," Binnington said.

It was a run for the ages by Binnington, who went 16–10 in the playoffs with a 2.46 GAA and a .914 save percentage. He led the Blues to a record of 10–3 on the road, and those 10 road wins in one postseason, in which they collectively outscored their opponents 42–30, tied an NHL record.

Along the way, there were other heroic performances from players like Jaden Schwartz, who had just 11 goals in the regular season but topped that with 12 in the playoffs, becoming the first Blue in history to have two hat tricks in one postseason. There was O'Reilly, who scored a goal in four straight games in the Cup Final, tying a record set by Wayne Gretzky, and there was the defensive pairing of Bouwmeester and Colton Parayko, who shut down the other teams' top lines throughout the four series.

The Blues had to overcome a record of 6–10 at home in the playoffs, a power play that converted at a rate of just 16.3 percent, and a controversial no-call by officials in Game 3 against San Jose, when Erik Karlsson's overtime goal stood despite a hand-pass by teammate Timo Meier. They took the next three games against the Sharks, outscoring them 12–2, to win the series.

In the postseason, the Blues won when it counted, compiling a record of 8–2 in Games 5,6, and 7 of all four series.

Now, after beating the improbable odds of winning Game 7 in Boston, the Blues were celebrating their first Stanley Cup.

"This is what we play for and coach for," Berube said. "I'm really happy for our town and our fans."

The current players were joined on the ice by many of the franchise's alumni, who had been yearning for this day.

"We all tried this for 52 years," said Bernie Federko, the former Blues center who is in the Hockey Hall of Fame. "Once you put on the sweater, you want to win the Cup for the city, for yourselves, and for the Blue Note. We weren't able to do it, and now to see that it's finally been done, that we have a piece of history now, that we are actually Stanley Cup champions, I can't be more proud of this group. They did it for us. What a job these guys have done."

"Regardless if you played five games or 500 games, you're a Blue forever," added Al MacInnis, the ex-Blues defenseman and fellow Hall of Famer. "This day is special for every player that's put on that jersey. Anybody that's touched this organization in any way, this is a special day for them. Is there any other season that a team has had that's even come close to this? Considering we were in 31st place in early January, it's remarkable. The comeback they had is… it's crazy."

Three days later was the Stanley Cup parade in St. Louis, the one that everyone had been envisioning on Market Street for decades. Fans camped out the night before for a spot up close, and by the time the procession began, they were standing 20 people deep, hanging from street poles and poking their heads out of holes in parking garages.

"This is what everyone told me it was going to be like, and I was like, 'Yeah, sure!'" Armstrong said. "But it shows you what a great fan base they are and how hungry they are."

The players had waited their entire lives for this moment, but knew St. Louis' history of hoping was even longer, so the Blues made the celebration about the city. Pietrangelo and Tarasenko were among many of them who yanked fans out of the crowd to walk side-by-side with them, hoist the Cup together, and even chug a beer simultaneously.

"You know what, although the St. Louis Blues won it on the ice, it feels like the whole community won the Stanley Cup," said the NHL's Philip Pritchard, whose title is the official Keeper of the Cup. "It's more than the team on the ice, and I think that's what St. Louis seems to be all about so far. Fifty-two years is a long time, but the community has stuck with them and, everywhere you look, everybody has a Blues shirt or Blues hat on. They're all in on this. It's really special."

The parade route ended at The Arch grounds, where there was a sea of blue singing "Gloria" in chorus and cheering at every glimpse of the Cup.

"There's a million people here... there's *a million* people!" former Blues player and broadcaster Kelly Chase said. "I mean, are you kidding me? It's unbelievable. Whatever happens in your life now, you got to experience it. It's all good now!"

2 MacInnis' Slap Shot

For a decade, Blues fans witnessed arguably the hardest slap shot in the history of the NHL.

The windup of Al MacInnis is a pose frozen in time, thanks to a statue outside Scottrade Center. And even more solid than the marble used to make the monument was the puck that came off the release.

"[MacInnis' shot is] very, very hard, and he puts it right in the best spot," former Montreal and Colorado goalie Patrick Roy once said. "His shot is hard to watch because it starts going faster as it comes at you."

MacInnis won the hardest shot contest at the NHL's skills competition seven times from 1991–2003, reaching 100.1 mph with his blast that won the contest in 2000. MacInnis edged Ottawa's Zdeno Chara for the title in 2003, hitting 98.9 mph.

"That guy's a freak," Jeremy Roenick said afterward. "I'm never getting in front of one of his shots, I'll tell you that."

Perhaps making MacInnis' power even more impressive was that in an era when many players were taking advantage of new stick technology, MacInnis, who played 13 seasons in Calgary before a trade to the Blues in 1994, was doing this with a wooden twig.

"I tried using the composite sticks last year, and I just couldn't feel comfortable," MacInnis said at the time. "I went back to [the wood]. They seem to have a little more give, a little more feel."

Upon hearing that, Boston's Joe Thornton quipped, "I wouldn't change that stick, either. He just has a rocket, and everyone knows that."

Al MacInnis connects on a slapshot during the hardest shot competition at the skills competition during the NHL All-Star weekend in Toronto on February 5, 2000. (CP Picture Archive/Kevin Frayer)

MacInnis' boomer was crafted in Nova Scotia. In a now-famous tale, MacInnis would lay down a sheet of plywood, grab a bucket of pucks, and rifle them off the wood at the side of the family's barn.

"I remember spending hours out there," MacInnis said. "I was just doing it to pass the time, never thinking it would end up the way it did and [that I would] be known for the slap shot. There's no question that's how the shot became what it is."

MacInnis began his career as a right winger, but his Midget coach in Nova Scotia switched him to defense and watched him take off from there.

"I had better hockey players, maybe five or six better than him on that team," coach Donnie MacIsaac said. "But I don't know if I had anyone more dedicated, more determined. He knew what he wanted."

MacInnis, chosen No. 15 overall by the Flames in 1981, played junior hockey with the Kitchener Rangers of the Ontario Hockey League. In his third season with Kitchener, MacInnis tied Bobby Orr's single-season junior record of 38 goals, which came in 51 games.

"My coach [Joe Crozier] was watching me shoot pucks after practice one day, and he came over shaking his head and said, 'Kid, that shot is going to get you into the NHL some day,'" MacInnis remembered. "And sure enough, it was a shot that gave me a chance to play."

In 1983–84, MacInnis joined Calgary full-time and netted 11 goals and 45 points in 51 games.

"He used to terrorize goaltenders with it back in junior hockey," Flames GM Cliff Fletcher said, "and he brought it with him."

Just ask former Blues goalie Mike Liut.

On January 17, 1984, long before his arrival in St. Louis, MacInnis knocked down Liut with a blister that broke his mask.

"Back then nobody pre-scouted, and when the Flames' lineup was posted, nobody in our room knew who this MacInnis kid was," Liut said. "We turned the puck over in the neutral zone, and MacInnis takes this shot from just outside the blue line—I'm thinking, *Can of corn. No problem.* But the puck explodes off his stick like a fastball.

"It's going to go about 2' over the net, but suddenly I'm trying to get out of the way. He shot it from 65' away, and it hits me in the wire before I can move 8". The joke was that nobody knew this guy—that's the first thing somebody should have told me. It's not like he developed this shot overnight."

The puck dropped and spun into the net for a goal.

"It made the papers all across Canada," MacInnis said.

MacInnis made his biggest headlines in 1989 when he led Calgary to a Stanley Cup. He set an NHL record for defensemen with a point in 17 consecutive playoff games en route to the Conn Smythe Trophy as the postseason MVP.

"You didn't have to coach Al MacInnis—just open the gate and let him go," said Terry Crisp, MacInnis' former coach in Calgary. "Everybody says what a shot he had. Yeah, he had a great shot, a booming shot, but he thought the game. He could set you up for the slap shot, he could wrist a shot off it, he could make the play to the side of the net to get it on net. He wasn't just a one-dimensional hockey player [like] everybody seems to think."

In 1994, on the Fourth of July, the Blues acquired MacInnis in a trade for defenseman Phil Housley. During a decade-long run in St. Louis, No. 2 continued to dominate on both blue lines.

In 1999, at age 35, MacInnis led all NHL defensemen with 62 points, including 20 goals, and he had a plus-33 rating. A five-time finalist for the Norris Trophy, he finally took home the award as the league's top defenseman. At age 39, he played in his 13th NHL All-Star Game.

"He was just a dynamic player, and he didn't get enough credit for his defensive play," said former Blue Dallas Drake. "He was great in his own zone."

On September 9, 2005, after an NHL lockout canceled the 2004–05 season, MacInnis retired because of an eye injury and a belief that he could no longer compete at a high level.

In the history of the game, MacInnis ranks third in goals (340), assists (934), and points (1,274) by a defenseman.

"Probably his biggest asset is, if you ever met him or if you know him, was the way he treated people and the way he respected the game," said former Nashville coach Barry Trotz, a teammate and roommate of MacInnis' in the minor leagues. "Those are things that are going to endure way past records or the guy with the big shot."

3 Gassoff Dies Tragically

The day had finally come.

"I got a call from my brother Barclay and he said, 'Let's go,'" Bobby Plager remembers. "He says, 'It's Diane. They took her to the hospital, she's going to have the baby, let's go. We said we'd be there.'"

Two months earlier, in the spring of 1977, Diane's husband, Bob Gassoff—arguably the toughest pound-for-pound player ever to wear the Blue Note—was tragically killed in a motorcycle accident. The horrific scene occurred on Memorial Day weekend in Gray Summit, Missouri, where many in the Blues' organization were gathered for a BBQ at the home of player Garry Unger.

Teammates loved the 5'10", 190-lb. Gassoff, who had been a third-round pick of the Blues in 1973.

In 1976–77, Gassoff posted six goals and 24 points, but he wasn't known for his offense. He amassed 254 penalty minutes in 77 games that season, or an average of 3.3 minutes per game.

Gassoff wasn't afraid of anyone. Two of his 10 fights in the 1976–77 season were against a Philadelphia Flyers rookie named Paul Holmgren, who stood 6'3" and weighed 210 lbs. Another was against Chicago's Grant Mulvey (6'4", 200).

"He was probably one of the most feared guys in the National Hockey League," former Blues teammate Bruce Affleck said. "Not big, 5'11" maybe, 200 lbs. maybe. But I tell the story, he got run over by a tractor when he was five years old and he lived. That's just the type of guy he was."

The Blues' annual end-of-the-season BBQ was a chance for players to wind down and relax.

"I was with Gasser on the four-wheeler going around the ranch," Plager said. "We came back and dropped off the four-wheel. We were getting ready to eat, and somebody had put the dirt bikes out there. Bruce [Affleck], another young kid, and Gasser—they picked up the bikes and away they went."

The Unger property was hilly. Affleck was in front, followed by the kid, and Gassoff was in the rear.

Driving toward them in a car was Douglas Klekamp, 19, who had been parking cars and running errands for Unger. Klekamp was returning to the party after making a trip for soda and ice.

"I was on a big bike, and they were on little dirt bikes," Affleck said. "I came over the hill and this car was coming by me, and then I heard the crash. But I couldn't see them because they weren't over the hill yet. So I turned around and went back. The car was speeding. It was fish-tailing a little bit when I came over the hill, but the car was on [its own] side of the road. However the accident occurred, [Klekamp] missed the 12-year-old kid somehow and then hit Gasser."

A lady from a nearby house came out to see what happened. She ran back inside, grabbed a blanket, and returned to drape it over the injured Blue.

Plager remembers he was chatting with his wife and Diane. "We're getting ready to eat the food, and it's a little quiet. Then Ungie says, 'Come on.' He is in tears. I go over there to talk to Ungie and he says, 'Bob, there's been an accident.'

"Here comes Diane. She had heard some rumbling. She said, 'What happened? What happened?' Ungie says Bob's been in an accident...the motorcycle. She gets in the truck with me, and we go to the accident. We get up there and the firetrucks are there and a couple of cops. I ask, 'How bad is it?' The cop looks and says, 'I don't know.' They put [Gasoff] in the ambulance and took him to Washington, Missouri. I look over and Bruce has his head down."

"I knew he was dead," Affleck said.

On May 29, 1977, at the age of 24, Gassoff was gone.

Still unaware, Plager and about 20 others rushed to St. Francis Hospital in Washington.

"I run in and [ask a nurse], 'There was an accident and they just brought somebody in, a friend of ours. Where is he?' Plager said. "She goes, 'Oh, he was DOA.' I don't even know what DOA is. I said, 'How bad is it?' She said, 'DOA.' Well, of course, that's 'dead on arrival.' Well, now Diane has lost it.

"I phone [my brother] Barclay and [Blues general manager] Emile Francis. Emile said, 'I'll be right there.' I turn and Diane is on the phone. I said, 'Who are you talking to?' She said, 'Bob's dad.' I grab the phone from her and go, 'Hello.' You can hear him say, 'Hello?' I said, 'Mr. Gassoff?' He said, 'What's going on?' I didn't tell him."

By then the owners of the Blues, the Salomons, had also arrived at the hospital. Everyone was focused on Diane, who had met Gassoff at Noel Picard's bar in Cuba, Missouri.

"People were saying they wished they never would have introduced them," Affleck remembered. "The Salomons were saying, 'If we hadn't drafted him, this wouldn't have happened.' None of it had anything to do with that."

Only one thing mattered.

"Diane was pregnant with Bobby Jr.," Affleck said.

Bob Plager said that Diane was in complete shock, but he and his brother Barclay tried to comfort her anyway.

"Barc said, 'Don't worry, we'll be in the hospital with the baby.... Bobby and I will be with you when you have your baby.... You won't be there alone,'" Bob remembers.

That day came on July 24, 1977.

"We go down to Barnes [Hospital], and she wants somebody to go in with her," Bob said. "Barc said, 'Oh Bob, you go in.' Barc had never seen one of his babies born. I said, 'Barc, it's you.' So Barc went in. She had the baby, young Bob, and we were there when he was born."

As he grew into an adult, Bob Jr. had familiar measurements—5'10", 190. The younger Gassoff didn't play in the NHL, but he had a successful career highlighted by a national championship at the University of Michigan and a season with the Peoria Rivermen.

But hockey is not where Gassoff Jr. planned to make his mark.

"He was telling his mother that he was training for hockey, and the whole time he was training for the [Navy] Seals," said former Blue Kelly Chase. "More than 400 guys tried out, and nine made it. He was one of them. You can talk about the character of hockey players and how tough they are—they man up. But [the Navy Seals] is a completely different level. That's the big boys, and for him to be a leader of the big boys, that's special."

On October 1, 1977, five months after Gassoff died and two months following the birth of his son, the Blues retired No. 3. It still hangs in the rafters today.

4 Picard Trips Orr

Former Blue Terry Crisp once joked that if he had known the picture of Boston's Bobby Orr soaring through the air after scoring the game-winning goal in the 1970 Stanley Cup final would become the most famous photo in NHL history, he never would have left the ice.

The expansion Blues had lost in the Stanley Cup final to Montreal in back-to-back years, and they were about to be swept by Orr and the Bruins, trailing the series three games to none.

On May 10, 1970, Game 4 went to overtime tied 3–3.

"I was on the ice when Bobby started his windup from behind his net," Crisp said. "With Bobby Orr, I knew full well that if I didn't cut him off, I wasn't going to see his number on the back of his jersey. Well, by the time I cut across the blue line, he was heading over the center-ice line. I figured I'm not catching Bobby—he's gone."

Crisp signaled to the Blues' bench that he was coming off the ice.

"In went Larry [Keenan], and the rest is history," Crisp said.

Orr, 22 years old at the time, penetrated the offensive zone and tossed the puck to Boston teammate Derek Sanderson in the corner. Sanderson waited and fed it back to Orr, who was charging the crease. With Orr already accounting for eight goals and 19 points in 13 playoff games that year, Blues goalie Glenn Hall realized what was developing in front him.

"You knew Bobby was coming, and you knew he was dangerous," Hall said. "It was a well-executed goal. I immediately knew I wouldn't have to put on that stinking equipment the next day."

Orr's game-winning goal 40 seconds into overtime lifted Boston to a 4–3 victory, capturing its fourth Stanley Cup but its first in nearly three decades. Orr was named the Conn Smythe Trophy winner as the MVP of the series.

Reliving the game-winning goal, Orr once said that Hall "had to move across the crease and had to open his pads a little. I was really trying to get the puck on net, and I did. As I went across, Glenn's legs opened. I looked back, and I saw it go in, so I jumped."

What happened next is best illustrated by the brilliant image captured by photographer Ray Lussier of the *Boston Record-American*. Lussier had moved from the East end of Boston Garden to the West end because that's where the Bruins would be shooting in OT. He surmised that the team would be "going for broke," trying to win at home instead of allowing the series to shift back to St. Louis.

On a 93-degree spring day in Boston, Russier claimed that a photographer for a competing newspaper stepped away from his position on the West side to buy a beer, and that's how he was able to line up the perfect angle for his famous shot.

As Orr leapt, Blues defenseman Noel Picard tripped him with his stick, propelling the talented Bruin into the air like Superman.

"He cut in front of the net and bingo, the puck was in," Picard said. "He was surprised that I lifted him up. But it was way too late."

"When Pic got him airborne, it was after the season was over," Hall said.

The only thing left to develop was Russier's frame, which includes Orr, Picard, and Hall.

"If I would have stayed on the ice, I could have been posterized in the most famous picture—Orr flying through the air, Glenn Hall sprawled, and me in the corner,'" Crisp said. "I missed my big chance. They'd say 'Crispy, can you sign this?' I'd say, 'Yeah, I'll sign it with Orr and Hall.'"

It might sound like a great idea now, being in the picture, but Hall actually lived it. And once when he was in Boston for a ceremony in 1996, he took a moment to remind Orr how many times he has been asked to sign the photo.

"I asked Bobby if that was the only goal that he ever scored because everybody had that picture," Hall laughed. "If you can't find something good in everything, then you're doing something wrong. We played as well as we were capable of playing. It wasn't good enough, but we had nothing to be ashamed of."

Picard, too, had a copy of the photo. It's signed by Orr and hangs on a wall in his home.

"The only difference with that picture is Bobby Orr probably made $2 million, and I probably made a penny," joked Picard, who said that Orr wrote on his picture, "Some day I will return the favor," "And he sure did," Picard said. "My daughter went to college in Boston, and he really took care of her, finding an apartment. He was pretty nice in general, Bobby Orr."

5 Greatest Blue in History

Bob Plager played 14 years in the NHL, but he still believes that his best year was his first season with the Blues in 1967–68.

"That year, I put five people in the hospital," Plager said. "One got his knee operated on, and four went to the maternity ward."

If you talk to Plager for five minutes and he hasn't told a joke, check his temperature. Dropping more one-liners than Richard Pryor and holding more titles than a Harry Potter series, No. 5 remains a regular at the rink every day, an ambassador who represents the rich history of the organization.

"Bobby is an original player and is still working with the organization after 52 years," said former Blues goaltender Glenn Hall. "He should probably be considered the greatest Blue in history."

Plager has been in St. Louis nearly as long as the Arch. He was acquired by the Blues in a trade with the New York Rangers on June 6, 1967. Along with Plager, the team received Gary Sabourin, Tim Ecclestone, and Gord Kannegiesser in exchange for Rod Seiling.

A few days before the trade, the NHL held its expansion draft and Plager didn't believe the Blues fared well, rating the team's picks as the worst. Then after the Blues acquired the defenseman, Plager quipped, "Hockey is a strange sport. It's amazing how with one good trade you can go all the way from last place to first!"

Plager took the first penalty in Blues' history just 64 seconds into the franchise's existence, but he made amends by assisting on the club's first goal, scored by teammate Larry Keenan. Almost everything Plager did in the organization was a first, which included being the first of three brothers to suit up for the Blues.

Barclay and Billy Plager joined Bobby in St. Louis, and in a milestone moment for the family, the three guys found themselves on the ice together one night in Montreal. Interestingly, they were each lined up at forward.

"I remember Scotty [Bowman] saying the lineup in the dressing room," Bobby said. "'Barclay Plager, center ice. Bob Plager, left wing. Billy Plager, right wing.'"

On the blue line, however, is where Bobby made his mark, patenting his famous hip-check. Listed at 5'11" and 190 lbs., he would crouch low and level opponents along the boards as they entered the offensive zone.

"He was awesome at that," former Blues teammate Terry Crisp said. "If you missed a hip check, you looked like you were out to lunch [because] they're going by you. Not very often did Bobby miss it. And he put a lot of guys out."

Even though Plager is known as a prankster, he was different on the ice.

"Bobby was a character, Barc was more of a serious guy," former teammate John Davidson said. "But when the puck dropped, they were the same. Bobby was just an unreal competitor, whatever he had to do."

Bobby Plager was willing to do anything to improve his game—well, almost anything.

After the Blues lost in the Stanley Cup final for the second straight season in 1969, the Salomon family took the team to Florida for a vacation. Bobby Plager remembered one time when everyone was sitting by the pool, including Coach Scotty Bowman.

"We were all by the pool, the whole team sitting by the cabana," Plager remembers. "Scotty is there, and the guys are saying, 'Look at him. What's he thinking? What's he going to do now?'

"The guys tell me, '[Coach] wants to talk to you, Bob.' You're still scared of Scotty, so you're walking over. Coach goes, 'I'm just out here thinking, Bob. You know they have these power-skating schools.' I thought, *Oh man, here goes my summer.*

"But he said, 'I was just thinking, if I was you, I would never go to one of those power-skating schools because if you ever learned how to skate, you might think you're a hockey player and you'd be no good anymore.' And then he walked away."

Plager walked away in 1978 after 11 seasons with the Blues, finishing as the franchise's all-time leader in games played as a defenseman (616), a record that stood until 2013. But Bobby was far from finished with the club despite hanging up his skates.

"I was a vice president, assistant general manager, director of player development, director of player personnel, Peoria head coach, pro scout, broadcaster, everything," Plager said. "I remember [former Blues owner] Harry Ornest said he was going to make me the assistant general manager. I said, 'Well, does it come with a raise?' He said, 'No, but it's a great title.'

"They'd call you a vice president or whatever, but it meant nothing. I was always the same thing. No matter what title I had, I did the same thing."

Plager held the title of Blues head coach for only 11 games.

After leading the Peoria Rivermen to the International Hockey League championship in 1990–91, Plager signed a two-year contract to replace Brian Sutter and become the 16th head coach of the Blues in 1992. But one month into his tenure, Plager abruptly resigned.

"I don't know if the game had passed me by, but it was different," Plager said at the time. "I think I did my best, but the game has changed, the players have changed. It wasn't right for me."

Not much else gets by Plager, however.

"One thing about Bobby, he knows where all the skeletons are in the St. Louis Blues," former Blue Kelly Chase said. "Anything that ever happened, Bobby Plager has got the best grasp on how it happened and what happened. He knows where all the bodies are buried."

But Plager doesn't tell those tales. He only shares the ones that make people laugh.

"Of all the people I've met in hockey, he is the most colorful, bar none," Crisp said. "I always tell people, the stories that I'm about to tell you are true, don't try these at home, and then I start talking about Bobby Plager. Before the night is over, their jaws are dropping. They're all going, 'These can't be true.' They're true."

Davidson still marvels at Plager, now in his seventies.

"He seems like he never ages," Davidson said. "And his heart, if you opened up his chest, there would be a Blue Note on his heart. For people to get into the sporting world at the age he did, and still be here now, that says a lot about what he does. You think of the Blues and you think of a few people, including Bobby Plager."

And that's why Blues fans were as thrilled for Plager as anyone throughout the team's run to the Stanley Cup in 2019. During the four rounds, he could hardly bear to watch the ice, opting to pace the rink to help rid himself of his nerves. Even in Boston for Game 7, he had to step away from the Blues' contingent in the visitors' suite.

"I started off in there, but I walked around the rink, and it was 1–0, and our goalie was making unbelievable saves," Plager said. "Then it's 2–0 and 3–0, so I leave the suite, I'm at the elevator, and all the [Boston fans] are starting to leave. There was a little noise and somebody said, 'That's not us scoring, it's not loud enough, it's the Blues.' So I give the little 'Yeah!'

"I asked them, 'Can you walk down these stairs five floors to the ice surface?' and they said, 'Yeah.' Well, I didn't walk down, I flew down, and went and stood behind our bench. When it was over, I got to go on the ice and celebrate, and when you're out there, you just can't believe it. It's unbelievable. And to win it in Boston; the last time that happened there [1970], I had to leave the ice when [the Bruins] were celebrating."

Back in St. Louis a few days later, Plager finally got the parade he'd been eager to experience for years. He rode with his family in a convertible car, waving to the weeping crowd.

"It doesn't seem real," he said. "You meet so many people over the years and a lot of them come up to me and say, 'We've got to do it soon, Bob, I'm not going to be here much longer. The best part about the whole thing to me—and there were so many great things—was to see the tears in their eyes. They're a bunch of hockey fans and this was the greatest thing for them."

6 Redhead Scores Six Goals

As far as hat tricks go, no player in Blues history can come close to matching Brett Hull, who is the franchise leader with 27. But Hull never had two hat tricks in the same game, unlike Gordon "Red" Berenson, who accomplished this feat on November 7, 1968.

Berenson's six-goal game against the Philadelphia Flyers is a Blues franchise record, and he remains the only player in NHL history to score six goals on the road. His half-dozen goals are seen by many as a share of the league's all-time record, but some refer to the sport's real benchmark as seven, which was set by the Quebec Bulldogs' Joe Malone in 1920.

On that November night in 1968, the Blues topped the Flyers 8–0 on a shutout by goaltender Jacques Plante, but the focus afterward was on the player known as the Red Baron.

"I can tell you I probably had better games but I just didn't have the numbers, the statistics, the goals to show for it," Berenson said. "You have good games, but sometimes they don't show up on the scoreboard. That game showed up on the scoreboard."

After winning a Stanley Cup in Montreal in 1965, Berenson spent time with the New York Rangers before being dealt to the Blues on November 29, 1967. In the deal, the club also acquired defenseman Barclay Plager, while Ron Attwell and Ron Stewart were sent to the Rangers.

Coming into the 1968–69 season, Berenson had managed 38 goals in 240 NHL games, but never did he dream of the night in which he'd score six goals, all at even strength, including four in a nine-minute stretch.

Before taking the ice against Philadelphia, Berenson had lit the lamp only three times in 11 games, and on his first shot against the

Flyers, goalie Doug Favell turned him aside. But it would turn out to be an evening to forget for Favell and defenseman Ed Van Impe.

"It was early in the year, and I hadn't scored in the previous couple of games," said Berenson. "When I scored the first goal, I went around [defenseman Ed] Van Impe and scored on my backhand. I remember saying to myself, 'Thank God I can still score.'"

Few could have predicted that it would be a game for the record books since Berenson had only one goal after the first period. But in the second, he scored on each of his four shots, handing the Blues a 5–0 advantage.

Legendary play-by-play voice Dan Kelly of KMOX radio in St. Louis was at the microphone for the call.

"Van Impe, who has broken his stick, is back to get it," Kelly described. "He lost it to McCreary. He's in with Berenson. Berenson shoots, he scores! Berenson has scored his fifth goal, and the Blues lead 5–0. What a night for the redhead!"

The four goals in a period matched the NHL record, which was shared by Toronto's Busher Jackson in 1934 and Chicago's Max Bentley in 1943.

"None of the goals were bad goals," Berenson said. "They were all five-on-five goals…a breakaway, a three-on-two, just good plays and the puck was going in."

Before Berenson capped off his magical night, the Blues picked up goals by Terry Crisp and Camille Henry, stretching their lead to 7–0.

Obviously that didn't sit well with the 9,164 hometown Philadelphia fans, but not for the reason one would think. They wanted to see history, whether it was their guy or not.

"I scored the seventh goal that night, and you know what's amusing? I got booed," Crisp said. "The crowd in Philly booed me because Red was on a roll. I only get four a year. That's one of my four, and they booed me. I said, 'This ain't right.' They should have been booing Red."

Berenson's Six-Goal Game

Here is a breakdown of Gordon "Red" Berenson's six goals in one game on November 7, 1968:

No. 1 (even strength)
Time: 16:42, first period
Assists: Noel Picard, McDonald
Score: Blues 1, Flyers 0

No. 2 (even strength)
Time: 10:26, second period
Assists: Unassisted
Score: Blues 2, Flyers 0

No. 3 (even strength)
Time: 14:42, second period
Assists: Henry, Noel Picard
Score: Blues 3, Flyers 0

No. 4 (even strength)
Time: 15:14, second period
Assists: Henry
Score: Blues 4, Flyers 0

No. 5 (even strength)
Time: 19:35, second period
Assists: McCreary
Score: Blues 5, Flyers 0

No. 6 (even strength)
Time: 14:04, third period
Assists: Unassisted
Score: Blues 8, Flyers 0

Instead, the Philly faithful cheered when Berenson reached six with 5:56 remaining in the game.

"Van Impe lost it to Berenson," Kelly announced on the radio broadcast. "Berenson has a break! One man back! Here he comes! A shot...he scores! Red Berenson has tied the record with six goals in one game! He gets a great ovation from this crowd at the Philadelphia Spectrum! Six goals in one hockey game, tying the record!"

Berenson tied the record set by Detroit's Syd Howe in 1944.

"I don't remember exactly what the chants were, but there was a lot of support from the Philadelphia fans," Berenson said. "We had a pretty good rivalry started with them, and it got even stronger as the years went on. I was probably the last player on St. Louis that Philadelphia fans ever cheered for."

The enthusiastic bunch nearly watched Berenson tie Malone's mark, but on a bid for his record-breaking seventh goal that night, "I hit a crossbar," said Berenson, who finished with 10 shots on goal.

Berenson claimed that he wasn't aware of the rarefied air he was breathing.

"I didn't have any idea that it was a record," he said. "I just thought I was lucky and I was having a good game. If you play long enough, you're bound to have a good game."

The mark still stands more than four decades later. In that span, only Toronto's Darryl Sittler has been able to duplicate it, reaching the six-goal plateau in 1976.

"I'm surprised there haven't been more six-goal games," Berenson said, "especially in the 1970s, when so many goals were being scored and you had guys scoring up to 100 goals a season and so many more gifted scorers—[Mario] Lemieux and [Wayne] Gretzky and others who could have scored seven or eight goals in a game. For one reason or another, it hasn't happened."

Berenson finished the 1968–69 season with 35 goals and 82 points. Those were totals he never matched again in his career, which took him to Detroit in the early 1970s before a return to St. Louis. He ended with 261 goals, six of which came on one memorable night.

"You get the hat tricks, okay, that's nice. Everybody gets a hat trick," Crisp said. "Then he gets the fourth goal and you're sitting there saying, 'Oh, that's pretty good, four goals in one game.' Then you're like, man, he's got five, then six…. At the given time, it's kind of neat, but you don't realize how long that [record] could last. So you're seeing part of history, and it doesn't sink in until years later."

7 Monday Night Miracle

Before the franchise finally got to hoist its first Stanley Cup in 2019, the "Monday Night Miracle" was the moment of glory most etched in the minds of Blues fans.

On May 12, 1986, the Blues trailed the Calgary Flames three games to two in the Campbell Conference finals, and they were behind 4–1 going into the third period of Game 6 at the Arena.

"It was a do-or-die situation for us, and we all knew that," Blues Hall of Famer Bernie Federko said. "We came in the locker room after the second period, and basically Coach Jacques Demers said, 'Guys, we've had a great year. Whatever happens in this next period, it's been a great year.' But you never know what can happen.

"We all knew that [Barclay Plager] had cancer, and Barc was in pretty bad shape. We were all pushing to try and do something for Barc. And it just happened the way it did."

Here's how it happened:

The Blues' Doug Wickenheiser scored a five-on-three advantage to pull the club within 4–2. But Calgary's Joe Mullen countered, beating Blues goalie Rick Wamsley on a slapshot that put the Flames back up 5–2 with 12:56 left in regulation.

Several folks in the crowd of 17,801 began to depart, including former Blues defenseman Bruce Affleck.

"I was in the real-estate business, and I had a presentation the next morning," Affleck said. "We left when they were down by three, thinking this was a chance to go home and get a good night's sleep and make a good presentation."

It wasn't as good as the presentation the Blues were about to make.

Like Wickenheiser, who had made the long road back from knee surgery, Blues captain Brian Sutter had been out since January with a shoulder injury, but he returned to the ice in the playoffs. Sutter showed a glimpse of his old self, scoring his first goal of the playoffs 62 seconds after Mullen.

The Blues' Greg Paslawski put the puck on net from the right circle, and Calgary's 22-year-old rookie goalie, Mike Vernon, broomed it to his right. Sutter charged the puck and hammered it home, cutting the Blues' deficit to 5–3 with 11:54 left.

"And the roller-coaster ride continues," Blues announcer Ken Wilson bellowed on the broadcast.

Five minutes, however, separated the Blues from their off-season. They could have used Brett Hull, but this was two years before his trade from Calgary, and Hull was a healthy scratch for the Flames, watching from the pressbox.

But the Blues would have other heroes rise to the occasion.

Doug Gilmour chipped the puck into the offensive zone in the right corner where Sutter hustled to fetch it. Sutter backhanded a pass in front of the net, and Paslawski didn't allow the Flames time to react, snapping a shot past Vernon for a 5–4 score with 4:11 to play.

"We didn't want to lose," Demers said.

Perhaps not, but the clock was in Calgary's favor as it ticked under 1½ minutes.

Photographers began leaving their ice-level spots to jockey for position where the Flames would be celebrating their conference championship.

"Boy, you get the idea if these Blues could come up with a miracle finish," Wilson said on the broadcast, "these Calgary Flames would have to crawl back to Alberta."

That miracle would need the help of one more goal to tie the game, and the Blues got it from Paslawski.

Gilmour again fired the puck into the offensive zone from just inside the red line. Vernon stopped it behind the net for Flames defenseman Jamie Macoun. Paslawski trailed Macoun undetected behind the net to the right side of Vernon. He then picked Macoun's pocket and, while spinning to his knees, let go of a surprise shot that knotted the game 5–5 with 1:08 to play.

"I made a line switch and got on the ice and just happened to swing behind the net," Paslawski said. "I just lifted [Macoun's] stick and turned around and shot, and it went in the net."

Was it luck?

"You've got to work hard to be lucky," Sutter said.

The Arena erupted after the Blues had erased Calgary leads of 4–1 and 5–2, but it was about to get louder. Regulation wrapped up with the teams deadlocked, and the teams went into their locker rooms for the overtime intermission.

"We were pretty positive that we were going to win the game. There was no question about it," Federko said. "Fate was on our side."

In OT, Mullen, a former Blue, nearly sent the Flames to the Stanley Cup final with the game-winner. But his shot hit the post, setting the stage a short time later for Wickenheiser, who was standing in the right place at the right time.

"Bernie made a beautiful pass, like he always does, over to Mark [Hunter]," Wickenheiser said after the game. "Mark shot, and the rebound came out to me. All I had to do was make sure it hit the net."

Pandemonium ensued as Wickenheiser scored the game-winner for a climactic 6–5 come-from-behind victory.

"Of all the times that I was in that building, nothing was ever louder than that," Federko said. "When Wick scored, I remember it was just before midnight when it happened. It was 12:30 or 12:45 AM and the building was three-quarters full and people were still standing and cheering. It was one of the few times that I've ever felt electricity like that in any building, and I'll never forget that."

The Blues didn't forget Demers' speech heading into the third period, either.

"All Jacques said was, 'Go out there and play with pride. A lot can happen in 20 minutes,'" Wickenheiser said afterward. "We proved that tonight. We got a couple of goals, a couple of breaks, and then the fans got behind us. We didn't want to let them down."

It was a miracle, even if only hockey fans in St. Louis felt that way.

"I don't know if it's one of the greatest comebacks in the NHL," Demers said, "but it's a great comeback for the Blues."

The Flames might have crawled back to Alberta after the loss, but two nights later Calgary edged the Blues 2–1 in Game 7, taking the best-of-seven series.

"The bummer about that whole thing, as great as it was, we were a goal away from going to the Stanley Cup final," Federko said.

There's no doubt that having an opportunity to play for the franchise's first Stanley Cup would have been even better, but had the Blues folded in Game 6, it's hard to fathom history without the Monday Night Miracle.

8 Consummate Competitor

As unbelievable as it might seem, the initial reaction to the trade that made Barclay Plager a St. Louis Blue was negative.

On November 29, 1967, just 19 games into the Blues' inaugural season, the club sent Ron Stewart and Ron Attwell to the New York Rangers for Plager and Red Berenson. At the time, Stewart had seven goals and 12 points and Attwell had seven assists.

"We traded our top two scorers for two guys in the minor leagues," Bobby Plager said. "We're getting a player who couldn't play in New York [in] Red, and we're getting a minor leaguer who has never played a game in the NHL in Barclay. Well, before the season was over, people didn't remember Ron Stewart and Ron Attwell."

Barclay Plager had played three seasons under legendary coach Scotty Bowman in junior hockey and Bowman, now coaching the Blues, knew that the defenseman could help the expansion club.

"For some reason, Barclay never really got a chance to prove himself in the NHL, despite his fine minor-league record," Bowman said. "We knew all along that he had fine puck-handling ability to go along with his reputation as a fighter."

Bowman paired Plager with Al Arbour to form the Blues' top defensive duo. Arbour had already won four Stanley Cups with Detroit, Chicago, and Toronto. Nine years older, the Blues' captain took Plager under his wing, and the two became roommates.

"Barclay Plager was a great player, my best friend," Arbour said.

In his first season, Plager had 20 points from the blue line and he led the entire NHL in penalty minutes with 153. For an organization looking to establish its identity, "Barc" sparked the Blues to three straight trips to the Stanley Cup final by wearing his heart on his sleeve.

"He was the consummate competitor," Bowman said. "Pound for pound, I don't think there was a better player that I've ever been able to coach. He wasn't small and he wasn't big, but he played very big. He just had the will to win all the time."

In 1970, Arbour took over the coaching duties from Bowman. Plager joked, "Does that mean we're not going to be roommates anymore?"

Arbour made Plager one of four alternate captains of the Blues, and in 1972, the club gave Plager the distinction on his own, making him the fifth player in the team's brief history to wear the "C."

"It won't be hard to be the captain of this team because it's a great bunch of guys," Plager said. "It's an honor to be captain, and if I didn't think I would help the team, I wouldn't be captain."

Plager continued to cement his reputation as a leader and an outstanding player. In 1973–74, he was named in a coaches' poll conducted by the *Toronto Star* as the best body-checker in the league. By then the defenseman had played in four NHL All-Star Games.

Returning to St. Louis after one of those All-Star affairs, Plager continued to justify the perception of his personality, offering Blues broadcaster Dan Kelly his memento from the game.

"Back then, they gave the players rings for playing in the All-Star Game," said John Kelly, Dan's son. "Barclay Plager gave my dad his All-Star ring and said to him, 'Because you're a broadcaster, you'll never get a ring. But you're an all-star broadcaster, so I want you to have this from me.'"

In 10 seasons with the Blues, Plager had 44 goals, 187 assists, 231 points, and 1,115 penalty minutes in 614 games. In perhaps a more telling statistic, he broke his nose 11 times—at least that's how many were documented.

Plager finished his playing career as a player-coach in the Blues' minor-league system in Kansas City and Salt Lake City. He was selected as a Central Hockey League All-Star at age 35 and was named by *The Hockey News* as the minor-league Coach of the Year.

"At his age, being a player-coach, that was not done a lot," said Blues Hall of Famer Bernie Federko, who played for Plager in Kansas City. "He was playing with a bunch of kids. He still didn't wear a helmet, but he blocked shots. Here was a guy who was a respected NHL player that gave up his NHL playing days to go down and actually play in the minors and coach at the same time. I've never had more respect for anybody than Barc."

In February 1978, Plager was named head coach of the Blues, replacing Leo Boivin. But after posting a record of 18–50–12 in his first full season, the worst mark in the franchise's history, Plager resigned in December 1979.

"I'm not getting the best out of the team," he said. "When a coach believes that, it's time to get out. I'm hoping whoever comes in here can get more out of this team than I did."

Unbeknownst at the time, Plager was dealing with health issues. He had undergone an exam for scar tissue on his brain that was reportedly the result of an injury suffered earlier in his career.

Meanwhile, Berenson, the player who came to St. Louis in the trade with Plager, took over the Blues and guided them to a record of 34–34–12 in 1979–80. Chicago swept the club in a best-of-three playoff round that year, but the Blues had two young emerging stars in Federko and Brian Sutter. Each player had an expired contract, and when training camp rolled around the following season, both were still unsigned.

"Barc came to us, and he was mad because neither one of us had signed," Federko said. "He made us go up and see [Blues GM Emile Francis], who was at an impasse with our agent. We went up and spoke personally with "The Cat," and he gave us what we wanted. He just wanted to hear it out of our mouths.

"Not many people know this, but after that Barc said, 'Okay guys, you are going to be here for a long time, so I want you to buy a house.' We said we didn't have enough money, so he gave us money for down payments on our houses. He said, 'You pay me back whenever you want.' He wouldn't take any interest or anything. So we did. We both built houses two doors apart in 1980."

With the severity of Plager's condition still unknown, the Blues held a ceremony on March 24, 1981, during which the defenseman's No. 8 was retired by the organization. It marked only the second number in club history to be raised to the rafters, following Bob Gassoff's No. 3.

"I have never met and worked with an athlete more dedicated and determined," former Blues GM Emile Francis said. "[Plager's] name is synonymous with the St. Louis Blues and the spirit this organization has developed with its history."

Four months later, Plager returned to the Blues bench as an assistant coach and even filled in as the interim head coach in 1982–83 before going back to his assistant position. But on November 3, 1984, it was announced that Plager had an inoperable brain tumor.

That night, the Blues, who were coached by Jacques Demers at the time, hosted the Calgary Flames. Demers showed tremendous emotion following the Blues' 5–2 win, which was dedicated to Plager.

"There was no way we were going to lose that game," Demers said. "We were motivated by a great man who is a great asset to our team. That's why I was pointing to the press box. He was sitting up there, and I wanted to tell him that this was for him."

Players rallied around Plager.

"He's had a lot of tough fights, and now he's in for the toughest fight of his life," Sutter said. "But Barc's as tough a man as I've ever met and also one of the most positive. He breeds that in other people."

His brother, Bobby, is one of them.

"Barc's attitude is that it's like a hockey injury," he said. "He's going to fight it and probably get back sooner than anyone else would. His biggest problem with the players now is he doesn't want anyone feeling sorry for him. That would hurt him more than anything else."

Plager was given six months to live but, like his hockey career, he stretched it out longer. He lived more than three years before succumbing to the cancer on February 6, 1988, at age 46. He was survived by his wife, Helen, and four children.

"Barclay Plager is not a normal person," Federko said. "His heart is so big that he's going to heaven in a rocket ship."

9 Ironman Streak Almost Never Started

The inspiration for the NHL's "Ironman" streak was Carol Ann Unger.

Five years younger than her brother, former Blue Garry Unger, Carol Ann was stricken with polio as a toddler. To witness Carol Ann's condition up close drove Garry every day of his life.

"I'm playing football and baseball and hockey and running around…and she was always in this wheelchair," Unger said. "So when I got an injury, it was really hard for me to say, 'Whoa, I feel sorry for myself,' knowing that my sister could never get out of this chair."

From 1967–79, Unger rode that attitude to a streak of 949 consecutive games played in the NHL, but that includes playoffs, which the NHL does not recognize in regard to the ironman streak. The forward suited up in 914 straight regular-season games, a record which was eclipsed by Doug Jarvis in 1985–86.

"If I'm signing autographs, people want me to write on their picture, 'Ironman,'" Unger said. "That's pretty special."

Despite Unger's motivation, or his pain tolerance, the streak almost never got started. He had been involved in a water-skiing accident and a basketball-related injury before his first professional camp with the Toronto Maple Leafs in 1967, leaving him with a leg that wouldn't straighten out.

Unger took a rather unique approach to fixing the problem.

"My friend had a Firebird with a four-speed," he said. "I thought if we traded cars and I used the clutch, one of those times my knee would pop back to normal and I would be fine.

"By the time I got to Peterborough, I almost had it straight. Then I got to camp. We took our medicals and the doctor said, 'What have you been doing with this leg?' I said I've been trying to straighten it. He said, 'Well, you've been tearing it.' I had surgery on my knee and missed training camp. It was a funny way to start an Ironman streak—to be hurt your whole rookie year."

After his knee healed, Unger eventually began his career with the Maple Leafs, one of six teams the forward played with during a 16-year career. He was dealt from Toronto to Detroit and then to the Blues in 1971 in a trade that sent Red Berenson to the Red Wings.

It wasn't until he was in St. Louis that Unger was even aware of the streak.

"We were playing in Long Island, and we lost a game," Unger said. "A reporter came to me after the game and said, 'Congratulations.' I said, 'What are you talking about? We just got killed.' He said, 'That was your 500th game in a row.' I said, 'That's what I do. I play hockey.'"

Unger still had quite far to go to break the Ironman record, which was 630 games at that time, held by longtime New York Rangers right wing Andy Hebenton.

"As it got closer to 630, it got more publicity," Unger said. "But again, I wasn't playing the games to try to break a streak."

But in 1976, as a member of the Blues, Unger eclipsed Hebenton's mark and established a new record with every game he played.

"They gave me a really nice Billy Cook saddle with an Ironman plaque on the back," he said. "I still have it. It's one of my prized possessions."

In 1979, the Blues traded Unger to Atlanta and, ironically, the streak came to an end against St. Louis, but not because the Ironman couldn't play.

The Flames had a lot of skill—maybe even the most talented team Unger had played with—but they were down in the standings.

"We were struggling, and every time we went into a city, because our record wasn't great, they would write about the Ironman streak," he said. "I didn't know this at the time, but I guess it was bugging the coach [Al MacNeil]."

Unger was recovering from a separated shoulder when Atlanta met the Blues on December 22, 1979. He was hurting, but considering the injuries he had played through in the past, he felt okay to suit up. Through two periods, however, Unger sat on the bench.

"He wasn't going to play me," Unger said of MacNeil. "With a couple minutes left in the game, we were winning 7–2 and the fans and players had realized that I hadn't been on the ice. Players were coming to me and saying, 'Take my shift.'"

Unger didn't budge.

Toward the end of the game, there was an incident where a few sticks came up near the Atlanta bench. Several players, including Unger, jumped to avoid being hit. MacNeil thought Unger was trying to get on the ice, but he wasn't going anywhere. If his coach wanted the streak to end, it would end. And it did.

Unger believes that he played in another 100 consecutive games following the incident, so had MacNeil not put his fingerprints on the scene, Unger could have surpassed the 1,000-game milestone. But he wasn't regretful.

With his sister Carol Ann on his mind, Unger said, "If there's one record that I would hope every player who laces on a pair of skates gets to break, it's an Ironman record, because that would mean they're not getting hurt."

Unger and MacNeil didn't cross paths again until several years after the streak had ended. Then in 2011, after Unger's playing days had ended, he was walking through the pressbox in Calgary when he ran into his former coach.

"It was really dark up [in the pressbox]," Unger said. "This guy walked by, and I thought I recognized him. I tapped him on the shoulder and said, 'Hello,' and he turned around and it was Al MacNeil. It was like shock. He just said 'hello' and scurried off. The look on his face was worth me not ever saying anything."

10 The Arena

The building that sat at 5700 Oakland Avenue from 1929–99 wasn't constructed for the Blues, but you'd have a hard time convincing someone who attended games at The Arena of that fact.

"It was a great spot," former Blues defenseman and head coach Al Arbour recalled.

The roof was actually put on 38 years before the expansion franchise opened up for business in 1967. However, after purchasing the Arena for $4 million, the Salomon family spruced it up with millions in upgrades.

The outer appearance received $1.5 million in attention, while inside the building, cushy seats, an Arena Club, and a scoreboard were added. Hallways were widened, concession stands were improved, and rest rooms were spit-shined.

"There were some basic things," said Sid Salomon Jr., the Blues' first owner, "that had to be done so we would not be embarrassed when our friends came to games."

Their attention to detail was impeccable, and the new ownership's desire to create a love affair between the city and its newest professional sports franchise was clear.

"The toilet bowls had blue water," former Blues public relations director Susie Mathieu remembers.

On October 11, 1967, the Blues christened the newly renovated Arena—a building that had previously hosted the Police Circus, National Dairy Show, and the Roller Dance Club—with the club's first NHL game. A crowd of 11,339 people filed into the 14,500-seat rink to watch the team skate to a 2–2 tie with the Minnesota North Stars.

"They were sitting right on top of the play," former Blues goalie Glenn Hall remembers. "It was a great place to play. I came from Chicago where the stadium was quite loud also, so I'd been a little bit used to it. But when they'd start singing at the Arena, I've often said we're at least half a goal ahead of them before they drop the puck."

Organist Norm Kramer used his keys to create a lively atmosphere at the Arena, and Kramer must have agreed that he helped trigger the offense.

"The first year, the team paid him $35 a night and he had instant fame," former Blues coach Scotty Bowman said. "So the next year, he went to sign his contract for about 39 games, and the owner of the team liked him, but [Kramer] wanted $10,000 a year instead of $35 a game.

"The owners said, 'No, we cannot afford that kind of money, Norm.' So Norm hauled out the newspaper and said, 'You've got some players who are being paid about $20,000. I'm worth half a goal a game, and they don't even score 10 goals in a season.'"

The Blues weren't the first hockey team to call the Arena home. The St. Louis Eagles played one year in the NHL (1934–35). The St. Louis Flyers were a minor-league organization that played in the American Hockey Association (1928–42) and American Hockey League (1944–53). The St. Louis Braves, the minor-league affiliate for the Chicago Blackhawks, also had a stint at the Arena in the Central Hockey League (1963–67).

But this was the NHL, and folks were arriving hours before the puck dropped for dinner and the filming of a live TV show called *Bowling for Dollars*.

In 1957, a 48-lane bowling alley was installed next to the Arena, adjacent to the roller-skating rink, and dubbed the Arena Bowl. Despite a tornado in 1959 that ripped through the property, causing damage to many of the lanes, they were rebuilt and became quite an attraction.

"The games were typically 8:00 back in the day, and you'd get off of work and park for free in Forest Park," said Jim Woodcock, a former Blues executive in the 1990s and 2000s, who had been a longtime fan of the club. "We would walk over the overpass, Highway 40, brutally cold, and then stop at the Arena Bowl, get a malted beverage, and watch people bowl.

"*Bowling for Dollars* used to be broadcast live around 6:30 or 7:00 PM on Channel 30. It was just something to do before the game and before I discovered Schmiezing's. You would go to Arena Bowl before the game and then walk literally 100' into the Arena for the game. The downside was always the walk after the game, when the temperature had dropped 20 degrees, back to Forest Park."

But the elements didn't matter to fans, who were now flocking to the Arena to watch the Blues.

"It was the place to be seen," remembered Claire Arbour, Al's wife. "You couldn't believe how well-dressed people would get. There was such an atmosphere in that building. We were the envy of the league.

"We always used to laugh, 'How many coats of paint did the Salomons have to put on?'" she added. "They were always painting and cleaning the place. It was immaculate in there. They took pride in that building."

Former Blues center Bernie Federko, who was drafted in 1976, toward the end of the Salomon reign, recalled that the painter stayed rather busy.

"He started on one end of the building and by the time he was finished, he started over again," Federko said. "They mopped the floors, too. When Mr. Salomon drove his Rolls [Royce] in, they had a guy behind with a mop, mopping over the tire marks."

The constant upkeep of the Arena caught the eyes of NHL officials, who awarded St. Louis the league's All-Star Game in 1970. The building hosted another type of goaltending in 1973, when Bill Walton shot and swatted UCLA to the NCAA basketball title over Memphis State, which had a starting point guard named Bill Laurie, a future owner of the Blues.

But by the time Laurie purchased the club in 1999, it had already moved into the spiffy new Kiel Center.

The Salomons had run into rough financial times, and after sinking a total of $8 million into the Arena, they were forced to sell in 1977. Ralston Purina, a local pet-food company, took over and renamed the building the Checkerdome.

"Ralston was the one that put in the air conditioning," Federko said. "And the acoustics were so bad, they put in all those chutes [canvases that draped from the ceiling]. But then the roof leaked, and they had all the stains on the chutes."

The team's third owner, Harry Ornest, bought the Blues and the Arena in 1983. The California businessman gave it both necessary upgrades and extra goodies, putting on a new roof and adding an electronic marquee outside. But the biggest improvement might have been restoring the rink's proper name—the St. Louis Arena.

Also under Ornest, the Blues' on-ice success was restored, and the building became a vibrant place to be once again.

"The one thing I'll fondly remember was when the team was coming on the ice, everyone would stand," Woodcock said. "It was very ceremonious and very moving. I don't know if any other clubs ever had that sort of entry on the ice as we did here. It was a sign of celebration, a sign of respect. Also, just the sense of community that existed between periods. I can't put my finger on it, but it was really cool."

When the Blues exited their dressing room and headed to the ice, fans were close enough that they could pat the players on the back.

"Out the chute, yeah, that was fun," said Michael Shanahan Sr., who attended games as a fan before buying the club in 1986. "I'd go down and do that some times—rev them up a little bit."

Shanahan didn't purchase the Arena because Ornest sold that to the city. While Shanahan wasn't financially invested in the building, however, the St. Louis native was emotionally invested.

"The intimacy was just terrific," Shanahan said. "I could sit in my box and talk to guys in the loge seats. 'Hey Mike, how are you doing? Hey, how are you doing?' It was kind of like a family thing there.

"One night, this man had a heart attack in the seats, and I ran over there. His name was Myron, and we always waved at each other. He died. One day his wife came to the box and said, 'My husband got these cufflinks from Sid Salomon way back when, and he wanted you to have them.' I wore them to most of the games, if not all. Then when I [sold the team] six or seven years later, I found her son and I gave them back to him. That's the Arena.... It was a family deal."

Despite a decaying appearance, sitting in obstructed-view seats was somehow not an issue for Blues fans elated to be at the game. The building was dirty, but it was clean. It smelled dingy, but it was distinctively home.

"Smoking was permitted back then, and it was pretty brutal at times, but it was part of the fabric of the Arena," Woodcock said.

The Arena wasn't built for the Blues, but the Blues wouldn't have been the same without it.

"It takes years and years to build character," Federko said. "The Arena had that character. It was really special. It was a fantastic place to play."

11 Sutter Wills Brothers and Blues

The Sutter name is synonymous with the NHL, especially in St. Louis.

Six of the seven Sutter brothers—Brian, Brent, Darryl, Duane, Rich, and Ron—all played in the league, and three of them were together in the Blues' organization. In the early 1990s, Brian was the head coach while twins Rich and Ron played for their older brother.

"Brian made the NHL first," Brent Sutter said. "That made us younger brothers think, 'If he made it, I can make it, too, and I'm going to be better than him.' It gave us some willpower."

If there is one characteristic that defined Brian Sutter in his career with the Blues, it was willpower. No. 11 stood not only on skates but on sheer determination. He was never projected to eclipse 40 goals in a season or 300 in his career, but hard work carried him past those totals.

"I don't have a bucketload of talent," Brian Sutter once said. "But if I tell myself I can knock somebody off the puck, I can."

The Blues selected Brian Sutter 13 spots behind Bernie Federko in the 1976 draft and assembled the "Kid Line." With the feistiness of the undersized Sutter, who weighed 180 lbs., and the skill of Federko, they were a perfect match.

"Brian was one of the ultimate competitors," Federko said. "There was no quit in Brian ever. He came to play. Whether he was feeling good or feeling bad, he put in the effort every night. He would go through the end wall. His desire to play the game was as good as it got. I think pound for pound, I don't know if there was anybody tougher. He was a great fit with me because he could get to the open spaces and I could find him. We were glued to the hip for years."

By his second full season, Sutter had netted a team-high 41 goals with the help of Federko's club-best 95 points. Meanwhile, Sutter led the Blues in penalty minutes each of his first three seasons in the NHL.

He was making a name for himself.

"Brian's first year in the league, he was saying, 'Mr. Affleck, Mr. Lefley, Mr. Unger, Mr. Whatever,'" former Blues defenseman Bruce Affleck said. "By the third year, it was '[Screw] you.' I mean, he took control. He wanted it to be his locker room. Not that he didn't respect you. But we got the real Brian Sutter."

In his fourth season with the Blues, the 23-year-old Sutter was named as the youngest captain in franchise history. It was not a difficult decision, said Barclay Plager, who previously wore the C and was now coach of the Blues.

"When you look for a captain, you look for somebody who is a hard worker and wants to win," Plager said. "Sutter works hard

Head coach Brian Sutter (center), Paul MacLean (15), and Brett Hull (16)
raise their arms in victory after defeating the Toronto Maple Leafs in St. Louis
on Thursday, April 12, 1990. St. Louis eliminated the Leafs to advance in the
playoffs. (AP Photo)

from the opening whistle until the game is over. The players respect
a guy who gives it everything he's got."

In 1982–83, the player nicknamed "Sudsy" had a career-high
46 goals and 254 penalty minutes, including 20 fighting majors. By
the end of the 1983–84 season, he had combined for 136 fights.

"He dropped his gloves with anybody, I don't care who it was,"
Federko said. "He didn't back down from anybody. If he had to
change the flow of the game, he would do it. If someone looked at
him wrong, he dropped his gloves."

When Brian arrived in the NHL, he received advice on fighting from Plager.

"It isn't as important to be a good fighter as for opponents to recognize that you're a willing fighter," Sutter said.

Opponents knew that Sutter was physical.

"Being in the same division as the Blues, we play them so often that I don't even have to turn around to see who's banging me into the boards or whacking at me in front of the net. I know it's Brian Sutter," Chicago defenseman Doug Wilson said. "I don't even know how many times I've felt like taking a two-hander at him. But every hit he gives you is an honest hit."

Unfortunately, Sutter's style led to injuries, and many of them. He suffered cracked ribs, a cracked pelvis, and a broken collarbone, but no injury was more serious than a broken shoulder on January 16, 1986, following a clean check from Minnesota's Dino Ciccarelli.

"When the Doc came in and told me, I cried," Sutter said. "The biggest thing is you feel you're letting the other guys down and you feel you're taking money for nothing. Everybody says injuries are part of the game, but they're hard to accept."

Sutter missed 35 consecutive games with the shoulder injury, then he re-aggravated it in his first game back. He played 76 games and had 37 points in 1987–88, his final season, but he was never the same after that injury.

The Blues were looking to replace Jacques Martin and made an offer to Mike Keenan, but at the last moment Keenan chose Chicago. The team had also expressed interested in Scotty Bowman and University of North Dakota coach Gino Gasparini.

"[Blues President] Jack Quinn called me in the office and said, 'Brian can't play, so we'd like him to coach,'" Federko remembered. "Jack said, 'Go talk to him and talk him into coaching.' Brian was my best friend, so I did. I said, 'What guy is going to get the opportunity to go from being a player in this league to a head coach and make the same amount of money?'

"[Brian] was [ticked] that he couldn't play anymore, but he took the job. From that moment on, he went from player to coach immediately. He cut the ties. There was no friendship with the players anymore. His wife wasn't even allowed to ride with my wife to the games anymore. That was his style, and I understood it. Whether I liked it or not, it was out of my control."

At the conclusion of his 12-year career playing with the Blues, Sutter registered 303 goals and 636 points in 779 games, all second in the Blues' record books to Federko at the time. Sutter exited with the franchise record for career PIMs of 1,786, a mark that still stands today. But on June 20, 1988, Sutter's time with the Blues took a new turn when he became the 15th coach in team history.

"Brian Sutter is an unquestioned leader," Blues GM Ron Caron said then. "He'll take pride in his new job because he has a Blue Note tattooed to his heart."

Sutter, whose No. 11 was retired in December 1988, led the Blues to a franchise-record 47 regular-season victories in 1990–91 and advanced past the opening round of the playoffs in each of his first three years. He also surpassed Scott Bowman in franchise coaching wins (153) and had the highest points percentage in club history (.545).

After the Blues suffered a first-round playoff loss to Chicago in 1992, however, Sutter was fired after 16 seasons with the team as a player and coach. He learned of the team's decision from his children, Shaun and Abigail, who saw the announcement on the TV news.

"It's not what happened, it's how it was handled," Sutter said. "Is that the right way to handle things? I've been here long enough that you expect the people you respect to talk to you directly, and when that doesn't happen, it hurts.

"No. 1, you want to continue in your job, but the last thing you want to do is leave the organization. I loved being part of the St. Louis Blues."

12 St. Louis Apollos

In 1967, after the NHL had played 24 seasons with the Original Six teams, the league was ready to double its size. There was fear of another league swiping up players, and more clubs could lead to a larger television contract.

St. Louis didn't initially put a formal bid on the table, but the Wirtz family, who owned the Chicago Blackhawks and the St. Louis Arena, held out its support for a franchise here. They wanted to sell the building to a local group, which could then use it to house its new hockey team.

Sid Salomon Jr., who was 55 years old at the time and had made a fortune in the insurance business, had inquired about being part of a prospective ownership group. At the urging of his son, 28-year-old Sid Salomon III, the father-son duo decided to post a $10,000 non-refundable application and bid for an expansion team themselves.

"He started thinking about it three or four years ago," Salomon Jr. said of his son, "and he finally got me interested in the project a couple of months back. At first I hoped some other group in St. Louis would take the lead and we could go in as minority owners. But no other group stepped forward, so we began looking into the matter more carefully.

"Our studies showed that it was a reasonable business proposition and [it was] also indicated that television revenues undoubtedly would pick up, so we formed our syndicate and made our bid."

On April 6, 1966, moments before making their presentation to the NHL's Board of Governors at the Plaza Hotel in New York City, the Salomons were said to be brainstorming ideas for the name of their unborn franchise. The St. Louis Apollos and Mercurys were under legitimate consideration.

The two space references were popular ideas at the time because McDonnell Douglas, an aerospace manufacturer and defense contractor, had been founded about that time and was headquartered in St. Louis.

"In the mid-1960s, the space race was on and McDonnell Douglas was at the center of that," said Jim Woodcock, a lifelong Blues fan and sports business executive who served in the Blues' front office for eight seasons. "The talk at the time was [to] do something that brings prestige to St. Louis and what we do here as a community, and those names were being bandied about."

Imagine history if legendary broadcaster Dan Kelly had described, "A pass from Bernie Federko to Brian Sutter, Sutter scores for the Mercurys!" Or how about Ken Wilson bellowing, "Oh baby, a hat trick for the Apollos' Brett Hull!"

Those names never saw the light of day, however. Shortly before the presentation, Salomon Jr. blurted out, "The name of the team has to be the Blues!"

It stuck.

"The name struck me as a natural," he said. "And when we announced the name [in the meeting], we got a tremendous reaction."

The origin of Salomon's idea was W.C. Handy, one of America's most influential songwriters who was considered the "Father of the Blues." In the early 1900s, Handy had spent some time in the Gateway to the West, where he produced the popular song, "Saint Louis Blues."

"It's part of the city where W.C. Handy composed his famed song while thinking of his girl one morning," Salomon said. "No matter where you go in town, there's singing. That's the spirit of St. Louis."

Salomon's attorney, Jim Cullen, recommended against naming the hockey club the Blues, expecting a lawsuit from the heirs of Handy, who died in 1958. But on the verge of acquiring a team and setting out to sell season tickets, the thought was that a negative reaction might not be the worst thing.

"I told [Cullen], 'That's the best publicity we could possible get," Salomon Jr. told reporters. "So, from now on, we're the St. Louis Blues. Sort of symbolic of the city."

The NHL didn't require its prospective teams to bring a nickname to the table in New York, but the Salomons figured it couldn't hurt. What helped more perhaps is that in addition to the $2 million for the expansion franchise, the family agreed to pay $4 million for the Arena. When the Salomons did that, the Blues were one of six teams added to the league, along with Los Angeles, Oakland, Minnesota, Pittsburgh, and Philadelphia.

"Both my son and I are elated, and all of our associates are happy," Salomon Jr. said. "We feel the Board of Governors has been extremely cooperative in this matter, and the governors have offered us all their help getting off the ground."

The next item on the agenda for the Salomons was designing a logo for the Blues. The younger Salomon quickly came up with the idea of a "flying" musical note for the crest. The Blue Note was born and immediately adopted by the inaugural roster, which was littered with many ex-Montreal players.

"The Blue Note was never ever to be stepped on, touched, or hit the floor," defenseman Bob Plager said. "The old timers from Montreal were the most steeped-in-tradition guys you could ever play with. The only time the emblem was ever touched was if players walked by and tapped it with their stick."

NHL Expansion

In 1967, the NHL doubled its size, adding six new franchises through expansion. It marked the first change to the league since 1942, when the Brooklyn Americans folded.

The Original Six Teams (date joined the NHL)
1. Boston Bruins (1924)
2. Chicago Blackhawks (1926)
3. Detroit Red Wings (1926)
4. Montreal Canadiens (1917)***
5. New York Rangers (1926)
6. Toronto Maple Leafs (1917)

The Expansion Teams of 1967
1. California Seals*
2. Los Angeles Kings
3. Minnesota North Stars**
4. Philadelphia Flyers
5. Pittsburgh Penguins
6. St. Louis Blues

Relocated to Cleveland, Ohio, as the Cleveland Barons in 1976 before merging with the Minnesota North Stars in 1978.
**Relocated to Dallas, Texas, as the Dallas Stars in 1993.*
***Founded in 1909.*

Plager remembers, however, one night during the 1967–68 season when the Blue Note did hit the team's locker-room floor. As you might assume, there were repercussions.

"That was Dickie Moore [who played 12 seasons with the Canadiens], and it happened in Oakland," Plager said. "Dickie was sitting there, and one of our younger players threw [the Blue Note] right by us on the floor. I knew something was going to happen, and in no time flat, Dickie Moore was choking him right against the wall. That was your life, the crest. That's what you played for."

The design of the Blues' jersey has been altered throughout the club's existence, but the crest has remained virtually identical and still stands today as one of the most cherished features of the franchise.

"The Blue Note is distinctly St. Louis and unmistakably the Blues," Woodcock said. "It represents tradition, [it] connects generations of Blues fans, and it's one of those rare team marks that I believe is respected and viewed positively even by rival fans. It's definitely fair to say there is no symbol like it in sports, or anywhere."

13 Inception of the Blues

The Salomons had their franchise. Now came the part of putting a competitive club on the ice.

The Blues hired general manager Lynn Patrick and assistant Scotty Bowman, whose options for building the club's roster were limited.

The top hockey players in the world at that time were under contract with the Original Six, so it was difficult for teams such as the Blues to get on an even playing field right away. The league kick-started the process with an expansion draft, in which the newcomers would take 20 players—two goalies and 18 skaters—off the rosters of the established clubs. However, the existing teams were able to put one goalie and 11 skaters on a "protected list," making them unavailable.

"Take Detroit, for example," Patrick said. "They took 45 professional players to camp. If they have to give up 20 of them in the expansion draft, that will leave them with only 25 for their big club, to stock their farm clubs, and have some available for recall.

Obviously clubs like Detroit are keeping every proven pro they can to hold the manpower at a high enough level to withstand the impact of the expansion draft."

"So I want the best players available, regardless of age. I want to put the best club on the ice I can."

The NHL held the expansion draft on June 6, 1967, in the ballroom of the Queen Elizabeth Hotel in Montreal, Quebec, Canada.

The Blues had the sixth pick in each round, and as Patrick had indicated, their selections did not reflect age. They took goalie Glenn Hall, 35, with their first-round pick and added defenseman Al Arbour, 34, with their fifth-round pick. The team had to talk each player out of retirement to come to St. Louis, and both men were major contributors in the early years.

In the 15th round, the Blues took Ron Stewart, 34, whom they later traded to New York to get Barclay Plager, 26. Terry Crisp, 24, who was taken in the eighth round, had been playing in the minor leagues.

"The biggest thing was you got a chance to play in the NHL," Crisp said. "There are only six teams and so many guys are buried in the minors [who] never had a chance to get up…. You couldn't crack the good ole boys.

"You wanted to prove you belong in the league, and everybody was in the same boat. We were a brand new expansion team, brand new city. It's like getting your first new bicycle. You take it out and you want to be on it all the time."

In their inaugural season, the Blues finished 27–31–16, which was good for third place in their division. In those days, the Original Six played in the East Division, and the expansion teams played in the West. Then the winners of the divisional playoffs met in the Stanley Cup final. So one expansion club, regardless if they couldn't beat the sixth-place team in the East, was guaranteed to advance to the championship.

Larry Keenan Nets First Goal

Now matter how long the Blues' organization exists, forward Larry Keenan can rest assured that he'll remain in the record books.

On October 11, 1967, just 3 minutes 22 seconds into the team's inaugural NHL game against Minnesota, Keenan netted the first goal in franchise history.

"It's something that will always be there. [It] can't be broken," said Keenan, who was invited back to St. Louis in 2010 on the anniversary of the goal. "I think it's just great that my family sees this."

There's no debating whether Keenan was the player who pulled the trigger on the goal, but like a fish story, the tale has grown over the years, and it's difficult to determine who's telling the whopper.

Bob Plager, another original Blue, assisted on the goal and has claimed in recent years that without a terrific setup, Keenan wouldn't be in the record books.

"We've got different versions of it," Keenan said. "I tell people that I went end-to-end, and he tells people that he made the play or I wouldn't have scored. Probably both of us are lying, but he did get the assist."

The Blues settled for a 2–2 tie with the North Stars. Keenan finished the season with 12 goals and 20 points in 40 games in the 1967–68 season. He played parts of four seasons with the club before leaving during the 1970–71 campaign.

Keenan said that the historic puck rests on his mantle at home in North Bay, Ontario, Canada.

"One of my kids will get it," he said. "They get everything else."

Keenan didn't come out empty-handed. He still wears a St. Louis Blues ring that was given to him and his teammates by former owner Sid Salomon.

"I've never tried it, but [the ring] was supposed to be a lifetime pass to every Blues' [home] game," Keenan said.

Even if it works, the piece of jewelry doesn't quite have the ring of "First Goal in Franchise History."

In the playoffs, the Blues beat Philadelphia in the first round and Minnesota in the second round, registering a monumental victory in Game 7 against the North Stars on Ron Schock's double-OT game-winning goal to send them to the Stanley Cup final.

"The fact was that somebody was going to win the West, but after a very slow start, we got our act together," said Bowman, who took over the coaching duties from Patrick after 16 games. "We were in the expansion draft to get a pretty good nucleus of defensemen, and we were fortunate to get a goalie like Glenn Hall."

In their first bid to win a Cup, the Blues faced the Montreal Canadiens, who had already won 14 of their NHL-best 24 titles. The Habs swept the Blues in four games, but all four were decided by one goal, and two were won in overtime.

"We forced them into playing their best," Hall said. "They wouldn't have won a mediocre game against us. They won them [all], but they were all close and they were good games. We played with emotion…. We really, really played well."

In 1968–69, the Blues swept Philadelphia and L.A. to make it back to the final, where the Blues met Montreal and were swept again. In 1969–70, the team won back-to-back six-game series over Minnesota and Pittsburgh for the right to face Boston, which handed the Blues their third consecutive sweep on Bobby Orr's memorable overtime goal.

Although the Blues were 0–12 in three consecutive appearances in the finals, the memories of the team's introduction into the NHL were positive.

"It was great," Crisp said. "Who would've expected that? We knew it was the West vs. the East, but what it took to get there and to be there for the hoopla…. You can't buy that experience. We were the best of a very poor [expansion] lot, but at least we were the best in the West. I think our organization did a fine job putting together the team it did. Our guys tried hard, as hard as they could. They wouldn't quit. It's not their fault we weren't good enough."

The success of those early clubs, Hall has claimed, laid a solid foundation for St. Louis' foray into the NHL and legitimized the league's decision to expand.

"I've always said, if the Blues hadn't represented that division as well," he said, "I don't think expansion would have been nearly as successful."

14 Wick

There was no escaping the obvious question when the Blues acquired center Doug Wickenheiser on December 21, 1983.

In 1980, Ron Caron was the director of player personnel for the Montreal Canadiens. He cast his vote in favor of drafting Wickenheiser with the No. 1 overall pick, ahead of defenseman David Babych or perhaps the more popular pick, French-Canadian center Denis Savard.

Caron wasn't alone in his front-office support of Wickenheiser. However, when the former Regina Pats star failed to live up to expectations in a couple of short years, the club executive was shown the door in the summer of 1983.

Caron quickly resurfaced as the GM in St. Louis. And when he sent Perry Turnbull to the Canadiens in exchange for Wickenheiser, Greg Paslawski, and Gilbert Delorme, Caron's intentions seemed transparent.

"I didn't get Wickenheiser because I want to prove that I was right," Caron insisted. "How he'll play, I don't know. But he'll be given every chance.... We're releasing the handcuffs."

Caron's comment was a reference to Wickenheiser's opportunities, which had been limited in Montreal. The Canadiens had a rich history of winning, and perhaps due to that, they also had a reputation of bringing along young players rather slowly.

"Wick" had the credentials to be an NHL star one day. In 1979–80, he led the Western Hockey League with 89 goals and 170 points, steering Regina to the Memorial Cup. The WHL named Wickenheiser its MVP, and the league selected him as a first-team All-Star. *The Hockey News* and *Central Scouting* both ranked Wickenheiser as the top available player in the draft.

"If Doug isn't the top selection, it's because the club doesn't need a forward badly enough," said longtime NHL coach and GM Bryan Murray, who coached Wickenheiser with the Pats.

Wickenheiser offered size up the middle at 6'1" and 195 lbs. Babych was clearly the best defenseman in the draft, standing 6'2" and weighing 200-plus lbs., and Savard rounded out the consensus top three.

"I know the Canadiens wanted a big center and I'm only 5'9" 157, but I'm going to prove to Montreal next year that I'm a better player than Wickenheiser," Savard said.

It didn't take long for Savard to have that chance.

Montreal took Wickenheiser No. 1, Babych went No. 2 to Winnipeg, and Savard went No. 3 to Chicago. The Canadiens and Blackhawks met on opening night of the 1980–81 season, a game that was televised nationally on *Hockey Night in Canada*.

Savard had a goal and an assist and was named the game's first star in Chicago's 5–4 win over Montreal. Wickenheiser, who at the start of training camp was handed No. 25, worn previously by Hall of Famer Jacques Lemaire, was a healthy scratch for the game.

"It definitely didn't help, not playing that first game," Wickenheiser admitted. "But the whole year was tough. Different things added up and had a bad effect on my confidence."

Wickenheiser played in 41 of Montreal's 82 games as a rookie, recording seven goals and 15 points. Savard posted 28 goals and 75 points in his first year with the Blackhawks.

"Denis had a great start to his career, and Wick was thrown into the fire in Montreal," Blues Hall of Famer Bernie Federko said. "He never got a chance because he was so under the microscope. Playing under that pressure, not being from Quebec, and having Denis Savard do so well in Chicago—I think it really affected his career."

In Wickenheiser's sophomore season in Montreal, he was switched to left wing, and he dealt with more injuries. He managed 12 goals and 35 points in just 56 games, while Savard climbed the ladder in Chicago, finishing sixth in the NHL scoring race with 119 points.

Longtime Montreal defensive star Larry Robinson acknowledged that Canadiens coach Claude Ruel, who wanted the team to take Savard in the draft, did not like Wickenheiser.

"Ruel didn't think he was a quality NHL player or a decent No. 1 pick," said Robinson, who questioned that Ruel's use of Wickenheiser might have been "a way to protest the team not picking Denis Savard."

By year three, Wickenheiser began to play better, but Montreal, which had won four Stanley Cups from 1975–79, failed to win the Cup for the fourth straight season in 1982–83. A change was needed.

First Caron became a Blue. Then Wickenheiser followed.

"Ron really loved him," Federko remembers. "[Wickenheiser] came to us, and it was a second chance."

That's the way Wickenheiser—still only 22—saw it, as well.

"Because of all the things that have gone on the last couple of years, there's always been a monkey on my back," he said. "In St. Louis, it'll be a lot different atmosphere. Now I can go out, be myself, and play relaxed, and maybe play the way I did in junior. Now I won't have to worry about making a mistake every time I step on the ice."

Arriving in December, Wickenheiser closed out the 1983–84 season with 28 points in 46 games. In 1984–85, he began to hit

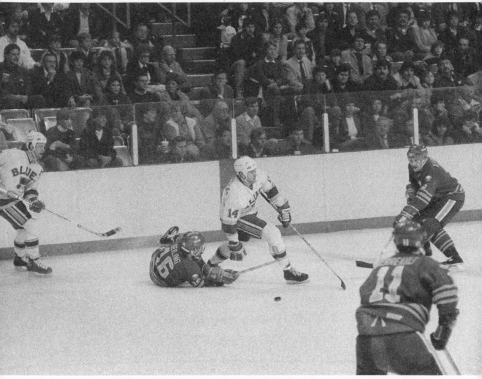

Center Doug Wickenheiser (14) skates around Buffalo Sabres winger Ric Seiling (16) while chasing the puck during the first period of a game in St. Louis on February 28, 1985. (AP Photo/Oscar Waters)

his stride with 23 goals, including two hat tricks, and 43 points through the first 68 games.

"Doug Wickenheiser was on the verge of being a star in this league," Blues coach Jacques Demers said.

But on March 13, 1985, it all came crashing down.

Several Blues players were in Eureka, Missouri, on a "snipe hunt," which was a code name for a plan to scare the daylights out of a couple unsuspecting teammates. A truck carrying the teammates pulled off the street, and Wickenheiser attempted to jump in the back. He lost his balance and stepped backward into the path of an oncoming car. The driver was a 17-year-old boy, and he was traveling about 10–15 mph.

"It could have happened to anybody," captain Brian Sutter said. "Everybody was there together. It wasn't that everybody was drunk or anything like that, because nobody was. The driver was going the normal speed. We're just thankful that [Wickenheiser's] not half-dead with two broken legs."

Wickenheiser tore two knee ligaments, requiring four hours of reconstructive surgery. The recovery time was estimated at nine to 12 months.

After five months, Wickenheiser said, "It's starting to look like a knee again."

He returned for the final 36 games of the 1985–86 regular season, but following the injury, "Wick was never really the same after that," Federko said.

Perhaps Wickenheiser was never the same, but because of his goal on May 12, 1986, Blues' hockey was never the same, either. In the conference finals against Calgary, trailing the series three games to two and Game 6 by the score of 5–2, the Blues rallied for an improbable 6–5 victory in overtime, with Wickenheiser netting the clincher.

Wickenheiser played one more season in St. Louis. He scored his 100th career goal with the club on March 27, 1987, but it would be his last as a Blue. Later that year, Wickenheiser was claimed in the NHL waiver draft, bouncing around the globe while wrapping up his career and eventually retiring.

In August 1994, Doug and his wife, Dianne, became parents of twin girls, Rachel and Kaitlyn.

Four days later, Wickenheiser underwent surgery to remove a malignant cyst on his wrist. In 1997, after ushering in daughter Carly, Wickenheiser was diagnosed with a tumor in his right lung. Then in 1998, his doctors discovered cancerous lesions on his brain. Wick underwent chemotherapy treatment at Barnes-Jewish Hospital in St. Louis and kept his spirits alive.

"Oh yeah, I'll always be optimistic," he said.

But on January 12, 1999, the Blues family went into mourning when Wickenheiser lost his life at age 37.

"You never expect something like that to happen," Federko said. "Why did something like that have to happen? He had so many rotten things happen to him. After starting out as the No. 1 pick, everything was like a black cloud. It was really disheartening to see something like that because Wick loved to have fun. He was always so full of life."

15 The Roots of the Blues' Community Efforts

Doug Wickenheiser's longtime friend, Dennis Hennessy, remembers when Wick's cancer returned.

"A lot of us didn't know it, but the prognosis wasn't good at all…. He never shared that," Hennessy said.

In the late 1990s, Wickenheiser was referred to an oncologist in New York, where he would receive a radical chemotherapy.

Wickenheiser and his wife, Dianne, were scheduled to fly to New York on Friday every fourth week. Doug would undergo treatment on Saturday, then the couple would return to St. Louis on Sunday.

"That's really how the 14 Fund got started. The alumni wanted to help him," Hennessy said. "I'll never forget, my phone rang in my office one day and it was Dianne and she was just in tears."

It was Thursday and the Wickenheisers were supposed to fly to New York the following day for the second round of treatment. But because of Doug's ongoing medical issues, he fell within Missouri's pool of uninsurables and the claim for the chemotherapy had been denied, Dianne said.

"Care provided outside the state of Missouri was not insured," Hennessey said. "I called the doctor's office [in New York] and said, 'What do I need to do for Doug to be able to come up tomorrow?' She said we need to know there's going to be payment. So I called Bruce Affleck.

"I had a short window. It was 1:00 pm and the doctor's office needed to know by 4:00. I told Bruce, 'If we can't get this covered by the insurance company, could [you] send the hospital something guaranteeing that the Blues will pay for the costs for Doug, [like] $5,000, $10,000?' He said, 'Absolutely.'" So Hennessy called the doctor's office again to see what they specifically needed.

"They wanted something on company letterhead that the [Blues would] guarantee they'll make the payment. So I called Bruce back and he whipped up something on Blues' letterhead. He faxed it to me and I faxed it to New York, and Doug and Dianne were able to go up there."

Prior to his untimely passing in 1999, Wickenheiser was aware of the groundswell of support that he received from his Blues family and the hockey community. Early in 1998, the organization unveiled the 14 Fund, dubbed that because Wickenheiser wore No. 14 for the Blues.

"Obviously it's a great thing they are doing," Wickenheiser said. "I'm flattered that they would put my number on it."

Former Blues executive Jim Woodcock developed the logo for the 14 Fund—a candlewick with the No. 14 above the flame. The fund was jump-started with identical donations of $5,000 each by the Blues alumni and Pizza World.

"This will be our charitable trust, just like the Cardinals Care for the baseball team," Woodcock said. "We'll have to get a board and organize it and all of that. But we wanted to name it in honor of Wick and his spirit."

Doug Wickenheiser Night was set for March 14—the No. 14 being key in the planning—and as Wick made his way to center ice for the pregame ceremonial puck-drop, the crowd at the Arena exploded.

"I don't know how to describe it," Wickenheiser said. "The support from people all over the country and all over Canada, it just makes you feel real good. To know that people who don't even know you personally take the time to send cards and prayers, it's almost overwhelming."

About three dozen ex-teammates and friends stayed after the Blues' matinee game to play in an alumni game. Along with a dinner and auction, they raised an additional $100,000 for the 14 Fund—money that continued to help offset the family's medical expenses.

Former Blues chairman Michael Shanahan made a donation of $10,000, and franchise icon Brett Hull quietly donated the proceeds from selling pieces of his personal memorabilia collection.

"Mike Shanahan was very supportive. He wanted to be a big part of it, making the donation to really get it going," Blues Hall of Famer Bernie Federko said.

When Wickenheiser passed away in January 1999, the Blues raised a banner with the 14 Fund logo to the rafters at what was then called the Kiel Center. In addition, the NHL held its All-Star Game there a few days later, and players wore the 14 Fund decal on their helmets.

Wickenheiser's memory remains lit in St. Louis. The 14 Fund underwent a name change several years ago, being placed under the "Blues for Kids" umbrella, but continues to contribute annually to the community. It impacts programs and services that "improve health and wellness of youth," much the way it began with Wickenheiser.

"The 14 Fund was originally started to help the Wickenheiser family," said Randy Girsch, the Blues' director of community relations and the fund. "You can't walk past any player who hasn't heard what type of guy or teammate Doug was. It's inspiring to everyone, and that's why they are always willing to help [keep] the foundation growing."

Blues for Kids has raised $5 million through team-sanctioned events such as an annual golf tournament in which current players participate, along with alumni greats such as Hull and Wayne Gretzky. They also sponsor a St. Louis Blues Casino Night, where fans can interact with the team.

"He was a tremendous person," Hull said of Wickenheiser. "It's not only for Doug Wickenheiser, but it's for a lot of people in the community, and when you can help people in need, that's what the St. Louis Blues and St. Louis are all about."

The board of trustees for Blues for Kids includes Tom Stillman, Bruce Affleck, Mike Caruso, Bruce Rubin, Phil Siddle, Scott McCuaig, Dennis Hennessy, Jim Woodcock, Chris Zimmerman, and Steve Chapman.

16 A Hull of an Era

In 1986–87, when Bob Plager headed up north to scout amateur players that the Blues might one day draft, general manager Ron Caron would make sure that Plager stopped in Moncton, New Brunswick, the home of the Calgary Flames' top affiliate.

"Ron would say, 'Let's see Moncton's schedule…. Oh boy, they're playing three games. I want you to watch that Hull,'" Plager said. "Ron was in love with Brett Hull when he was drafted by

Calgary. He'd say, 'Oh Brett Hull, Oh Brett Hull. This guy is a goal scorer.'

"But Brett was already under contract [to Calgary], so you wonder why you're going there—a trade?"

Few knew much about Hull, other than he was the son of Hall of Famer Bobby Hull and he was putting up big numbers in Moncton. Even fewer knew that Caron was attempting to acquire the potential sniper.

Calgary was in the midst of contending for a Stanley Cup, and Caron realized the Flames needed a goalie and a defenseman to have a legitimate shot. So Plager continued to monitor Hull and his shot.

"I phoned Ron one day, and he said, 'How was Brett?'" Plager remembered. "I said, 'Ron, he'll drive you crazy. He was out there one time, he never came back [to the defensive end]. He broke a stick one time and just looked at his stick. He's a coach killer.'

"Ron said, 'Well, how did he do?' I said, 'Oh, he's good. He got three goals and one assist, but he'll drive you crazy.' He said, 'I don't care if he drives me crazy if he gets me three goals and one assist.'"

Driving Calgary crazy was the fact that in 1987, their rivals in Alberta, the Edmonton Oilers, won another Stanley Cup. That was good news for Caron, who knew that after watching the Oilers hoist the Cup again, the Flames' interest in Blues goalie Rick Wamsley and defenseman Rob Ramage might heat up.

"Ron said, 'Now I'm going to get my guy,'" Plager said. "I said, 'What do you mean?' He said, 'Calgary and Edmonton hate each other. I've got the two players they need to win. I have their two players. They know it.'

"But Calgary was being ho-hum. They didn't want to make the trade because they knew Brett Hull was a pretty good hockey player. So it went back and forth. [The trade] was going to get made and then it wasn't going to get made."

In 1987, Cliff Fletcher was the Calgary general manager and Terry Crisp, who coached Hull in Moncton, had been promoted to the Flames' bench. They were part of internal meetings that discussed the trade proposal.

"There were seven of us in the room, and we all knew that Brett Hull was a goal scorer," Crisp said. "We knew full well what he was capable of. I think somebody in the room said, 'You know we're

Brett Hull takes control of the puck as the Toronto Maple Leafs Dave Ellett battles to steal it from Hull in first period action between the Blues and the Maple Leafs on November 27, 1990, in St. Louis. (AP Photo/ Mark Butkus)

trading a 40-goal scorer?' But we felt at the given time that we were close to what we wanted to accomplish.

"We all discussed it and I think the [vote] went 6–1 to trade Brett, to get the pieces we needed to win the Stanley Cup. The funny thing is today, all seven guys in the room claim that they were the one who voted to keep him. Brett Hull became one of the greatest goal scorers, one of the greatest players, in the game."

On March 7, 1988, the Blues traded Ramage and Wamsley to Calgary for Hull and Steve Bozek, a swap that was immediately seen as a lopsided deal—in the Flames' favor.

"Caron must have a job lined up in Calgary," joked Edmonton general manager Glen Sather. "It's a helluva deal for the Flames."

Indeed, Calgary had acquired two proven players, and a year later, the Flames' thinking was justified when the club won the organization's first Stanley Cup. A decade later, while the Blues hadn't hoisted the Cup with Hull, his presence had created the most entertaining era of hockey ever seen in St. Louis.

In 11 seasons, Hull scored a franchise-record 527 goals, including 27 hat tricks, in 744 regular-season games. An underrated passer, he produced 409 assists for a total of 936 points, second only to Bernie Federko in team history in those two departments. Hull was better than a point-per-game player in the playoffs with 67 goals and 117 points in 102 postseason games.

"When I came, I knew I was at home the minute I stepped on this ice," Hull once said. "Ron Caron, 'The Professor,' we all know and love.... He saw my potential when a lot of people didn't."

Two weeks after the trade, still reconciling the deal in Calgary, Fletcher told reporters, "It wouldn't surprise me if [Hull] scored 190 goals over the next four years."

Fletcher was wrong. Over the next four-plus seasons, including the end of 1987–88, Hull netted 275 goals in 322 regular-season games and another 40 goals in 51 playoff games. His first four full seasons witnessed goal totals of 41, 72, 86, and 70, respectively.

Hull's 86 goals still stand as the third-most in a single season in NHL history. Only Wayne Gretzky amassed more in a year, with 92 goals in 1981–82 and 87 in 1983–84.

"[Playing with] Hullie was like playing with Babe Ruth," said former Blues teammate Brendan Shanahan. "It was like having Babe Ruth in the prime of his career. He was funny, he was brash. He would do things and say things that you thought couldn't be said and then…he would just sort of call his shots."

Kelly Chase, another former teammate and close friend, remembered one night against Los Angeles when Hull did, in fact, call his shot. The Kings had scored in the third period, tying the Blues 3–3, and the time left in regulation was dwindling.

"Brian [Sutter] wanted to get us into OT and he didn't want Brett on the ice because he didn't trust his defense," Chase said. "He put out Richie Sutter and Dave Lowry. Hullie jumps over the boards and goes right out on the ice. He's standing at right wing and Brian is yelling at him to come off and he ain't coming off.

"Don Koharski is reffing the game and he said, 'One of you guys needs to get off the ice,' and Brett—I can't repeat what he said—but he told Richie Sutter to get off the ice. Richie said, 'Brian wants you off.' But Brian realized Brett wasn't coming off the ice, so Richie came to the bench."

Play continued and Blues goalie Vincent Riendeau turned aside a flurry of L.A. shots, and then with 26 seconds remaining in regulation, Hull found the back of the net.

"The [Kings] defenseman couldn't make a decision how to stay with Brett, and he just ripped the puck over [goalie Mario Gosselin's] right shoulder and scored," Chase said. "[Brett] didn't even let the guys congratulate him. He literally made a U-turn, came right back to the bench, stopped, looked at Brian and said, 'Yeah, like we're playing overtime in L.A.'

"He just decided that the game was going to be over. He probably had something to do afterward, like go hang out with Gretzky."

Hull sent the teams to the showers in the regular season with 70 game-winning goals, another one of his team records, which was 25 more than second-place Pavol Demitra.

"When I see Brett Hull in my mind, I see a late-minute situation in a game where you need a goal and Brett's out there at the

Brett Hull in the NHL

Hull's NHL Records
741 career goals (ranked fourth in NHL history)
86 goals in one season (1990–91; third highest single-season total)
One of five NHL players to score 50 goals in 50 games (1990–91)
Led the NHL in goals (1989–90, 1990–91, 1991–92)

Hull's Awards
First Team All-Star (1989–90, 1990–91, 1991–92)
All-Star Game (1989, 1990, 1992, 1993, 1994, 1996, 1997, 2001)
Lady Byng Memorial Trophy (1989–90)
Hart Memorial Trophy (1990–91)
Lester B. Pearson Award (1990–91)

St. Louis Blues Records Held by Hull
Regular season:
Games played: 744 (4th)
Goals: 527 (1st)
Assists: 409 (2nd)
Points: 936 (2nd)
Hat Tricks: 27 (1st)
Game-Winning Goals: 70 (1st)
Power Play Goals: 195 (1st)
Short-Handed Goals: 18 (2nd)
Shots on Goal: 3,367 (1st)

Playoffs:
Games: 102 (1st)
Goals: 67 (1st)
Assists: 50 (2nd)
Points: 117 (1st)

faceoff, on the rim of the circle, and somehow he comes up with this unbelievable goal to give you a victory," said former Blues play-by-play voice Ken Wilson. "With all due respect to Brett, and I certainly have respect for what he accomplished, there were so many games where he wasn't very visible. And then you get down 2–1 with three minutes to go and you knew Brett was going to score.

"The headline is 'Hull scores two in the Blues' overtime victory,' and you say to yourself the next day this guy was the star of the game [but he] didn't do much the first 56 minutes. But that's the kind of ability he had, and he did that a lot of times. He could just turn it on. 'We need a goal? Okay, I'll get you a goal.'"

After the 1988–89 season, in which Hull broke out with 41 goals, he had a famous end-of-the-year meeting with Sutter. Hull admitted that he expected to be praised by the head coach. Instead, Sutter implored Hull to make himself better.

"Brian Sutter, he made me realize and reach the potential… that 'The Professor' saw," Hull would say years later when the Blues were retiring his No. 16 sweater. "Without that meeting, I'm not sure that I would be standing here today."

Even though Sutter believed that Hull possessed more inside him, the Blues coach and former club captain admitted to being like everyone else in that he didn't know what was coming next.

"You never knew what you were going to get, or what you were going to hear, or what you were going to see," Sutter said. "Over the next 11 years, the NHL watched along with all of his teammates in total awe. You never knew how good he could be, and what he did was absolutely unbelievable."

Hull couldn't go anywhere without a mob scene ensuing.

"You didn't see many fans standing outside after the game looking for autographs in the pre–Brett Hull days, and then you had lines of them," former Blues chairman Michael Shanahan Sr.

said. "When the team went on the road, we had to smuggle Brett on the plane."

But many nights Hull would stay until he signed every last autograph.

Bruce Affleck, who doubled as the Blues' salesman and broadcaster, remembered, "Brett's clothes would have marks all over them because of the markers he was using."

Hull would continue to leave his mark on the Blues, but not all of it was on the ice. He was as colorful off the ice as anyone who ever played the game. From his criticism of the NHL's ruling on Scott Stevens to his daily bickering with ex-Blues coach Mike Keenan, Hull said what he wanted, when he wanted.

"What's funny is that I had come from New Jersey where it was very Lou Lamoriello, from no one player is bigger than the team to a team where one player [Hull] was bigger than the team," Brendan Shanahan said. "I used to say to him, 'Hullie, you can't say that,' and he would say, 'Yes, I can.'

"It was just so entertaining to go to the rink every day, whether it was practice or a game. He was pure entertainment, with his mouth and with his skill. I remember not playing with him anymore and thinking, *This is not as much fun.*"

In 1994 the Blues moved into a new building. Originally called the Kiel Center, it has often been referred to as "The House that Hull built," and for good reason. His popularity had pushed a group of local businessmen who called themselves the Kiel Center Partners to purchase the Blues in 1991 on the premise of constructing a downtown arena.

"Maybe I'm biased because I'm good friends with [Hull], but I don't think the St. Louis Blues franchise, or this building, would be here today had he not been traded to the Blues," said Gretzky, who briefly became teammates with Hull in 1995–96. "He's one of the best, best people that I've ever met in my life, as far as his enthusiasm and his love for the game. I always told him I don't know if I

71

knew a guy who knew more about the game than Brett Hull. He truly knows a lot about the sport, loves the sport, loves the game."

But by the late 1990s, Hull had become a polarizing figure in St. Louis. Despite all of his heroics, there were some who believed that the team couldn't win a Stanley Cup with him.

Hull became a free agent in the summer of 1998, and after general manager Larry Pleau declined to give Hull a no-trade clause, Pleau decided to part ways with No. 16.

"Hullie called me and said, 'You know what, they don't want me back,'" Chase recalled. "I said, 'No, no. They just want you to take less money.' He said, 'No, I accepted what they offered, and they didn't want me.' It hurt him.'"

Pleau called it a "tough decision."

"I always thought Brett was the best goal scorer I had ever seen in the NHL," Pleau said. "But I think, like we all do sometimes, we wear out our welcome. When I went in there and met with Hullie and his agent, it just didn't look like anything was going to get worked out. Sometimes it's better for everybody to move on. It was time for a culture change, and unfortunately I had to be the one to do it."

Hull signed with Dallas, and in 1999 he scored the game-winning goal in triple overtime of Game 6 to clinch the Stanley Cup, the first of his career. Three years later he went to Detroit where Shanahan, Steve Yzerman, and Nicklas Lidstrom each deferred $1 million in salary so that the Red Wings could sign Hull, allowing Hull to add another Cup.

"He proved the naysayers wrong," said former Blue Peter Stastny. "I was in St. Louis a couple of seasons with [Hull], and a lot of people were saying that he would never win. And it was the best answer when he went out and won two Stanley Cups. He did so much for the Blues, more than anybody else, single-handedly. He's the No. 1 player the Blues have, No. 1 face."

Hull's days in St. Louis were a magical time in Blues' history. How else do you explain a player scoring three goals in the first period, which Hull did on April 16, 1995, for a hat trick on Hat Day at the Arena? Fans appropriately littered the ice with their souvenirs.

"There were so many moments," Caron said. "The fans were also expecting some magic every time he would get in the zone to shoot the puck. Every time I saw him play, he excited me."

Teammates got excited, too.

"You had to focus…. Sometimes it was hard to believe what he was doing," Chase said. "When someone asked us what time it was, Garth [Butcher] would say, 'It's the time of your life. Don't miss it.'"

Hull, who was inducted into the Hockey Hall of Fame in 2009, wasn't able to truly appreciate it all until after his career.

"We never really took any time—or at least I didn't—to soak anything in," Hull said. "I just lived by the seat of my pants. It was just one big never-ending circle of fun."

17 Picard Takes Break in Enemy Territory

Blues defenseman Noel Picard was winded, and he had reason to be after helping teammate Bobby Plager kill off the majority of a two-minute penalty. What happened when Picard finally went to the bench to rest, however, is an embarrassing moment that will have a long shelf life.

The game was played on November 5, 1970, and the Blues were visiting the Boston Bruins.

"In Boston, you were killing penalties against Bobby Orr and [Phil] Esposito and [Ken] Hodge," Plager said. "We were killing a penalty that night. They had the puck and I think they had it in our end for the whole two minutes, passing it around, taking shots, hitting the goal posts. Our bench was at the other end, so we couldn't get off the ice."

The puck went to the corner of the ice where Picard fell on it, leading to a merciful stoppage in play.

"I couldn't even move, or get my breath. Noel, same thing," Plager said. "Finally, the refs blow the whistle and we get the line change. I go to the bench and I'm bent over. In the meantime, Noel gets up and skates toward the Boston bench."

In today's NHL, the team benches are uniformly on the same side of the ice. But in those days, many of the rinks, including the Boston Garden, had benches on opposite sides. The Bruins' penalty box was on the same side of the rink as their bench.

"I'm going, 'Ah [shoot], did they give Noel a penalty for falling on the puck? Did he really get a penalty for falling on the puck?'" Plager said.

Nope, Picard didn't receive a penalty. Instead, it appeared that the defenseman might have been injured and was heading to the Blues' locker room, which could only be accessed by going through the Boston bench.

"I'm going, 'Oh, he got hurt. He's going to our dressing room,'" Plager said.

But when Boston trainer Frosty Forrestal opened the door to his team's bench, Picard didn't continue on to the dressing room for stitches or ice. He plopped down on the pine and took a seat, attempting to catch his breath.

By that time, Bruins players had caught on to what was happening and, hardly able to contain their laughter, they scooted down the bench to make room for Picard.

"We're all looking, and all the Boston players move down," Plager said. "Noel, because his head is down, hasn't looked up. The whole building in Boston is laughing. Noel finally looks up."

Picard saw that everyone on the bench is wearing a different jersey than him and said, "Can you believe this? What am I going to do now?"

Picard was a rugged defenseman who would have been a welcome addition to the Boston lineup, and at least one Bruins player was telling Picard to stay put.

"Gerry Cheevers was saying, 'We'll make a trade. We'll send a player over to their bench,'" Plager said.

On the opposite side of the rink, Blues coach Scotty Bowman was none too pleased, so Picard acted quickly. When the puck went into the Bruins' zone, he made a mad dash 85' across the ice to rejoin his teammates.

"He jumped over the boards on the Boston bench and skated all the way to our bench," Plager said.

An alert referee, who caught Picard trying to cover up his mishap, blew his whistle. The Blues were flagged for having too many men on the ice, sending them back on the penalty kill.

The Blues skated to a 4–4 tie with Boston that night. But a few nights later in Pittsburgh, the Blues got the idea that few were going to forget the blooper any time soon.

"We're doing the warmups, we're getting ready to start the game," Plager said, "and the players in Pittsburgh put up a big sign that read, 'Noel Picard, This is Your Bench.'"

18 "Meat on the Burner"

Brett Hull once proclaimed that Ron Caron was "the most passionate St. Louis Blues fan" that would ever grace the Earth.

Caron, the flamboyant Blues general manager who had two stints with the club (1983–94) and (1996–97), was perhaps best known for his acquisition of Hull from the Calgary Flames in 1988.

"Ron kept saying, 'I'm going to get my guy, I'm going to get my guy,'" former Blue Bob Plager remembered.

Caron did get his guy, and his hunch on Hull proved to be accurate. The right winger went on to score a franchise-record 527 goals with the Blues, becoming an organizational icon. But "The Professor"—as Caron was called because of his uncanny memory—was known for more than orchestrating the most profitable trade in club history.

There was so much involved in the caricature of Caron. His animated and emotional personality, witnessed by many during his frequent pressbox tirades, made Caron a wildly popular figure in St. Louis.

A few months after Caron was fired by Montreal in 1983, former Blues owner Harry Ornest hired Caron. During his time in Montreal, Caron was part of six Stanley Cups as the director of scouting and player personnel.

"Ron Caron is a winner," Ornest said. "He knows how to win, and he knows what it takes to win. This is a proud day for the St. Louis Blues."

For three seasons under Ornest, Caron turned dimes into dollars. He hired Jacques Demers as coach and acquired Doug Wickenheiser, Greg Paslawski, Rick Meagher, and Rick Wamsley in trades.

The Blues had their first winning record in four years during Caron's second season (1984–85), and the Blues won the Norris Division.

In 1986, despite being forced to deal Joe Mullen because Ornest wouldn't pony up the necessary money, Caron's club came within a whisker of playing in the Stanley Cup final. However, after a dramatic win over Calgary in Game 6 of the conference final— also known as the Monday Night Miracle—the Blues lost Game 7.

"When Ron came here, he hired Jacques to coach and my brother Barclay was the assistant," Plager said. "We had Ted Hampson as a head scout. We had a trainer and we had Susie Mathieu doing public relations. That was our whole staff. You had to get rid of your top players every year because they were making too much money and Harry Ornest wasn't going to pay them. When you consider the budgets we had, the things he went through…. Ron Caron did an amazing job."

A group led by Mike Shanahan bought the Blues in 1986, and with the trade for Hull in 1988, it was a new era for both Caron and the club. With a new centerpiece in place and more payroll flexibility, there was more "meat on the burner," a phrase he often used in reference to trades.

Caron acquired Adam Oates and Jeff Brown. Then he signed Scott Stevens to a four-year, $5 million deal, handing over five first-round draft picks to Washington in return.

"Not too many people in the game have accepted the risk of mortgaging the future," Caron said. "We are criticized for not raising our own vegetables, but those days are gone. You can't wait. To me, this is the new formula for success."

Going more than two decades without a Stanley Cup, Blues fans were hungry. With Hull and Oates piling up goals and Stevens standing up opponents on the blue line, the club was as close as ever to a Cup in the early 1990s. But then Caron seemed to outsmart himself in a devastating trade with Vancouver.

In March 1991, despite having the best record in the NHL, Caron dealt Geoff Courtnall, Sergio Momesso, Cliff Ronning, and Robert Dirk to the Canucks for Garth Butcher and Dan Quinn. That year the Blues lost in the second round of the playoffs.

That off-season, Caron signed New Jersey free agent Brendan Shanahan, and in a controversial arbitration ruling, Stevens was awarded to the Devils as compensation.

"[Caron] was kind of miscast here a little bit," former Blues chairman Mike Shanahan said. "We were in a position where we had to win now to keep the fans coming. We couldn't afford to take years to build a winner. I think if [Caron] would have been in a position to build something from the ground up, that's where he would have been an especially successful guy."

Whatever the stakes, Caron was never at a loss for emotion.

During the Blues' first-round playoff series against Detroit in 1991, he was fined $10,000 for nearly getting into a fight with Red Wings third-string goalie Glen Hanlon. Detroit's Bob Probert had slashed Garth Butcher and jabbed Vincent Riendeau. Probert did receive a double-minor penalty, but Butcher also got two minutes for roughing.

Caron was irate, charging out of his private box and voicing his disgust with Probert. Caron came into contact with Hanlon, who took exception to Caron's raving and yanked the GM's tie before the two were separated.

"I get it all out," Caron once said.

Even one of his own players experienced the fiery side of Caron.

"On New Year's Eve [1993], we played in Winnipeg," Brendan Shanahan remembered. "Caron and I were great with each other except after losses. We were down by a goal in the third period and [a Jets player] had given Garth Butcher a cheap shot. I came over and retaliated and got a penalty, and Winnipeg scored the clinching

Blues GMs

Lynn Patrick	1967–68
Scotty Bowman	1968–71
Lynn Patrick	1971–72
Sid Abel	1972–73
Charles Catto	1973–74
Gerry Ehman	1974–75
Denis Ball	1975–76
Emile Francis	1976–83
Ron Caron	1983–94
Mike Keenan	1994–96
Ron Caron	1996–97
Larry Pleau	1997–2010
Doug Armstrong	2010–present

goal on the power play. I had taken an undisciplined, poorly timed penalty that cost us the game."

On more than one occasion, Caron had warned Shanahan about staying disciplined.

"He'd always say, 'Well, you're Irish and you Irish can't control yourself,'" Shanahan said. "I was only 22–23 years old thinking, *I don't think he's supposed to say this to me.* So we're in the locker room after that game against Winnipeg and it's real quiet. We haven't even taken our jerseys off yet, and Caron came busting in the room and he was red [and] angry.

"He's looking around the room, and I know he's looking for me. And then he finally sees me and he goes, 'You.' and I said, 'What?' And he said, 'You [expletive] Irish.' He didn't even get the sentence out and I jumped from my chair and lunged at him. Garth Butcher and Kevin Miller tackled me and I was lying on the floor with them on top of me. I remember the rest of the night the guys were kidding around that I had played my last night with the Blues."

After a day off for the club, Caron was waiting for Shanahan to arrive at the front door of the Arena.

"He put his arm around me and said he never should have said that about the Irish," Shanahan said. "He said he loved the Irish and he was wrong, but he hates losing as much as me and he apologized. I just loved the man."

In 1994 when Mike Keenan was hired, Caron took a backseat with the Blues, calling himself the "consultant who was never consulted."

Caron returned to the GM chair in 1996 after Iron Mike was terminated. When asked how he felt at age 67, Caron replied, "Good. I've been resting for 2½ years."

But this time Caron's tenure was brief. He helped find his successor, Larry Pleau, a guy Caron had signed as a player in Montreal in the late 1960s.

In 2012, following an extended illness, Caron died while living in Montreal. The timing of the Professor's passing didn't go unnoticed, as the Blues were making a rare appearance in Montreal the following night.

"I can definitely say—and I mean this in only a most special and kind way—that the good Lord broke the mold when he made Caron," former Blues captain Brian Sutter said. "And when he did, the Big Guy upstairs said, 'We're never going to do that again.' Ron Caron was a very special man."

19 Blues-Blackhawks Rivalry

The memory of Chicago goaltender Ed Belfour slashing his stick on the crossbar and right post before storming off the ice at The Arena is an image that may never be forgotten by Blues fans.

On April 25, 1993, Craig Janney intercepted a clearing attempt by the Blackhawks and flung the puck into a wide-open net. While returning to the crease, Belfour had collided with Brett Hull. After arguing that he was interfered with, to no avail, Belfour took out his frustration on the net and later a coffee machine and an electric fan.

Janney's goal—scored 10 minutes, 43 seconds into over-time—propelled the underdog Blues to a 4–3 victory in Game 4 of the Norris Division semifinals and completed a clean sweep of Chicago. A crowd of 18,012 fans declined to leave their seats until they were completely hoarse.

"What a great feeling," Janney said afterward. "It's hard to describe. We're all pumped up. The fans are pumped up."

If you're a fan of the Blues, it's imperative to loathe the Blackhawks. It's been that way since day one with the club's chief opponent just 300 miles northeast in the Windy City. Whether it's due to proximity, historically hostile arenas, or the compilation of continuous events, it's a rivalry that has few equals in professional sports.

"When we came here [in 1967], it was already in place as far as a city rivalry," former Blues defenseman Bob Plager said. "We got caught up in it. [We didn't want to] disappoint our fans, [so] we'd get pumped up and play as hard as we could against Chicago. They were always hard-hitting, hard-fought games."

A franchise series—which began with a 5–2 Blackhawks win over the Blues on November 12, 1967—has witnessed its share of competitive hockey in the 300-plus meetings since 1967. But we've always been reminded of the existence of the affair because of the signature scenes, such as the Belfour postgame fit, Brent Johnson's NHL-record three consecutive playoff shutouts in 2002, and six Sutter brothers squaring off, three per side, in 1991.

"I don't know if it's because of the closeness [of the cities] or what, but Chicago–St. Louis was the toughest, grittiest of any of them," ex-Chicago forward Jeremy Roenick said. "It was a war, especially in the old buildings. Those buildings had their own character, their own smell, their own sounds. I could close my eyes and hear that organ play in St. Louis, and I knew where I was."

Every good show needs a big stage, and the Blues and Blackhawks had two of the best in the Arena and Chicago Stadium. Each built in 1929, they had age wrinkles that made them unique, but neither one needed a hearing aid to gather the sound.

"In the old buildings, it seemed like everybody was on top of each other," former Blues enforcer Tony Twist said. "You had hard-drinking, cigarette-smoking fans who wanted to see how loud and obnoxious things could get."

An unfriendly exchange on the ice only intensified the crowd, and with ruffians like Twist and Kelly Chase and Chicago's Bob Probert, there was always potential for that.

"If they start losing control out there, we'll have problems," Officer Arnold Miller, who had been working games at the Arena for 10 years, once told the local newspaper.

Former Arena superintendent Fred Corsi would sometimes hire 10 extra policemen and add more ushers for the tilts between the Blackhawks and the Blues in St. Louis.

"These are always the toughest games," Corsi said in 1990. "When the Blues and the Blackhawks play, the atmosphere is always pretty intense, but Saturday night games are the most intense. Because it's the weekend, a lot of Blackhawk fans travel from Chicago on Friday. That means they could drink Friday night and get juiced all day Saturday."

The majority of the Blackhawks fans were seated by the south end of the rink, and many eyes were glued there, including those of the players.

"We couldn't compete with the number of fights that occurred in the stands," former Blue Brendan Shanahan said. "The police had a room down by our locker room. After the game we would stop by there and get the stories from them. We'd say, 'You saw all of our fights, but tell us how yours all went.' We'd sit around and have a beer and listen to their stories."

The story was similar in Chicago.

"The atmosphere was something, sometimes scary," former Blues center Bernie Federko said. "The one memory that stands out about any particular game is the time at Chicago Stadium when they were throwing Heineken bottles at Mike Liut."

But Shanahan said that he enjoyed playing in Chicago.

"I loved that feeling of being a little bit sick to your stomach with fear," he said. "It brought out the best in you. If I could have played every game against them, I would have been up for that. It was so much fun."

The Blues-Blackhawks' rivalry, however, has endured its down days.

Beginning in the 1990s, the league switch from the Norris Division to the Central Division limited the number of times the Midwest teams played each other. The NHL also went away from scheduling home-and-home series, so when the clubs played a back-to-back set on December 9–10, 2000, it was their first since April 3-4, 1993. And following the Blues' playoff sweep in 1993, they did not see the 'Hawks in the postseason again until 2002.

Meanwhile, the Blues and Chicago had moved into new arenas—the Kiel Center and United Center, respectively—and things just weren't the same in these new homes.

"It's like if you get into an alley fight, and there's people hanging out windows overhead, and people lining the sidewalks watching, there is a lot more intensity," said the Blues' Adam Creighton, also an ex-Blackhawk. "If you have the same fight in the middle of Caesars Palace, it's not the same."

The home-ice advantage seemed obsolete as the Blues went 0–5–1 in their first six home games against Chicago before finally winning at Kiel Center in 1997.

But in between, showing the signs of a true rivalry, there were moments when the Blues continued to push the Blackhawks' buttons.

On February 9, 1995, club president Jack Quinn flew in Wayne Messmer, Chicago's famed national-anthem singer before he was unceremoniously dumped by the 'Hawks, to belt out the pregame tune in St. Louis. The stunt failed, though, as the Blues were dumped 5–0.

Although he had been traded to Hartford six months earlier, Shanahan rammed Chicago defenseman Chris Chelios into the boards on January 20, 1996—at the NHL All-Star Game.

"When you see that Blackhawks helmet, you can't help yourself," Shanahan said. "He and I had a special thing going the last four years."

The last four decades, the Blues and Blackhawks have had that "special thing" and the players have all played their parts. But in the end, the annual meetings between the clubs come back to the energy in the building.

"I always think of it as a rivalry because the fans think of it as a rivalry," former Blue Brett Hull said. "They're the ones who create the excitement."

20 Courtnall Calls His Shot

You've heard of Babe Ruth famously calling his shot in the 1932 World Series, blasting a ball into the center-field bleachers at Wrigley Field just seconds after pointing in that direction.

Well, the Blues' Geoff Courtnall isn't as famous as the Babe, and he may never admit to calling his shot, but in 1998 he changed the course of the Western Conference quarterfinals against the Los Angeles Kings.

The Blues were leading L.A. two games to none, but they weren't in total control of the series, falling behind the Kings 3–0 in Game 3. In the Blues' locker room during the second intermission, Courtnall told teammates that if he had a chance to take a shot at opposing goalie Jamie Storr, he wouldn't pass it up.

"We didn't look like we were in a very good spot in the second period, but I know the dressing room was very positive," said Blues forward Terry Yake, Courtnall's former teammate. "There were some things said that I will leave in the dressing room, but they indicated we were going to make a comeback. I've got to say that everything played out almost as perfectly as it could possibly play out."

A first-round pick participating in his first playoff series, Storr was having what he felt was a perfect game to that point, and he acknowledged that L.A. was fortunate to be holding a three-goal lead against the more talented Blues.

"When you're lining up against Al MacInnis, Grant Fuhr, Pierre Turgeon, and Geoff Courtnall—we were honored to be on the ice with those guys," Storr said. "When you talk about that series, they had such a good team and something would have had to give for us to be in that series. In that game, we had actually taken advantage of a couple of mishaps, found a couple of goals on Grant Fuhr. And I remember vividly, it was almost like that was my night. But looking back, that's the greatest thing about sports—you don't know what's going to happen."

Courtnall did.

With less than 12 minutes left for the Blues to mount a comeback, the right winger chased a puck behind the Kings' net. Storr went to stop the puck, leaving it for defenseman Sean O'Donnell.

In different fashion than the Babe, Courtnall sized up his shot.

"You realize the guy is on you, but you don't think he's going to hit you," Storr said. "It's almost a little bit of a blindside. You step out and all of a sudden, he's right on you. To be honest with you, it's blatant why it would happen. There was an urgency to change the momentum. Do you just let the last 10 minutes of the game run out and just accept losing 3–0? Or do you try and make something happen?"

The hit alone didn't even up the score, but the retaliation from O'Donnell, jumping on top of Courtnall and pummeling him, earned the Kings defenseman a five-minute major, putting the Blues on an extended power play.

"The [referees] obviously treated things differently back then," Yake remembered. "If you jumped on a guy and just started beating him, and the guy didn't fight back, one guy got five and the other guys didn't. Courts took enough punches that they gave [O'Donnell] a five-minute major and we didn't get anything."

Oh, the Blues got something.

In a span of 3 minutes, 7 seconds, they netted four power-play goals, rallying for a 4–3 victory to take a commanding 3–0 lead in a series that they soon swept.

Pascal Rheaume trimmed the Blues' deficit to 3–1 with 10:01 left in regulation. Brett Hull made it 3–2 with 8:57 to play. With 8:01 remaining, Pierre Turgeon tied it 3–3, beautifully deflecting a shot by Al MacInnis for MacInnis' second assist in the spree.

"We just kept the pressure on," MacInnis said. "It's just one of those things where they kind of lost their composure and you kind of sniff those things out."

At that point, it wasn't a question of which team would win the game. It became which Blue would score the game-winner.

With 6:54 to play in regulation, Storr gloved a shot by Blues defenseman Steve Duchesne, but the puck somehow popped out. Yake was standing on the doorstep.

"Kid in a candy store," Yake said. "That was about as easy a goal as I had in my NHL career, but it was probably as rewarding as any one I've ever scored in my life."

Storr, who had stayed in Game 3 but did not play in Game 4 because of the effects of the Courtnall hit, couldn't believe his eyes.

"It was one of those moments where it was like, 'Did this really happen?'" Storr said.

Courtnall has yet to publicly acknowledge his intentions, only saying that he was playing aggressively, as one should in the postseason.

"That's the whole idea in the playoffs—antagonize and create a problem for teams and get them to lose their concentration…[and] that's exactly what happened," Courtnall said. "I was going in full speed for the puck, and he stepped out a bit. It wasn't one of those things where I thought, *Okay, I'm going to be able to hit this guy and take him out of the game.* But that's sort of what happened."

Teammates who played in the game, however, have confirmed Courtnall's plan, which he told them before the start of the third period. Either way, Storr insisted that he doesn't blame the Blue.

"I don't think he set out for me," Storr said. "If I was standing in my net, I probably wouldn't have been touched. I just think it arose at the right time and it happened. That's why there's no anger toward it. If they were up 3–0 and I was Geoff Courtnall, I wouldn't regret doing anything. I don't think he should. It was part of the game. It's just a play that happened."

Storr may not have been playing the blame game, but Courtnall's brother, Russ, who was playing for the Kings that night, sure was. After the players showered and changed, Russ and Geoff passed each other while leaving the arena.

"It was the old [L.A.] Forum and the Kings, to get out, always had to walk by the visitors' dressing room and up the stairs after the game," MacInnis remembered. "Courts and I were leaving, and Russ walked by and called him [an expletive] and kept going. It wasn't a brotherly exchange by any means."

Geoff vividly recalled the exchange.

"Russ said to me, 'That's [expletive] brutal.' I said, 'You don't teach that.'"

While the footage of Ruth's home run is somewhat grainy and his intentions weren't quite clear, there's no mistaking Courtnall's shot.

"The funny part is that my [10-year-old] son tried to look up his old man on YouTube, looking for some saves, and the first thing that pops up is the hit," Storr said. "He was like, 'Oooh, you didn't do too good in that one.'"

The incident may not register with all NHL fans, but fans in the two cities don't need the Internet as a reminder.

"It was one of the most interesting incidents that I've seen in my career," MacInnis said. "Whether it's Blues fans or Kings fans, that's certainly one of the instances that's etched in everyone's memory, without a doubt."

21 Original Captain

An original Blue selected in the NHL expansion draft, Al Arbour was also the original captain of the franchise.

At 35 years old, Arbour was a veteran of 395 games in the league. The Blues gave Arbour the "C" prior to their inaugural season in 1967, while Ron Stewart, Jimmy Roberts, and Noel Picard were chosen as alternate captains.

"I was honored to be the captain of the team, no question about it," Arbour said. "I had been around a long time. I knew what to do."

One of Arbour's first acts as captain might have been the jump the expansion Blues needed as they tried to successfully break into the NHL.

After recording the organization's first victory, a 4–2 win at Pittsburgh on October 14, 1967, the Blues were 12–20–3 at the end of December. The inauspicious start included a seven-game losing streak.

The players were off on New Year's Eve, so Al and his wife, Claire, planned a party.

"We hardly knew each other," Claire Arbour said. "With Al being the captain, he had the whole team come to our little house in Florissant. We had a team party and that's where we all kind of met each other, and they never looked back after that. I remember the headlines at the time: 'The Blues Sink Lower in the Basement.' After that, you could just see [that] they were meshing together. They did extremely well."

Arbour had already won Stanley Cups as a player—with Detroit, Chicago, and Toronto—making him one of only 10 players in league history to win the Cup with three clubs. That pedigree is what drew the Blues to the defenseman in the expansion draft, plucking him from the Maple Leafs with their fifth pick.

"I drafted him not only as an outstanding defenseman but also as a team captain," said former Blues general manager and head coach Lynn Patrick. "I told Scotty [Bowman] when I picked him that Al was going to be our captain. He was that kind of guy."

Like goaltender Glenn Hall, Arbour was on the verge of retirement.

"I really wanted to quit, but Lynn kept after me," Arbour said. "He kept telling me just to come to St. Louis and look things over.

Blues Captains

Al Arbour	1967–70
Garry Unger	1970–72
Frank St. Marseille	1970–72
Bob Plager	1970–72
Barclay Plager	1970–76
Jimmy Roberts	1971–72
Red Berenson	1970–71, 1977–78
Garry Unger	1976-77
Barry Gibbs	1978–79
Brian Sutter	1979–88
Bernie Federko	1988–89
Rich Meagher	1989–90
Scott Stevens	1990–91
Garth Butcher	1991–92
Brett Hull	1992–95
Shayne Corson	1995–96
Wayne Gretzky	1996
Chris Pronger	1997–2002
Al MacInnis	2002–04
Dallas Drake	2005–07
Eric Brewer	2008–11
David Backes	2011–16
Alex Pietrangelo	2016–present

So two weeks after the season started, I came. It was the best thing that ever happened to me."

Arbour added 231 NHL games to his career total of 626, and he wasn't just going through the motions with the Blues. The last player to wear glasses on the ice, Arbour was named to the West Division's starting lineup for the NHL All-Star Game in back-to-back seasons.

"He was never out of position," former Blues defenseman Barclay Plager said. "I like to think that's one thing I learned from him. You have to play your position. He was such an inspiration to everyone on the team. How could you not go out there and give it everything you had when you looked over at this guy who seemed to have to struggle just to skate, wearing glasses, going down to block shots?"

Arbour said he had more than 300 stitches in his career, and he had pucks hit his frames but never his lenses.

"I never got one square in the eye," he said. "Once when I was wearing steel rims, I got hit and the puck drove a piece of the frame into my eye. That's when I started looking around for plastic that wouldn't break."

After three seasons with the Blues, and three failed trips to the Stanley Cup final, Arbour was ready to retire with the Blues. Bowman wanted to concentrate on his GM duties, so he talked Arbour into moving behind the bench.

"We selected Al as coach for the same reason we selected him as a player three years ago," Bowman said. "He has a lot of leadership qualities. I think Al's main problem will be replacing himself as a player. No. 3 was a pretty valuable man."

At first some people wondered if Arbour could be tough enough as a coach.

"Arbour not tough?" Bowman responded. "You don't know him. He may not seem it, but he's tough under the skin. As a player, he had the ability to dig deeper when he had to, to make himself go harder when he was hurting or when the team needed it. That's toughness. And because he was that kind of player, the guys who are playing for him now will have to give 100 percent. They know what he expects of them because they know what he demanded of himself."

Arbour coached the Blues in the team's first 50 games of the 1970–71 season, but ownership wanted Bowman to return to the bench. And as Bowman had already predicted, the team missed Arbour on the blue line so he laced up his skates for 28 more games. Once the Blues bowed out in the first round against Minnesota, however, Arbour retired as a player for good.

Bowman wanted Arbour to be re-installed as the head coach for the 1971–72 season, but the club turned to Sid Abel instead. When Abel and Bill McCreary didn't work out, Arbour returned to the Blues' bench one more time.

"When I took over again, the team wasn't as close as the Blues club I played for," Arbour said. "The important thing was to stress upon them that if they were going to do anything, they had to do it together."

The Blues advanced to the second round of the playoffs in 1972 but fell to Boston in a sweep. Thirteen games into the following season, the club replaced Arbour with Jean-Guy Talbot, continuing the game of musical chairs.

Of course, Arbour went on to the New York Islanders, with whom he won four straight Stanley Cups (1980–83). He was the second-winningest coach in NHL history (782) before being passed by Joel Quenneville and Ken Hitchcock. But Al and Claire retained fond memories of their time with the Blues.

"I enjoyed St. Louis very much," Arbour said. "They were great people. It didn't turn out right, but still it was a good team. I enjoyed my stay there. It was our favorite spot."

22 Patrick Gone Too Soon

The first employee of the Blues' organization, Lynn Patrick, was lost in an automobile accident while returning home after a game.

A member of the prestigious Patrick family, he attended the Blues' 4–4 tie with the Colorado Rockies on January 26, 1980. Then, while driving on a side street near the Checkerdome, he had a heart attack that caused him to hit a fire hydrant.

Patrick, who had left the game because he was feeling ill, was pronounced dead at nearby Deaconess Hospital. He was 67.

"It was really a shock," said Blues public relations director Susie Mathieu at the time. "I think it was kind of fitting that the last thing he did was see a hockey game."

Patrick, the son of famed former New York Rangers coach Lester Patrick, had witnessed hundreds of hockey games throughout his life. A left winger for the Rangers during his playing days, Lynn coached that club for one season before working in Boston as the Bruins' head coach and GM.

Patrick spent the 1965–66 season as the coach of the Western Hockey League's Los Angeles Blades, who were owned by L.A. Rams owner Dan Reeves. Reeves had indicated that Patrick would be his hockey man if the city was awarded an NHL team.

"I had gone to L.A. the year before because I knew expansion was coming and I was to be the coach and general manager of the new Los Angeles franchise," Patrick said.

Indeed, the NHL expanded to L.A. in 1967, but the league awarded the team to Jack Kent Cooke, not Reeves, leaving Patrick out of a potential job. That, however, didn't last long.

Sidney Salomon Jr., the new owner of the expansion Blues, asked Rangers owner Bill Jennings for his recommendation on who to hire in St. Louis. Jennings got input from Emile Francis, who later worked in St. Louis but at the time was the coach and GM of the Rangers, and Francis suggested Patrick.

On May 5, 1966, Patrick was hired by Salomon as the Blues' first head coach and GM.

"I in turn hired Scotty Bowman and Cliff Fletcher, and we were the only three employees until the draft the next year," he said.

Patrick had enjoyed only one winning record in five regular seasons in the NHL and was 22–48–2 as the coach of the L.A. Blades, but he said he looked forward to coaching the Blues.

"My record is so lousy the last six years that I'm beginning to wonder," he said. "I want to prove something to myself."

In the Blues' inaugural season, however, Patrick would stand behind the bench for only 16 games, going 4–10–2 before he decided to hand over the reins to Bowman.

"Lynn was a very good man," said former Blues defenseman Al Arbour, who played for Patrick on the original team. "He was very quiet. He had a lot of experience, a lot of hockey knowledge. But he didn't coach very long. He was too good a guy to coach. He had a hard time with discipline."

Patrick stayed on as GM in 1967–68 and remained a front office executive for 11 years with the club. He twice returned to the bench as the Blues' interim coach. He coached two games (1–0–1) during the 1974–75 season and eight more (3–5) in the 1975–76 season.

Patrick was 63 when he started his third stint as the Blues' coach. Leo Boivin, who would eventually replace Patrick, ran the practices because Patrick said he hadn't been on skates in eight years.

"And I'm not about to buy any, either," he said. "I don't want to be the permanent coach."

Patrick was a VP with the Blues until he was let go in 1977 because of what was labeled an economy crunch.

"I could see this coming," he said. "The team was short of money, and something had to be done. I know the situation, and I know it isn't good. I feel very fortunate to have enjoyed the 10 years I've had in the Blues organization."

Ironically, the person who connected the Blues and Patrick was the same person who notified Patrick of his dismissal. By then, Francis had left the Rangers and joined the Blues.

"I guess our paths have crossed a few times over the years, and now he's the one who told me I was *fini*," Patrick said. "Emile runs the whole thing now, and I think he does an excellent job of it. He's a one-man front office and there just isn't that much for me to do. I was getting ready to retire anyway."

Following his fatal accident, Patrick was inducted into the Hockey Hall of Fame posthumously in 1980. He had two sons, Craig and Glenn, who continued the family tradition by playing in the NHL.

"Just a great family," former Blues defenseman Bruce Affleck said. "[Patrick was] a guy you wanted to be around, a good guy. You could sit down and talk to him for hours about hockey and you'd never get tired of it."

23 Francis Revitalizes Franchise

Emile Francis had an extra incentive to revitalize the Blues after taking over as general manager and head coach on April 12, 1976.

Part of the deal that brought Francis to St. Louis after a 10-year run with the New York Rangers was an agreement with owner Sidney Salomon to make him a stockholder in the Missouri Arena Corp., the parent company of the Blues.

"As a shareholder, I'm fooling around not only with someone else's money, but my own," Francis said. "It's a secure arrangement, as far as I'm concerned, to involve my own money."

Francis, whose nickname was "The Cat," scratched and clawed for seven seasons like the Blues were his own personal investment.

When the Blues broke into the NHL as an expansion team in 1967, their preference was experienced players, and the success of guys such as Glenn Hall, Jacques Plante, and Doug Harvey proved to be key in three consecutive trips to the Stanley Cup final. But by the 1970s, the club's roster was aging and it needed an overhaul.

Six weeks after being hired, Francis turned his attention to the NHL draft. Three of his first five selections in the summer of 1976 were Bernie Federko (No. 7 overall), Brian Sutter (No. 20), and Mike Liut (No. 56). In 1978, Francis nabbed Wayne Babych (No. 3), and in 1979 he added Perry Turnbull (No. 2).

"[Francis] always said that you build through the draft, and his philosophy was you always draft the best player available," Federko said. "You don't draft by position. He said if you have too many of one thing, it's a good thing because you can make a deal to get what you want. He always had a plan, there's no question about that."

Also part of Francis' plan was taking over for Leo Boivin as head coach, making him the Blues' 10th coach in as many years. Francis inherited a club that had a record of 29–37–14 in 1975–76, but he quickly made his players forget about that.

"I told them that I'm starting fresh and they're starting fresh," Francis said. "I don't know what their standings with the organization were before I arrived and I don't care. They're all starting with clean slates."

Despite the clean slate and the new additions, though, the Blues would continue to take their lumps. They went 32–39–9 in Francis' first season, and he returned the coaching keys to Boivin before hiring Barclay Plager. But Plager's team went 18–50–12 in 1978–79 and started 7–14–3 in 1979–80, leading to Plager's resignation.

Just when it became uncertain which way the Blues were headed, Francis hired former Blues standout Red Berenson. Berenson seemed to be a natural fit behind the bench, as did the players Francis provided.

The Blues traded for right winger Blair Chapman, center Blake Dunlop, center Ralph Klassen, and defensemen Ed Kea, Rick Lapointe, Bryan Maxwell, and Joe Micheletti. By the end of the 1979–80 season, only six players who finished the previous year with the club were still on the roster. The team suddenly had 10 first-round picks in the lineup, and seven of them were acquired from other teams.

"When 'The Cat' started making all of those deals," Federko said, "that's when we knew we were going to be a heck of a hockey club."

It all came together in 1980–81.

The Blues posted a record of 45–18–17 for 107 points—a franchise record at the time—nearly equaling the point total of the two previous seasons combined (128). The club went from having the second-worst record in the NHL to having the second-best mark in the league in just two years.

Federko eclipsed the century mark for the first time in his career with 104 points, Liut broke his own franchise record with 33 victories, and Babych netted 54 goals, becoming the first 50-goal scorer for the Blues.

"The Blues are a young team; their future looks bright," said John Baird, a senior vice president with Ralston Purina, which had bought the Blues from the Salomons. "This is no accident. Emile Francis has executed the blueprint he drew up five years ago, and he is on schedule. He has shown himself to be one of the outstanding executives in professional hockey."

The Hockey News named Francis the NHL's Executive of the Year, and *The Sporting News* selected him as its GM of the Year.

What made Francis' dealings even more impressive is that he was operating on strict budgets, first under the Salomons and then under Ralston Purina. In fact, it was Francis who helped orchestrate that deal, as well, keeping the Blues in St. Louis in the late 1970s and making the 1980–81 season possible.

Shortly after Francis came aboard, the Salomons could no longer afford to run the club. The night before an NHL finance committee meeting, where the Blues' future was to be discussed, Francis found out that a prospective buyer had backed out. But at the meeting he fudged the truth to buy the Blues more time.

"I stood up and told everyone we had a prospective buyer and that I was sure everybody would work out," Francis said. "And I looked around that room and told everyone, 'Just because we're down right now, don't think we're not going to make it. The St. Louis Blues are going to be in the National Hockey League long after a lot of you are gone and forgotten.'"

Later, a chance encounter between Francis and Ralston Purina's Hal Dean led to the company's purchase of the Blues.

"For a guy of his stature, he exuded respect," Federko said. "He had that kind of fire in him. I've never met a man that I had more respect for. He knew hockey."

Unfortunately, the Blues couldn't sustain the success they created. In 1981–82, the team struggled, so Francis fired Berenson and returned to the bench himself. He stayed with the organization until 1983, but with the Blues again for sale, Francis was released from his contract and signed with Hartford as the team's president and GM.

So what became of Francis' stock in the Blues? Well, when Ralston Purina, a huge animal feed company headquartered in St. Louis, took control, they mandated that everyone turn in their stock.

"I've got a lifetime supply of dog and cat food," Francis quipped. "That's where my 10 percent went."

24 Federko Proves to Be Fabulous

On his third call-up to the NHL, Blues rookie Bernie Federko finally made his home-ice debut on February 5, 1977.

In a 6–5 win over the Buffalo Sabres, Federko had a hat-trick, sending the crowd at the Arena into a tizzy.

"It became a love affair with the Blues fans right off the bat there," Federko said.

It was a 13-year love affair in which Federko became the franchise leader in points, reaching the milestone on the day his second child was born. If not for an unexpected trade to Detroit, it would have had a storybook ending, too.

Bernard Allan Federko was a top NHL prospect in the 1976 draft. In his final season of junior hockey with the Saskatoon Blades, the center produced 72 goals and 187 points in 72 games. Despite those totals, Federko lasted until No. 7 in the draft, becoming the first selection by new Blues general manager Emile Francis.

"We were lucky as hell that Bernie was still there when we picked seventh," Francis said. "Detroit drafted a center [Fred Williams] from the same team that Bernie played on, and Oakland surprised everybody by drafting a guy [Bjorn Johansson] from Sweden. We had Bernie rated the No. 1 player in the draft but never thought we had a chance at getting him."

Motivated by the snub of the six teams, Federko flew to St. Louis, ready to prove he could play in the NHL. But with a broken bone in his foot, he came to training camp early, looking to learn more about the town he would call home.

"Growing up in Canada, we followed either the [Toronto Maple] Leafs or the [Montreal] Canadiens," Federko said. "I didn't have a clue where St. Louis was. It was a total change in my life. But within a month, just through training camp, I knew how special it was. Getting to meet the Plager boys, Bobby and Barclay. Barc took me under his wing right off the bat, and I think from that moment on, I knew that it was going to be special playing for the Blues."

But first Federko went to the minors, playing for Barclay Plager with the Kansas City Blues of the Central Hockey League. Federko led the club in goals (30) and points (69) and was named the CHL's Rookie of the Year. But it wasn't until his third call-up that he stuck with the Blues.

"Barc called us into his office," Federko remembers. "It was Brian [Sutter], Rick [Bourbonnais], and myself. He said, 'You're going up [to St. Louis], and you're going to play a regular shift. You guys are going to be part of the team now.'"

Federko's first hat trick, on February 5, was just the start of his success. Playing on the "Kid Line" with Sutter and Bourbonnais, Federko rang up three hat tricks in his first month in the NHL. In all, he had 14 goals and 23 points in 31 games with the Blues.

By Federko's third season in the NHL, with Barclay Plager now coaching the Blues, the center's career took off. Still playing on a line with Sutter but swapping Wayne Babych for Bourbonnais, Federko posted 31 goals and 95 points in 74 games despite playing on a team that finished 18–50–12.

"That's when I knew I could play in this league and do well," Federko said. "Brian got 40 and I got 95 points—and I missed the last five games of the season with a broken wrist, or I might have gotten 100 points."

In 1980–81, with Red Berenson coaching the Blues, Federko would eclipse the century mark with 104 points. He finished with 31 goals and 73 assists, ranking fourth in the NHL in assists.

"He could score a helluva lot more goals—50 for sure—if he weren't such a generous centerman," Berenson said. "He threads the needle with his passes."

Federko did score a career-high 41 goals in 1983–84, making Blues history with a goal against Chicago on December 13, 1983. As part of a two-point night, he became the franchise's all-time scoring leader with 577 points, surpassing Garry Unger who had 575 in 150 more games.

The record-breaking performance came just hours after Federko's wife, Bernadette, delivered the couple's second son, Dustin Patrick Federko.

"I tried to score a goal for the little one and Berna," he said. "It was a very exciting day on both fronts."

Federko finished with 107 points in 1983–84, also a personal best, and it was the start of three consecutive 100-point campaigns, all under Blues coach Jacques Demers.

"I know there are a lot of great centers in this league, but having seen Bernie Federko play all out every night for the last three seasons, I have to believe he belongs right there with the best," Demers said. "You know, I think I could go out there and score 20 goals playing on the wing with Bernie."

Well, one might not go that far, but Federko did thrive with anyone who was put on his line.

"I was always given the guy who was struggling, to try to get him out of a slump," he said. "Then I would get somebody else. That bothered a lot of guys, but that never bothered me. I thought that was a compliment. I didn't like to see anybody fail."

On March 19, 1988, Federko set up a teammate and reached another milestone. His assist on a goal by Mark Hunter made him the 22nd player in NHL history to reach 1,000 points. He was proud of the accomplishment, but Federko never got too caught up in his own personal statistics.

"Records are great, but the ultimate thing is trying to win a Cup," he said. "All the personal glory that I've had is not fulfilled because we don't have a Cup here. One has to go with the other."

Federko calls the Monday Night Miracle of 1986 his greatest achievement as a Blue because the club was one win away from the Stanley Cup final. He didn't have another chance to play for a Cup in St. Louis.

On June 15, 1989, the Blues traded Federko and Tony McKegney for Adam Oates and Paul MacLean.

Weeks earlier, Federko had learned of the Blues' desire to deal him. The team captain was cleaning out his locker after a playoff loss to Chicago when former general manager Ron Caron approached him and arranged a meeting for later in the week. Federko firmly believes that even when the meeting was set, Caron had planned to talk about an extension.

"Caron came to me and said, 'Bernie, we're going to talk about your contract,'" Federko said. "I said, 'I can come Friday but I have a golf tournament up by Alton [Illinois] at noon.' He said, 'Come here at 9:00 on Friday and we'll be done by 10.' I didn't have an agent at the time, but [Caron] knew what I wanted. We talked about it—one year and an option. Then I would be 35 and retire."

Federko showed up at Caron's office at 9:00 AM sharp.

"I was dressed in my golf attire," Federko recalled. "I walked in and Ron was sitting behind a desk and he said, 'Sit down.' I sat down. He said, 'Well Bernie, we had our meetings this week and we decided that you are no longer part of our plans.' I said, 'What?'"

Caron told Federko that he could decide his destination, but he should take the weekend to think about it.

"I remember Ron saying, 'Go home and have a great weekend,'" Federko said. "Oh yeah, I'm going to have a really great weekend."

Federko made a pit stop at home to deliver the news to his wife, but eventually he made his way to the golf tournament.

"I must have done two or three interviews at this golf tournament, and everything [the reporters] were saying was, 'Longtime Blue….will be here for the rest of his career…blah, blah, blah,'" Federko said. "I couldn't say a word. I bit my tongue. It was killing me that I couldn't say anything."

On Monday, Federko returned to Caron's office and before he could discuss his own preference of where to play next, the GM said, "We think we have a place for you, and I know you'd like it."

Federko knew it was Detroit. Demers was now coaching the Red Wings and coveted him. The Blues and Federko agreed on contract terms, which Detroit had required, and the deal was executed.

"It's extremely tough to part with people who've done so much for a franchise," Caron said. "But because we were below our objective in terms of achievement, the only way you can find new assets is to go to the top element and change. Changing the 17-rated player on a team isn't going to help much. We needed to do things faster, quicker, and different."

While in St. Louis, Federko played with more than 170 Blues players, went through eight coaching changes, four different ownerships, and nearly watched the team move to Saskatoon.

"I had a lot of great times here," Federko said at the time. "I've gone through a lot of ups and downs. You become such a part of the team you feel you're never going to leave. I have to feel lucky for being in one place so long. I feel I always gave 100 percent to the St. Louis Blues."

Federko lasted only one season with Detroit before retiring with exactly 1,000 games played in the NHL. More than two decades later, Federko remains the Blues' franchise leader in games played (927), assists (721), and points (1,073). He ranks No. 2 in goals (352) and hat tricks (11), as his records were later broken by Brett Hull.

25 From "Problem" to Playoff MVP

Believe it or not, there was a time when Ryan O'Reilly wondered whether he was the problem.

A second-round pick of Colorado in 2009, O'Reilly spent six seasons with the Avalanche before a trade to Buffalo in 2015. In three years with the Sabres, the club went 93–118–35 and didn't finish higher than 23rd in the NHL standings.

In 2017–18, Buffalo was last in the league with just 62 points, and during a locker room interview with the media, O'Reilly admitted there were times when he'd lost his passion for hockey.

"It's disappointing... sad," O'Reilly said. "I felt throughout the year I've lost the love of the game multiple times. You need to get back to it because it's just eating myself up."

After one of the best trades in Blues' history, O'Reilly redis-covered that zeal in St. Louis. From worst to first, the renewed commitment of the centerman led to an NHL All-Star selection, the Stanley Cup, the Conn Smythe Trophy as the playoff MVP, and the Selke Award as the league's best defensive forward.

"It's tough to describe," O'Reilly said moments after the Blues' 4–1 win over Boston in Game 7. "The Cup is the ultimate goal. You're just trying to go out and be a spark and be a difference maker. Looking at the names on this thing, most of these guys on here I pretended to be as a kid, and now to be here on that with them is just an incredible feeling. There's just so many people to thank."

The Blues had Buffalo to thank.

The club desperately needed help up the middle and heavily pursued O'Reilly, who was 27 at the time, coming off a 61-point season and entering the third season of a seven-year, $52.5 million contract.

Blues general manager Doug Armstrong was seen conversing with Buffalo GM Jason Botterill at the 2018 NHL Draft in Dallas.

"We were hoping to get it done at the draft," Armstrong said. "The draft is an area where you have assets. We had a first-round pick. We weren't able to get anything done there."

The club continued conversations with the Sabres leading up to the first day of free agency, July 1, but on that morning, the deal was dead.

Armstrong responded by signing free-agent center Tyler Bozak to a three-year, $15 million contract and David Perron to a four-year, $16 million deal, moves that might not have been made had the team acquired O'Reilly.

But later that day, somewhat surprisingly, Botterill re-engaged the Blues, and the two sides worked out a massive trade package: O'Reilly in exchange for a first-round pick in 2019, a second-round pick in 2021, Patrik Berglund, Vladimir Sobotka, and prospect Tage Thompson.

"It fell apart a little bit this morning and we went in a different direction and we were able to pick it up after that—add and subtract some pieces that made everyone comfortable in the end," Armstrong said. "We got it done tonight."

One important aspect of the deal is that O'Reilly's contract called for a $7.5 million signing bonus that night. The Blues were aware of that and knew they would be on the hook for it once everything was finalized.

"I'd like to give a lot of credit to the Blues' ownership group," Armstrong said. "When you have to go to a group and tell them about a $7.5 million signing bonus that is due and you get nothing but a quick 'You do what you have to do to make us a better team'… it's a great feeling."

The Blues were thrilled to have O'Reilly in the fold, and even more so after a phone call between he and Armstrong. The club released a video of that call on its social media accounts, which would later make O'Reilly look like a prophet.

"From knowing a bunch of guys on the team and looking at the roster, I was so amped up and I said, 'Let's go win a Cup,'" he recalled.

The O'Reilly era, though, didn't start off well for the Blues. Oh, he was fine—more than fine, in fact. He had 50 points in the club's first 49 games of the season, including a 10-game point-streak, and led the team in goals, assists, and plus-minus. That earned him a trip to his second NHL All-Star Game on January 26.

"To get to go to the All-Star Game is obviously something special," O'Reilly said. "I look forward to it."

Shining for the Central Division, which lost to the Metropolitan Division in the championship game, O'Reilly finished with seven points (two goals, five assists) in two games and was one of four finalists for the MVP Award that went to Pittsburgh's Sidney Crosby.

Though appreciative of the All-Star opportunity, O'Reilly was frustrated with the state of the Blues, who had been last in the league standings in early January and, with a record of 22–22–5, were still in the bottom 10 at the time of the All-Star Game.

"I'm thinking, 'Gosh, I feel I'm a cancer'... like I've just destroyed a team kind of thing," O'Reilly would later say. "I was just worried. You go through those things. I remember talking to my dad [Brian]. He's the one that said, 'Be patient with this. This is a really well-built team. There's so many [new] faces. It's going to take a while to click."

From the day Armstrong brought in O'Reilly, the GM never had any worry about the center being a problem.

"I've worked with Ryan in the past in international events, and I know he has a great passion," Armstrong said before addressing comments in Buffalo after the 2017–18 season. "I've certainly been guilty of saying things I was thinking and wishing I didn't say them. He probably would add that to the list of things he wished he would have kept internal, but it was out there. He's got great passion for the sport, he's got great passion to compete and to win."

O'Reilly was just as stellar in the second half of the season and would finish with 28 goals and 77 points, which were both career highs. In the playoffs, he had eight goals and 23 points in 26 games, despite playing with a significant injury that occurred in the second round.

"I think against Dallas I kind of cracked a rib," O'Reilly said. "It was manageable. Then I got bumped in San Jose and kind of locked up some stuff. But we have a great medical staff. Once you get going, the adrenaline takes over and I didn't really notice it."

In the Stanley Cup final, O'Reilly had five goals and nine points in the seven games. He became the first player since Wayne

Gretzky in 1985 to score in four consecutive games (Nos. 4–7) and took home the Conn Smythe Trophy.

"He's an absolute stud," Blues center Brayden Schenn said. "He's a beast, all playoffs. Does it in both ends. Selke winner, Conn Smythe winner, Stanley Cup champion all in one year. The guy is an absolute beast."

Meanwhile in Buffalo, Sobotka, Berglund, and Thompson combined for just 14 goals and 29 points all season. Sobotka and Berglund were both healthy scratches and Berglund actually went AWOL, which led to the termination of his contract.

And that first-round pick that the Sabres received from St. Louis? Well, with the Blues winning the Stanley Cup, that selection slid all the way down to the last pick of the first round, and they took defenseman Ryan Johnson. So while the jury will remain out on him, the verdict has already been turned in on the trade and the Blues came out as the winners.

"I remember being on an exercise bike when I was told of the trade," Blues owner Tom Stillman said. "We thought that was a very important piece in putting together a true contender. That turned out to be the case."

O'Reilly was far from being a concern. He was one of the main reasons they won the Cup.

"I still can't believe this," he said. "I can't believe I'm here right now as a Stanley Cup champion with this group of guys."

26 Old Man

Not long into Brett Hull's career in St. Louis, the question became *when* and not *if* his No. 16 would be retired.

After many thrills, a delicate departure, two Stanley Cups wearing an opposing uniform, and the mending of his fractured relationship with the Blues, Hull finally had his night on December 5, 2006.

The evening in which Hull's number was raised to the arena rafters could not have been more memorable. It was just as his father, Bobby Hull, knew it would be.

Three decades earlier, the "Golden Jet" had his No. 9 retired by both the Chicago Blackhawks (1983) and Winnipeg Jets (1989). During the week leading up to the ceremony for Brett, who was fittingly called the "Golden Brett," Bobby spelled out what the moment would be like for his son.

"The night they retired my number in Winnipeg, my friend Gordon Howe was there," Bobby Hull said. "He said to me, 'In a few minutes when the lights go out and everything goes quiet and the spotlight goes on that No. 9 flag, you're not going to be able to talk.' He was absolutely right. I was choked up, and I bet that Brett will feel the same way."

Before that moment unfolded, Brett Hull first stepped to the podium during the lavish pregame ceremony and was greeted with a thunderous ovation from the overflow crowd of 19,646 at Scottrade Center.

In addition to the fans, Hull was joined by his family, his children, former coaches—including Brian Sutter, who was making his first appearance in St. Louis since being fired in 1992—and dozens of ex-teammates, including Wayne Gretzky, Garth Butcher, Adam Oates, Kelly Chase, Geoff Courtnall, and Curtis Joseph.

"I had no idea that it was going to be this difficult," Hull said. "You are the greatest people, and I feel very privileged to be standing here in front of you. I would first like to thank [Dave] Checketts and John Davidson for bringing me back into a family that I have missed for many years. Unfortunately I wasn't able to retire here, but I can tell you what—my heart never left."

Hull, who went to Dallas as a free agent in 1998 after the Blues chose not to re-sign him, spent his night thanking others. He specifically named former Blues chairman Mike Shanahan and general manager Ron Caron, who brought Hull to St. Louis in a trade with Calgary in 1988. Hull claimed Caron was "the most passionate St. Louis Blues fan" that would ever grace the Earth.

Hull then acknowledged former Blues publicist Susie Mathieu, who was the club representative who picked him up from the St. Louis airport and drove him to the arena. "I knew I was at home the minute I stepped onto the ice," he said, gaining steam with the crowd.

Moving on to his family, Hull talked about his son, Jude, who was then a 13-year-old aspiring goaltender. "I don't know where he got his genes from," Hull joked. "His grandfather and his father have more than 1,300 goals…and he's a goalie."

Much like his career, Hull's timing was impeccable. During his speech he covered ground like he covered the slot during his heyday. And when he was finished, the time clock read "16" minutes.

After Hull was done, Oates, perhaps the person most responsible for Hull's success in St. Louis, addressed his former wing man. "It's hard to believe that it's been 15 years since we've been here playing together…. It seems like yesterday."

The Blues announced that a statue of Hull would be placed outside Scottrade Center. Former club president John Davidson

Brett Hull (left) puts his arm around his father, Bobby Hull, as he watches the banner with his retired No. 16 raise to the ceiling on Tuesday, December 5, 2006, in St. Louis. (AP Photo/Tom Gannam)

Remembered Forever

Here is a list of the numbers that have been retired for the St. Louis Blues:

Number	Player	Date Retired
No. 2	Al MacInnis	April 9, 2006
No. 3	Bob Gassoff	October 1, 1977
No. 5	Bob Plager	February 2, 2017
No. 8	Barclay Plager	March 24, 1981
No. 11	Brian Sutter	December 30, 1988
No. 16	Brett Hull	December 5, 2006
No. 24	Bernie Federko	March 16, 1991

added that the city would change the name of a portion of Clark Street, between 14ᵗʰ and 15ᵗʰ Streets in front of the arena, to Brett Hull Way.

Not missing a beat, Hull responded, "It's definitely a one-way street."

If there is one person who Hull defers to, it's his father, Bobby.

When he was dreaming up the script for his jersey retirement in St. Louis, Hull was asked to come up with a song to play during the ceremony.

"He picked it right away—Neil Young's 'Old Man,'" Chase said. "He just said, 'Don't you think that's what we should have?' I said, 'Buddy, I think that's great.'"

Blues executive Mike Caruso then mentioned the idea of the night culminating with Brett and Bobby standing side by side, the jersey climbing to the roof, with "Old Man" blaring on the sound system.

"That was Hullie picking the song," Caruso said, "and then you start listening to it, and you're thinking, *What if…*"

After much planning, the moment finally came.

"Never in the history of pro sports has a father and son had their numbers retired," former Blues chairman Dave Checketts said. "That's all about to change."

The No. 16 banner rose into the air, and the lyrics began. "Old man look at my life, I'm a lot like you were…"

"I think when you look at that jersey going up, and you hear that song, and it shows the backside of Brett and Bobby, I think it's awesome," Chase said. "For sports teams, that's part of their history now, how they pull off events like that. If you're going to do it, do it right or don't do it. Make it memorable, or don't do it. That night certainly was [memorable].

"It meant a lot to have Bobby there. You plant a potato and you get a potato. Brett is a product of his father's genes. Brett has always respected his father, and Bobby has always gone out of his way to make sure that the credit of the best goal scorer ever was given to Brett."

Only the presence of one other person could have intensified the emotion. The Blues made inquiries about getting Neil Young, the Canadian singer-songwriter and an NHL fan, to come to St. Louis to play "Old Man" in person, but a scheduling conflict prevented it from happening.

"We tried to get Neil Young here to surprise Brett. [Young] ended up signing a guitar to Brett, but we wanted [Young] to actually come in and play that song," Caruso said. "Because of his schedule, it couldn't get done. That would have been over the top."

Over the top, indeed. Instead the Blues settled for perfect.

27 Mayhem in Philadelphia

Former Blues defenseman Bob Plager had a reason for being the last player on his team to leave the ice after each period.

"[I did that] in case something happened in the stands, I wouldn't be sitting in the dressing room, missing something," Plager said. "There was a time in the minors where I did leave and I was in the dressing room when a fight started outside. So I said, 'I'll make sure everybody is in the dressing room safe before I ever come in.'"

But even Plager might not have envisioned what transpired between two NHL expansion rivals—the Blues and the Philadelphia Flyers—on January 6, 1972, at the Spectrum. After the second period, with the Blues trailing 2–0, head coach Al Arbour confronted referee John Ashley about a few questionable calls.

"The first period, the referee was very bad," Plager said. "The first goal shouldn't have been a goal. The second goal, same thing. Al is going crazy. When the period ended, Al opened the door and our players went up to the dressing room. Al steps on the ice, and he's going after the referees. In those days, you were allowed to do that. So I'm skating behind Al [because] I want to make sure nothing happens."

As Arbour followed Ashley up a ramp toward the officials' dressing room, still exchanging words, a fan doused Arbour with a beer.

The reaction was one that would put any on-ice hockey brawl to shame. It was a chaotic scene that lasted 25 minutes, required the response of 200 police officers, and ended with four people from the Blues organization spending the night in jail.

"Someone dumped a beer on me, and then I tripped over a policeman," Arbour said. "As I started to get up, another policeman hit me over the head with a club. When I started to get up again, a fan conked me."

Several Blues players climbed into the seats at the Spectrum, including all three Plager brothers, leading to a melee with the fans.

"I go up in the stands after the fan, and the next thing I know Barclay is behind me and Billy is behind him," Bob Plager said. "We go up there and start pushing and shoving. The police pull me down and people are swinging at me. That's when our players came in and our guys started swinging sticks. Then the police came in. Al is pushing one of the policeman, who whacks him over the head with the billy [club]. Now I grab the policemen with the billy and I'm fighting the policeman—not punching him but pulling him. It went on for quite a while."

More authorities rushed to the area, and according to a report, Detective Lt. Matthew Veasey told the Blues to return to the ice level or they would be arrested. The battle between the players and police continued, but the team eventually made its way back to the dressing room.

John Arbour, who was recalled by the Blues the morning of the game, was struck on the back on the head, and the cut required 30 stitches. Al Arbour (no relation) also required roughly a dozen stitches. A 14-year-old boy, a middle-aged woman, and two cops suffered minor injuries.

"It's the worst case of police brutality I've ever seen," Blues owner Sid Salomon said. "We'll get the tape from TV."

There was talk about canceling the game, but it was decided that they would play the final period. Arbour was left to wear only a T-shirt under his blazer because his dress shirt was bloodied.

Meanwhile, authorities stood outside the Blues' locker room as the players returned to the ice and wrote down the jersey numbers of those involved, indicating that action would be taken after the game.

"We got the big policeman with the white shirt, and he's got the big yellow pad and pen," Plager said. "So we open the door and I'm watching the guys going out. Here goes Garry Unger, and they're pointing at him. Phil Roberto, Floyd Thomson…they're taking the numbers down.

"Well, I knew they were going to get me. But like I said, I'm the last one off the ice and I'm the last one on the ice, too. So I told Tommy Woodcock, our trainer, 'Lock the door when you go out and come back and get me when the cops are gone.' I hid in the dressing room. Tommy locked the door and the police said, 'That's everybody?' And Tommy said, 'That's everybody.'

That wasn't everybody.

Minutes later, Woodcock returned to get Plager, who went to the bench unnoticed. It was a busy day for Woodcock, who also had to sharpen as many skates as he could between periods because they were dulled by the players climbing into the concrete stands. But it was worth it as the Blues rallied for a 3–2 victory.

"I was one of the stars of the game," Plager said.

After the game, Plager was hoping the Blues' lineup was the only lineup he'd be in that day. Looking at their yellow pad of numbers, the police started nabbing players.

"They let our players shower and get dressed, and then they handcuffed them behind the back," Plager said. "Here I'm walking with my head down, just waiting, and they go, 'No. 5, nope.' They brought the paddy wagon right in the back, loaded up all the guys, and took them to jail."

Al Arbour and John Arbour, along with Thomson and Roberto, were hauled off and charged with disorderly conduct and assault and battery on policemen. In jail, Al Arbour, who smoked at the time, pulled out a cigarette and pandemonium ensued among inmates seeking a puff. Later that night, each of the Blues was released on $500 bail.

Plager, who admitted that he was the first one in the stands and "started the whole thing," was not taken into custody—at least not until decades later.

"I went back a few years ago, and they arrested me," he said. "I was talking about it on TV and in comes the cop. He said, 'We didn't get you then, but we got you now.'"

28 Blues Help Create Broad Street Bullies

A Philadelphia newspaper was credited in 1973 with nicknaming the Flyers the "Broad Street Bullies," but it was the Blues who created the need for a nickname.

The Blues and Flyers, who both entered the league as expansion franchises in 1967, met in the first round of the NHL playoffs during their first two years of existence, and the results were eye-opening for Philadelphia's management.

The physical play of Blues brothers Barclay and Bob Plager—along with their partner in crime, Noel Picard—led to a bloodbath in both series, and Flyers' chairman Ed Snider vowed that his team would never be bullied again.

"One thing the Philadelphia Flyers were going to be known for was that no one was going to out-muscle us, beat us up, or be tougher than us," Snider said.

The first playoff series for both clubs, in 1968, went seven games before the Blues literally fought their way into the next round.

Barclay Plager led the entire NHL with 153 penalty minutes during the 1967–68 regular season, and he seemed focused on raising that total in the postseason.

The Blues and Flyers split the opening two games in the series, and then as one newspaper described him, Barclay Plager became a "one-man wrecking crew."

In the first period of Game 3, Plager appeared to time his exit from the penalty box so that he could lay a heavy hit on Philadelphia's Art Stratton. A recap of the game said, "Stratton went down like a 30-30 rifle and was removed from the action."

Plager was far from finished. In the second period, he dropped the gloves with the Philadelphia's Gary Dornhoefer, who suffered a broken ankle during the ensuing brawl.

Philadelphia recalled Simon Nolet from its farm team in Quebec for Game 4, but Plager promptly sent Nolet back to Quebec with a vicious check. The Blues won 5–2, and they went back to St. Louis with a 3–1 lead in the series.

The Flyers had a sensational young goaltender named Bernie Parent, who led the playoffs that year with a 1.35 goals-against average, but they didn't have an answer for the physicality of the Blues.

Plager led the NHL playoffs in penalty minutes with 73, several of which came during Philadelphia's 6–1 victory in Game 5. In the third period, Picard and Philadelphia's Claude Laforge triggered a brawl that cleared the benches.

"Picard hit Laforge from behind," Flyers GM Bud Poile contested. "That doesn't take much guts."

After the fracas, Barclay Plager received a 10-minute misconduct and a game misconduct. He was fined $275 by NHL president Clarence Campbell, along with fines for Blues coach Scotty Bowman ($400) and Flyers coach Keith Allen ($500). In the end, both clubs were fined a combined $3,800.

"[Bowman and Allen] have failed completely to maintain discipline and control over the players so often that their failure is inexcusable," Campbell said.

The Flyers won 2–1 in double overtime in Game 6, evening up the series, but the Blues won Game 7 by a score of 3–1.

A brash style paid off for the Blues, who were the lower seed. Four Blues players led the NHL postseason in penalty minutes that year, with Barclay Plager followed by Bob Plager (69), Picard (46), and Gary Sabourin (30).

A year later, in the 1969 playoffs, the extracurricular activity continued between the Blues and Flyers.

The Blues won the first two games in the first-round matchup, outscoring Philadelphia 10–2. In Game 3, the Flyers coach was upset after a second-period melee led to the ejection of captain Ed Van Impe.

Bob Plager crushed Van Impe into the boards and received a minor penalty. Van Impe retaliated by swinging his stick, which almost hit Picard in the head, earning a five-minute major. Needless to say, Picard went after Van Impe.

"He only takes advantage of small men who can't defend themselves," Picard said. "I keep telling him, if you want to fight, fight without a stick.... You've got no guts."

Bob Plager replied, "I don't blame [Van Impe]. If Picard was chasing me, I would use a stick, too."

Poile boiled over, arguing that Bowman sends out his team to "intimidate people."

Whatever it was, it worked. The Blues swept the series in four games, knocking the Flyers out of the playoffs for the second year in a row.

Snider had seen enough.

"In the old days, prior to the Blues terrorizing us, teams had what they called one policeman," Snider said. "I asked my [staff],

'Is there any rule that says you can't have more than one?' We sort of changed the philosophy at the time."

Snider instructed Poile, and later Allen after he replaced Poile as GM, to import toughness.

In the 1969 NHL Draft, the Flyers selected Bobby Clarke (No. 17 overall), Dave "The Hammer" Schultz (No. 52), and Don "Big Bird" Saleski (No. 64). In 1970, they took Bob "Hound" Kelly (No. 32), and in 1972 they acquired Andre "Moose" Dupont from the Blues.

Fred Shero, who took over as head coach in 1971, promoted Philadelphia's new strategy, often saying, "If you can't beat 'em in an alley, you can't beat 'em on the ice."

In January 1973, following the Flyers' penalty-filled win over Atlanta, the headline in the next day's Philadelphia Bulletin read, "Broad Street Bullies Muscle Atlanta." Piggybacking on an actual street named Broad Street, a 13-mile major artery in Philly, the nickname was born.

During the 1973–74 season, the "Bullies" led the NHL with 1,740 penalty minutes, 600 more than any other team. In 1975, Schultz set an NHL record with 472 PIMs.

To be sure, the Flyers had skill, but they intimidated their way to back-to-back Stanley Cup championships in 1974 and 1975, becoming the first expansion team to hoist the trophy.

"But before we did it, the St. Louis Blues were worse," Snider said. "We didn't invent it. We just did it a little better than everybody else."

29 Bowman Was "Great, Great Coach"

Before becoming a Hall of Fame coach in the NHL, William "Scotty" Bowman wanted to be a left winger in the league. And he might have been if not for a serious injury suffered on March 6, 1952.

Bowman, then playing for the Montreal Junior Canadiens, was struck on the head by the stick of Jean-Guy Talbot of the Trois-Rivieres Reds in a junior hockey playoff game.

"I was never the same player afterward," Bowman said. "I just didn't have the confidence. I had a lot of headaches and blurred vision."

But a new career was born.

After a dozen years working in the Montreal organization as a scout, coach, and administrator, the NHL finally came calling in 1966. Blues general manager and head coach Lynn Patrick was looking for an assistant.

"I was coaching a junior team in Canada, and Craig Patrick, Lynn's son, was playing junior for me," Bowman said. "When the Blues got the expansion team, he wanted to know if I wanted to get into the NHL with the Blues. That's how it happened."

Patrick had forecasted that his tenure on the Blues' bench would be short, and after just 16 games, with a record of 4–10–2, he handed over the reins to a 34-year-old Bowman.

On November 22, 1967, Bowman coached his first game in the NHL. It came against his former employer, the Montreal Canadiens, who dealt the Blues a 3–1 loss in Bowman's debut.

The first of his 1,244 regular-season victories, the most in league history, came on November 29, 1967, in a 3–2 win over Los

Angeles. In his first 33 games, he coached the club to a respectable record of 15–12–6.

"A happy team is usually a good team," Bowman said then. "You can't treat adults like children. You also can't treat older veterans like raw rookies. You treat them like good people, and they usually act like good people. I have rules. I set curfews. I just don't believe in overdoing it. I try to get the most out of them."

Still, it took time for Bowman's Blues to figure out their new boss.

"Every day with him was a mystery," former Blues forward Terry Crisp said. "Every day was a new page because you never knew where his mind was coming from, but he kept you thinking, he kept you on your toes. Everybody said he played head games. Yeah, he played head games. But you didn't get mired into a freaking rut. He was a master at that."

Bowman had a reason for everything, according to former Blue Bobby Plager.

"But we didn't know what it was. We thought he was stupid," Plager said. "We'd say, 'Scotty, who's going on the ice?' He'd say, 'Any five dogs! The way you guys are playing, just put five of you dogs out there.' So we'd say, 'We're going to show Scotty.' We'd score a goal, and you'd hear guys barking on the bench. Now he's got the guys going. Scotty knew how to handle us."

Bowman says today that the Blues' trade with the New York Rangers for forward Red Berenson and defenseman Barclay Plager "is what made our team." Bowman's handling of Berenson is perhaps the best illustration of his abilities.

"Scotty would yell at Red, and Red would pout," Bobby Plager said. "You'd lose Red for a couple of games. Scotty would come in and say, 'Red, let me tell you something. I want to win so badly, and I know you want to win bad. It's my fault. I've got you killing penalties, power play. I'm tiring you out.'

"Scotty said, 'These other guys are getting paychecks. Let's see if they can kill a penalty. Tonight, you'll play a regular shift, but don't kill penalties. Let's see if these other dogs, they get paid, let's see if they can do it.' Red would say, 'I'm okay.' Scotty would say, 'No, you're tired, but it's my fault.' Red would say, 'I'm good,' and he would come out flying. He should've been benched, but Scotty made him feel like he was the best."

Berenson would say later, "When I came to St. Louis, I felt like a kid's bicycle that has two supporting learner's wheels. Scotty took the supports away and gave me a chance to prove I could do it alone. When I knew he had the confidence in me to do a lot of things, I responded to it."

Berenson wasn't the only example of Bowman's coaching skill. Bowman got under Noel Picard's skin, too.

"Scotty would walk by Noel and say just loud enough, 'Big tough Noel Picard, you're the talker of the league,'" Plager said. "Noel said, 'What did you say?' Scotty said, 'You're a talker. That's what everybody says. Who have you hit in the last week?' Noel said, 'I'll kill…' Scotty would say, 'Here you are talking again…'"

"He's got Noel so pumped up, Noel won't even talk to us. We're playing Philly, first shift, Scotty says, 'Bob and the Talker go out.' Noel's hitting everything, of course. Well, the scouting report was don't wake up Noel. They didn't wake him up. Scotty woke him up."

Coaching an expansion team, Bowman had to employ different tactics to get a wide-ranging roster of players to gel.

"Scotty brought in his team here," Crisp said. "He had a mixture of veterans, the Montreal Canadiens he brought in, and a lot of young kids. Scotty blended us together, and we were a good hockey team. We were a damn good hockey team."

Bowman guided the Blues to three consecutive appearances in the Stanley Cup final where they were beaten by Montreal in 1968 and 1969 and by Boston in 1970. He handed the reins to Al

St. Louis Blues Head Coaches

Lynn Patrick	October 11, 1967–November 22, 1967
Scotty Bowman	November 22, 1967–June 5, 1970
Al Arbour	June 5, 1970–February 8, 1971
Scotty Bowman	February 8, 1971–April 30, 1971
Sid Abel	May 7, 1971–October 31, 1971
Bill McCreary	October 31, 1971–December 25, 1971
Al Arbour	December 25, 1971–November 9, 1972
Jean-Guy Talbot	November 9, 1972–February 16, 1974
Lou Angotti	February 16, 1974–October 30, 1974
Lynn Patrick	October 30, 1974–November 4, 1974
Garry Young	November 4, 1974–December 14, 1975
Lynn Patrick	December 14, 1975–January 5, 1976
Leo Boivin	January 5, 1976–September 14, 1976
Emile Francis	September 14, 1976–August 5, 1977
Leo Boivin	August 5, 1977–February 16, 1978
Barclay Plager	February 16, 1978–December 8, 1979
Red Berenson	December 8, 1979–March 8, 1982
Emile Francis	March 8, 1982–December 14, 1982
Barclay Plager	December 14, 1982–April 11, 1983
Jacques Demers	August 17, 1983–June 13, 1986
Jacques Martin	June 26, 1986–May 17, 1988
Brian Sutter	June 20, 1988–May 1, 1992
Bob Plager	May 1, 1992–October 29, 1992
Bob Berry	October 29, 1992–July 17, 1994
Mike Keenan	July 17, 1994–December 19, 1996
Jim Roberts	December 19, 1996–January 6, 1997
Joel Quenneville	January 6, 1997–February 24, 2004
Mike Kitchen	February 24, 2004–December 11, 2006
Andy Murray	December 11, 2006–January 2, 2010
Davis Payne	January 2, 2010–November 6, 2011
Ken Hitchcock	November 6, 2011–February 1, 2017
Mike Yeo	February 1, 2017–November 19, 2018
Craig Berube	November 19, 2018–present

Arbour the following season so he could focus on his GM duties, but Bowman was asked to return to coaching after 50 games.

Bowman's relationship with the Salomons, the owners of the Blues, began to deteriorate not long after that.

"They came to me one day, and Mr. Salomon said, 'Red Berenson is not going to be here when we win the Stanley Cup,'" Bowman said. "He said there's a goalie in Philadelphia, Bernie Parent, and they asked about trading for Berenson. I said, 'Oh, they're not going to trade Bernie Parent. Impossible.' So I called [Flyers GM] Keith Allen, and he laughed at me.

"I came back and told Mr. Salomon. He was insistent. He said, 'You know, Detroit's got a young centerman, Garry Unger. He's 22, he's really going to be great. Berenson is 31, on the downside, blah, blah, blah.' So we made the trade, but I was reluctant.

"Then later, for whatever reason, they didn't like Al Arbour as the coach. I had put in Al as coach my fourth year to concentrate on being the manager. They made me come back and coach because they felt we were short on defense." With Bowman as coach, the Salomons felt Arbour could return to playing defense. "I said only if Al Arbour gets the job next year as coach. They said okay, and then they reneged," Bowman said.

"There were things that I didn't agree with, and I got mad at a year-end meeting. They tried to say that was a resignation. That was the beginning of it. I just couldn't operate with those people."

Bowman left in 1971, taking over in Montreal, where he won five Stanley Cups. In the history of hockey, Bowman ranks No. 1 in Stanley Cups (9), regular-season wins (1,244), and playoff wins (223).

"He knew the game better than anybody else," former Blues goalie Glenn Hall said. "It's not surprising to me that he won so many Stanley Cups. He made his players better. I don't think there was a player he ever coached that didn't leave Scotty as a better player than when he came in. He was just a great, great coach."

30 Craig Berube to the Rescue

It was November 20 and Craig Berube was staring into a crowd of reporters, repeating as the newly named interim coach of the Blues that his chief concern was restoring the team's confidence.

Mike Yeo had been fired just hours earlier, and Berube, who they call "Chief," was being promoted to replace him. He was inheriting a roster that had high expectations at the start of the season but stumbled to a start of 7–9–3.

Many understood that the Blues needed time to gel after adding players like Ryan O'Reilly, Tyler Bozak, David Perron, and Pat Maroon over the summer. But two months into the season, the club had already put itself in jeopardy of missing the playoffs.

"It's a good hockey team, we've got good players, and we've got to get moving in the right direction," Berube said at the time. "Early on in the season, we played some pretty good hockey and ended up on the losing side of things, and that wears on players a lot of times. It can go the other way then, right? We've just got to get that confidence back, build them back up. We're going to be a demanding coaching group, and it starts in practice."

The eternal Blues' optimist might have thought that was possible, but perhaps few could have predicted Berube would lead the Blues to the Stanley Cup, something the best coaches in the history of the game couldn't accomplish.

The 53-year-old played 17 seasons in the NHL from 1986 to 2003, most notably with Philadelphia and Washington. An enforcer who scored 61 career goals, Berube also finished with 3,149 penalty minutes, the seventh-highest total in the history of the game.

"When I think of Craig, 'character' just jumps right out at me," said Jim Schoenfeld, who coached Berube in Washington. "He spent a career doing the heavy lifting for his teammates. He was a tough, hard-nosed player. If there was someone on the other side that was of the same ilk, they usually tangled.

"He never shied away from the role, but Craig could play the game, too. He wasn't solely an enforcer. He had a good understanding of the game. He was a good reliable hockey player, and you could see the hockey sense he had back then. He was a leader in the room, a leader on the bench. He had that."

Following his playing career, Berube coached 11 seasons with Philadelphia at the minor-league and NHL level before he was fired by the Flyers in 2015. He was hired by Doug Armstrong for a scouting job with Team Canada in preparation for the 2016 World Cup of Hockey, which led to the Blues' GM putting him in charge of his club's AHL affiliate, the Chicago Wolves, in 2016–17.

In that one season with the Wolves, Berube went 44–19–13, impressing the organization with his ability to communicate with his players, holding them accountable, and being someone to whom they could relate.

"He would talk to everyone, after practice, before practice, just walk by and say, 'Hey, good morning, how are you?'" said Blues forward Ivan Barbashev, who played for Berube in Chicago. "Especially after the game, the next day, he'll come talk to me and say, 'Hey, you're doing a really good job. Just keep going.' He's a good talker."

When St. Louis severed ties with the Wolves after the '16–17 season, Berube joined the Blues as an associate head coach under Yeo and had been on the bench for a little over one full season when the change was made. Berube's rapidly growing reputation made him an easy choice for Armstrong to become the interim coach.

"I'm excited to work with Craig," Armstrong said in November. "Craig's career speaks for itself as a player, and he's put his time in as an NHL head coach before. He's worked in our organization with some of our younger players. He's in tune with today's game, and he's in tune with today's athlete. We're going to support Craig and his staff."

One of Berube's first moves as head coach had a lasting impression.

"We had a meeting way back when we were five games below .500," Maroon said. "He took the standings down off the wall and said, 'I believe in you guys, and we're going to make the playoffs!' It was during those times where we'd win two, lose two, and he would still come in and just say, 'Be positive! Keep finding ways to battle through these things because I believe in you, and if I still believe in you, then you guys should believe.'

"He had faith in us, and it goes a long way when someone believes in you so much. Then the players start to believe and everyone in the room is buying into each other and sticking up for each other, doing the little things that make you a good hockey team. So the belief system just got stronger and stronger."

Armstrong admitted that Berube's idea to remove the standings from the wall was not one that would have dawned on him.

"I thought that was a really strong idea," he said. "When you come in in October and you look at the standings, you're excited that you're at the top. Then as you're going lower and lower and lower, it gets depressing coming in on a Tuesday morning and looking up at 28 teams ahead of you. I thought it was a great idea to take those down. And really what he stressed to everyone in our group is, 'Let's live in the moment. You're not going to change yesterday, and tomorrow is going to come soon enough. Let's work on today.' I really appreciated that approach."

But while Berube held his players in high regard, he had to treat the stars and role players alike, with the same sternness.

Craig Berube hoists the Stanley Cup as the team cheers. (AP Photo/Michael Dwyer)

"You just hold people accountable, whether it's through ice time or where you fit in the lineup on a nightly basis," Berube said. "It's just the team-first mindset and drilling it into the team. It takes a lot of work, it's every day, but it's getting that team-first mindset. I think that's the simplest way I can put it: conversations and holding players and people accountable, including myself. When you do that and have good players, you have a chance to win."

It didn't happen right away. The Blues went 3–5–1 in Berube's first five games, but from December 11 until the end of the regular season, April 6, they were 35–14–5 for 75 points. That was the the second-most in the league during that stretch behind Tampa Bay (79).

"He's done a helluva a job for us," Armstrong said in April. "I just think the embarrassment factor was at a level where these guys, they have a lot of pride and they were tired of hearing about how bad we all were. I really think what happened was collectively, the embarrassment level got so high that the laser focus set in."

Individuals were playing as a team, rookie Jordan Binnington was giving the Blues the goaltending they needed, and with a second-half surge, that playoff spot that seemed impossible to reach a few months prior was now theirs. But to their credit, the club didn't want the story to end there.

"They wanted to be a good team, and that obviously happened and they became a good team," Berube said at the time. "It's a special group, it really is. I think what they've accomplished in two months is pretty good, but by no means are they satisfied. That's the feeling I get from them and that's good. They want a lot more."

The Blues accomplished much more in the postseason, and in large part because of Berube. He pushed all the right buttons, moving players such as Brayden Schenn, Jaden Schwartz, and Alexander Steen around in the lineup, and inserting others like Zach Sanford and Sammy Blais. Berube showed some passion walking off the ice in Winnipeg and jawing with the Jets, which rubbed off on his players. And he had the perfect response to San Jose winning on a hand-pass goal in the conference final, imploring the club to move on immediately.

During the Sharks' series, Armstrong acknowledged that the coaching search had now become a 'list of one.' The two sides agreed to get through the season before removing Berube's interim tag and making him the permanent coach.

That was a mere formality, though, even before he led the Blues to their Stanley Cup win over Boston, which neither Scotty Bowman, Al Arbour, Joel Quenneville, nor Ken Hitchcock could do during stops in St. Louis.

Berube did it with a no-nonsense approach, which was witnessed by Blues fans on many of the pregame speeches that were recorded by the club.

"He's pretty straightforward," Blues defenseman Vince Dunn told the *St. Louis Post-Dispatch.* "He doesn't try to mess with you. He doesn't send you mixed signals. I think you can get the message pretty clear with a voice like his."

"Demands a lot of his players, but that's what you want as a player," Schenn also told the *Post-Dispatch.* "You want your coach to be able to go up to talk to you and say, 'How's it going?' At the same time, when it's game time, to be hard on you. I think guys respect that."

On June 26, two weeks after Berube led the Blues to their Cup win over the Bruins, the team rewarded him with a three-year contract extension.

"We had a long list, but we never got past the point of compiling a list," Armstrong said. "Once we got into January, we were certainly going to allow Craig to guide the team for the rest of the year. The wins started to accumulate, and quite honestly, I don't think I've looked at that list since January. I don't even know where it is.

"It just became evident that he's the pulse of our group. Our relationship was growing and becoming extremely comfortable, [as was] the belief that we had. Then as the season progressed, it became evident to everybody that he was going to be the next head coach."

Berube set out to restore the confidence in the 2018–19 club, and by putting an historic season in the books, he did so throughout the entire organization.

"I just want to thank the Blues' organization," he said. "It takes everybody. The players did a tremendous job, the coaching staff, management, everybody that was involved, and you need everybody to be part of it. Everybody bought in and fortunately we came out on top, which was great, and I just want to thank Doug for giving me the opportunity moving forward on the new contract to guide the St. Louis Blues to hopefully more championships."

31 Here Comes Cheveldae

Curtis "Cujo" Joseph made many brilliant saves for the Blues in the 1990s, but perhaps his lasting legacy will be the shots he took on January 23, 1993.

The Blues and Detroit have had many memorable battles in their rivalry, but the second game of a home-and-home series in 1993 may go down as one of the best: the night Joseph fought Red Wings goalie Tim Cheveldae.

Following the Blues' 5–3 loss two nights earlier in Detroit, tempers were off the charts when the teams came back to St. Louis. Fifty-four seconds after the puck dropped, the Blues' Kelly Chase and Detroit's Jim Cummins dropped the gloves.

"The Joseph-Cheveldae fight, it was funny how it started. I thought I was going to have to fight [Bob] Probert," Chase said. "I went out on the ice and initiated a cross-check to [Probert] and thought, *Well, he's going to fight me, and I'm going to get this over with early in the hockey game.* I don't know if Bob had a bad hand and he didn't want to make it worse. But he played the body and skated away from me. All of a sudden, Jimmy Cummins came right across the ice and dropped the gloves."

As the Chase-Cummins tilt in the corner concluded and the players were taken toward the penalty box, Probert went after Chase and the melee began anew. Probert was tangled up with the Blues' Dave Lowry, and then teammate Rick Zombo skated in to help. When Zombo was tackled by Detroit's Brad McCrimmon, Bob Bassen jumped in to aid Lowry with Probert.

What happened next almost instantaneously became one of announcer Ken Wilson's most famous calls for the Blues:

"Here comes Cheveldae! He'll be thrown out of the game," Wilson bellowed. "Now Joseph gets into it…. Curtis Joseph grabs Cheveldae, and the two goalies go at it."

Cheveldae darted out from his crease and attempted to pull Bassen off Probert. When he did, Joseph made a beeline to Cheveldae and tugged him from behind. Cheveldae's mask came off during the scrum for positioning, and then he pulled off Joseph's mask.

"Joseph with three great rights to Cheveldae!" Wilson shrieked.

With sticks and gloves and two goalie masks on the ice, the crowd of 18,104 nearly blew the roof off the Arena. They cheered each of Joseph's bare-knuckle shots, including one that caught the eye of Cheveldae, leading to immediate swelling.

Meanwhile, the Blues had an extra body on the ice because Cummins had already been escorted to the penalty box. But that was no deterrent since Cummins came out of the box to rejoin the fray. There were three pairs of players tied up near center ice, including Joseph and Cheveldae.

"For those of you watching [the goalie fight] on television, we'll try to update you on everyone else," Wilson continued to narrate, sounding more like a police dispatcher than a hockey announcer.

As officials chauffeured Probert to the penalty box, some semblance of sanity finally began to take hold. But that was far from the end of it.

"As soon as [Probert] got put in the penalty box, a guy sitting in the stands started giving him a bunch of crap," said Blues public-address announcer Tom Calhoun, who was stationed next to the visiting penalty box. "Well, Proby starts going up the glass after this guy and I'm sitting there thinking, *I guess I better do something.*

"I reach up and I grab Proby by the trunks and start pulling him back down off the glass. He looks down at me and goes, 'You don't want to do that.' I said, 'Okay, no problem, no sweat.' One of the linesmen skated over and said, 'Proby, get off that glass. You'll get kicked out of the game.'

"So he sat back down, right next to me, and after I make all the penalty announcements and things finally calm down, he tapped me on the shoulder and goes, 'What the hell were you thinking?' I said, 'Proby, I had no idea what I was thinking.'"

Four players were ejected—Probert, Cummins, Lowry, and Zombo. And Cummins was hit with a double-game misconduct for leaving the penalty box.

Somehow Joseph and Cheveldae avoided being booted from the game, despite Rule No. 54e: "A game misconduct penalty shall be imposed on any player who is assessed a major penalty for fighting after the original altercation." Instead, referee Dan Marouelli handed out only minor penalties to each of the goalies for leaving their crease.

"It was his judgement," Will Norris, the NHL's officiating supervisor that night, told reporters. "He felt he didn't want to throw out the goalies. That was it."

The decision perhaps helped the Blues, who were outshot 42–21 but won the game 4–3 on two goals by Brett Hull, one from Brendan Shanahan, and the game-winner by Kevin Miller.

If Joseph had been ejected, the Blues would have been forced to play Geoff Sarjeant who hadn't played one minute in the NHL and was only on the roster because the other half of the team's tandem, Guy Hebert, was injured.

"It's a very satisfying win," said a smiling Joseph after the game.

Teammate Garth Butcher chimed in, "Don't get too close, boys. He'll drill you."

Just ask Cheveldae.

"I played in Saskatoon with Tim Cheveldae," Chase said. "And after everything settled down, they were tossing me out of the game and I looked over at Cheveldae and I could see that his eye was swollen up shut. You could see in the fight if you watched the tape he kind of holds his eye when it's over.

"I said, 'You're an embarrassment to the Saskatoon Blade alumni.' He went crazy. He said, 'You idiot, you started all of this.' I tell Cujo all the time the only reason that he was able to beat up Cheveldae was because he went and played in Western Canada for a year and we toughened him up."

32 Gilmour Traded after Civil Suit

On the same day the Blues announced the trade of point-producing center Doug Gilmour, they stressed the point that a $1 million civil lawsuit filed against him a week earlier had nothing to do with the deal.

However, even Gilmour, who was shipped to Calgary in a seven-player trade, acknowledged that the move was necessary because he faced sexual allegations from a 13-year-old girl who was the babysitter for his 3-year-old daughter.

"Although I did not request the trade, I know it was done in my best interest," said Gilmour, who was 25 and married to wife Robyne at the time. "I would love to stay in St. Louis and prove that these allegations are false, but that would not be fair to my family or my teammates."

The affair allegedly occurred in the summer and fall of 1987. The girl, who was not identified, never revealed the relationship, but her parents learned of it after discovering their daughter's diary under her mattress while she was out of town.

"We laid in bed that night 'til 4:00 AM trying to figure out what to do," her mother said in an interview with the *St. Louis Post-Dispatch*.

"There was one page in the diary," her father said in the same interview, "where she asked for help. I thought about the celebrities involved. I felt safe confiding in an attorney. I just wanted advice."

The couple waited two weeks before confronting their daughter about the descriptions in the diary, which she acknowledged were true. They contacted St. Louis attorney Richard Schwartz, who advised them not to go through the criminal court system and "expose their daughter to all the publicity."

Instead, Schwartz contacted Blues owner Mike Shanahan and indicated they would be willing to settle if the club agreed to a structure of compensation for psychiatric expenses for the girl and her parents. At that point, the estimated costs were $1,500 to $2,000.

"We did not necessarily want to see the player's head cut off," Schwartz said. "I felt it was better for the team, better for St. Louis."

According to media reports, Shanahan contacted St. Louis County prosecuting attorney George "Buzz" Westfall, who believed the Blues were the target of an extortion case.

The family filed a $1 million civil suit on August 30, 1988, bringing the case to light in the St. Louis community.

"Doug has consistently denied any involvement with the girl," said Gordon Ankney, Gilmour's attorney. "I understand why Mr. Schwartz wants to fight this in the press. He does not have enough of a case to go to a jury or grand jury."

Schwartz demanded that Westfall withdraw from the case and a special prosecutor be appointed, claiming that Westfall's personal ties to the Blues' Shanahan would show bias.

Meanwhile, the Blues moved quickly in trading Gilmour to Calgary on September 6, 1988. A seventh-round draft pick who netted 42 goals and 105 points in 1986–87, he was sent along with Mark Hunter, Steve Bozek, and Michael Dark to the Flames for Mike Bullard, Craig Coxe, and prospect Tim Corkery.

"It just so happens a deal was made," said Blues rookie coach Brian Sutter, who had been roommates with Gilmour for five seasons. "It had nothing to do with the suit."

Calgary was glad to be on the receiving end of the deal.

"I know we weren't the first team the Blues were talking to about a trade [involving Gilmour]," Flames GM Cliff Fletcher said. "The Blues were very strong in their feelings that there was no substance to the suit. We did some checking on our own over the last 72 hours, and we feel there was no reason not to make the trade."

Gilmour was gone, but the case was not.

In December 1988, a St. Louis County grand jury heard testimony from the girl and Gilmour and discussed the issues for more than an hour.

Gilmour missed two games with his new team in order to meet with the grand jurors.

"Any time you go in front of a grand jury, you don't know what to expect," Gilmour said. "Everything went well. I just want to go on with my hockey and go on with my life."

On December 27, the grand jury declined to indict the ex-Blue.

"It's like Christmas and New Year's Day all wrapped up in one," Gilmour told the *Calgary Herald*.

"The civil suit is still there, which is why I'm not making too many comments, but this is the thing we wanted to get through and it all worked out well."

His Blues' teammates were thrilled, as well.

"All the guys felt he was innocent," goaltender Greg Millen said. "Everybody supported Doug all through this. I'm happy for Doug and his family that it's resolved at the criminal level."

On March 10, 1989, a St. Louis County circuit judge dismissed the civil suit against the Blues and president Jack Quinn. Unfortunately, the Blues could not rewrite history.

Bullard played only 20 games for the club before he was dealt to Philadelphia for Peter Zezel. Coxe dressed in 41 games but was sent to Chicago as compensation for the Blues signing Rik Wilson. Corkery never played in the NHL.

As far as Gilmour, he spent four seasons in Calgary and, including time with five other clubs, lasted in the league until 2003. He recorded 1,414 points in 1,474 games and was inducted into the Hockey Hall of Fame in 2011.

33 The Building Went Silent

On March 22, 1989, the Blues' matchup against Buffalo became a matter of life and death.

In one of the most horrific scenes in the history of the NHL, Buffalo goaltender Clint Malarchuk had his neck cut by the skate of the Blues' Steve Tuttle after Tuttle and Sabres defenseman Uwe Krupp crashed the net late in the first period. Some 14,000 fans at Buffalo's Memorial Auditorium, or the "Aud" as it was called, collectively gasped. A six-inch gash opened the carotid artery in Malarchuk's neck and blood was gushing out, creating a red pool in the crease.

"It was unbelievable," said the Blues' Greg Paslawski, who was on the ice at the time. "The ice melted. It was like it went right down to the cement. I remember people puking when they saw it."

Buffalo trainer Jim Pizzutelli raced onto the ice carrying a towel, making it to Malarchuk in 10 seconds. The building went silent. No one cared that the Blues were leading 1–0, or anything else about the game.

"I thought I was dying then. I really did," Malarchuk said later. "I thought I didn't have long to live."

Malarchuk might have died that March day if not for one factor working in his favor. The incident occurred at the end of the rink where the players exited the ice and not behind the benches. The shorter distance allowed medics to move Malarchuk to the locker room faster, perhaps saving the life of the 27-year-old goalie.

"I thank God it didn't happen at the other end of the ice," Buffalo coach Ted Sator said.

The game was on TV in the Buffalo area, and Malarchuk's mother was reportedly watching.

"Oh! Look at the blood! Take the...oh man!" said Niagara Frontier Sports Network color commentator Mike Robitaille. "Please take the camera off and don't even bring it over there. Please! Just keep it away! Oh, terrible! Oh my God, what happened?"

There weren't any pictures being broadcast back in St. Louis.

"Fortunately we weren't on TV. We were just on radio," said former analyst Bruce Affleck. "When we came back, it was silent in the building. We didn't know what to say. We didn't know how he was.

"It was a pretty eerie feeling in the building. They were still cleaning up the blood on the ice. It was the ugliest incident I had ever seen. I know they were talking about whether they should even continue playing the game."

Meanwhile, in the locker room of the Aud, Buffalo's team doctor Peter James gained control of the situation and stopped the bleeding. But Marlarchuk wasn't out of the woods yet, so he was rushed to Buffalo General Hospital.

"Can you have me back for the third period?" Malarchuk reportedly asked a paramedic.

The teams decided to resume the game. Although Buffalo tied the score 1–1 on a goal by Mike Foligno 6½ minutes into the second period, the Sabres weren't really in the game mentally.

"Our guys were visibly shaken," Sator said. "There was a lot of emotion between periods."

There was tangible emotion on the Blues' side, too.

Tuttle, a sixth-round pick of the Blues in the 1984 NHL Draft, was in his first season with the club.

"I just felt so bad for Tuts because he didn't mean it," Paslawski said. "You know, he didn't mean it. I know he called Malarchuk a couple of times to say that he was sorry, but that's just part of the game."

The Blues won the game 2–1, clinching a playoff spot in the Norris Division, but a day after the incident, Tuttle said that was insignificant.

"At this time of the season, it's an important game, but a life is so much more important," he said. "I hear he's okay, and I feel much better. Hopefully everything will work out with him."

Malarchuk required 300 stitches to help close the wound. He returned to the rink two days after the incident, and he was recognized by the fans during an emotional standing ovation that lasted two minutes.

Malarchuk played three more seasons in the NHL—all in Buffalo—before wrapping up his career in the International Hockey League. He has since worked as a goalie coach for the Florida Panthers, Columbus Blue Jackets, and Calgary Flames.

34 Iron Mike

The team's plane touched down at Lambert International Airport, and because they lived close to one another, Blues head coach Mike Keenan hitched a ride home with assistant Bob Berry.

Keenan had consumed some beer on the flight and had a can with him when he jumped in the passenger's seat of Berry's car, which was bound for Brentwood, Missouri.

"We had started home," said Berry, "and as we got off the freeway to go to his house, there was a stop sign. It's 1:30 or 2:00 in the morning and it's snowing, and Mike opened the window and threw out the beer can. I take off and I said, 'Oh Christ, Mike, there's a cop behind us.' We pulled over and the cop knew I hadn't been drinking.

"Mike tells him, 'I'm Mike Keenan. I'm the head coach of the Blues,' but the cop tells him to get out and get the can. Like I said, it was snowing a little and Mike said to me, 'Bob, can you go out and get it?' The cop says, 'No, you get out and get it. I don't care if you're [expletive] Mike Keenan or not. Get out of the car and get the [expletive] can.'"

Hiring Keenan on July 17, 1994, fresh off his championship with the New York Rangers, was a move that many people hoped would bring the Blues a Stanley Cup. But it didn't take long before "Iron Mike" wore out his welcome in St. Louis and was eventually canned himself.

In two-plus seasons with the Blues, Keenan's record was a combined 75–66–22. His brief stint included winning just one of three playoff series, most notably falling in Game 7 of the 1996 Western Conference semifinals on Steve Yzerman's double-overtime goal.

But much more memorable than the games during Keenan's tenure were the ice capades in the locker room.

From Keenan's infamous feuds with Brett Hull to his trade of Brendan Shanahan as well as alienating other fan favorites, there was never a dull moment from the day Keenan was hired until December 19, 1996, when Blues chairman Jerry Ritter pulled the plug, saying, "This has been a learning experience for all of us."

It's rare that an NHL team looking to hire a coach can find one who just won a Cup, and Keenan's availability should have been a red flag. However, after carrying the Rangers to their first title in 54 years, Keenan wanted to hold the dual titles of head coach and general manager, and the Blues, who had Berry on the bench and Ron Caron as their GM, were willing to oblige.

"I was very open," said Keenan after signing a five-year, $5 million deal. "I could have been a coach, a general manager, or a coach and a general manager. This is the right situation for me at the right time."

Despite the reputation that preceded Keenan's arrival in town, the Blues' staff had good things to say about his demeanor behind the scenes.

"There were a lot of great qualities in Mike," said Bob Plager, a former player and head coach. "He had an ego and all this, but you could always sit down and talk to him and he'd listen to you. He trusted us."

Added Berry, "When he first came to St. Louis, he was very nice to me. I had funny things in my head about Mike Keenan, but I'll never forget he said, 'I want you to remember one thing—I only have one rule.' I said, 'What's that?' Mike said, 'There are no [expletive] rules.'"

Keenan had rules, but he seemed to make them up on the fly.

On October 23, 1995, one week after praising Hull as the "biggest convert" to the coach's hard-working style, Keenan stripped No. 16 of his captaincy.

"He's just a hockey player now," said Keenan, adding that the decision was not personal.

"It's not personal?" Hull responded to reporters. "The heck it's not personal. It's a complete slap in the face."

Later that season, the Blues dropped to 16–17–5 following a 4–3 overtime loss to Toronto, after which Keenan called the team disappointing and inconsistent. Then in typical fashion, he took it a step further.

"It's very frustrating...[but] two of the critical pieces of the puzzle I had nothing to do with—Brett Hull and Al MacInnis," he said. "I had nothing to do with them in terms of them being here. Ultimately, it is my responsibility, but it's not entirely my team."

Once again, Hull fumed.

"He's blaming everyone else again," Hull said. "That's like saying you're not responsible for your stepkids if you get remarried."

Keenan, who even tried to trade Hull, put many Blues up for adoption. He dealt Curtis Joseph. He left enforcer Kelly Chase eligible for the waiver draft, and Hartford claimed him. Keenan traded Brendan Shanahan for Chris Pronger in a deal that eventually worked out okay for the Blues, but at the time it was viewed strictly as an ego-driven trade.

"Mike wanted to take on everybody," Chase said.

Everybody who wasn't a Blue when Keenan arrived, that is.

"I really liked Mike on the bench," Shanahan said. "I really thought he was one of the best bench coaches I had. I liked being coached by him in the sense that I felt like it gave us an edge over many teams. But I also felt like there was sort of a disdain for the players that were already in St. Louis [when he arrived].

"Mike was just coming off a Stanley Cup victory in New York, and I think that he resented that we were popular [even though we hadn't] enjoyed any playoff success. I think systematically, one by one, we each had an expiration date with him. I remember him coming into the locker room once and he just said in a mocking voice, 'Cujo, Shanny, Hullie—why do these people like you so much? It makes me sick. You've never won anything.' To be honest, I was buying in, thinking, *You're right, let's win something.* But like I said, one by one, we were all sort of going down."

Keenan was even responsible for Wayne Gretzky not re-signing with the Blues. Hull was one of the few players to outlast Keenan.

"I'm not saying it's a relief, that's for sure," Hull said after his boss was fired. "We had our differences, but no matter what, you have to respect a guy for wanting to win and doing whatever he thought it took to win, no matter what. Never did I consider it a showdown. But everyone knows how much I love it here. It's over now."

In recent years, Keenan has said that he regrets how he handled some of those situations with Hull and the Blues. He's even made up with Nos. 16 and 99.

"I know it's healthy to move on," Chase said. "But Mike's responsible for not bringing Gretzky back and trying to get rid of Hullie…. And now I laugh. Wayne invites Mike to his fantasy camp, and Brett's always there. I give Wayne and Brett a lot of grief over it. It's great to let bygones be bygones, but Mike certainly didn't endear himself to the city of St. Louis."

35 Stevens Awarded to New Jersey

When it was all said and done, there were veteran soap opera writers who didn't believe the twists and turns of Scott Stevens' brief stop in St. Louis. No one died and came back to life, but the plot surrounding the defenseman was just as thick.

All within a 15-month period, Stevens went from a revolutionary free-agent signing to controversial compensation, a tale that to this day infuriates Blues' fans, many of whom still ask the question, "What if?"

The club was coming off a second-place finish in the Norris Division and a second-round playoff loss to Chicago when they went looking for a franchise defenseman. They believed they had found one in Stevens, a 26-year-old free agent with the Washington Capitals. A first-round pick (No. 5 overall) in 1982, the hard-nosed blue-liner had 98 goals, 429 points, 1,628 penalty minutes, and a plus-88 in 601 NHL games.

The Blues, who had the lowest payroll in the NHL the previous season at $3.5 million, were seeking to make a bold move. After signing franchise cornerstone Brett Hull to a four-year, $7 million contract in June, they inked Stevens to a four-year offer sheet worth an estimated $5.1 million, including a $1.4 million signing bonus. Not only did the Blues ante up, they gave the Capitals five first-round draft picks, the required compensation for signing the free agent.

"This shows the level of the Blues' commitment to winning a Stanley Cup," said Stevens' agent, Rick Bennett.

Bennett was a relative unknown in the hockey world. His clientele included mainly NFL players until one day he received a call from Stevens asking him to represent the defenseman. Unfamiliar with Stevens' talents, Bennett phoned former Blues defenseman Bob Plager, whom he had roomed with as a law student at Washington University.

In fact, it was those conversations that led to Stevens landing in St. Louis and, some suspect, his quick departure, too.

"I got a call from Ricky and he said, 'I don't know why [Stevens] called me, but he wants me to be his agent,'" Plager recalled. "I said, 'You've got a good one there.' He said, 'Maybe you can help me out. How would you rate him?' I said, 'He's right there at the top.'"

According to Plager, Bennett envisioned Stevens signing with Detroit or Chicago "because they've got some money." Always looking out for the Blues' best interests, Plager tried to steer the Stevens camp away from the Blues' division.

"I said, 'No, you want to get him in New York or Philadelphia. They would pay big money to get him away from Washington. That's where you want to get him,'" Plager said. "Then I phoned our people and said, 'I'm with my friend and he's got Scott Stevens. He's telling me Detroit and Chicago, and I'm telling him New York, Philadelphia.' Our people said, 'What's the matter with St. Louis?'

"I said, 'Well, we don't have the money here. We just signed Brett Hull to that big contract.' They said, 'Wait, we're going to talk to [head coach] Brian Sutter.' They phoned Brian and said, 'How would you like Scott Stevens on your team? Brian said, 'Get that [expletive] guy, get that guy.' Sutter went crazy. They said, 'Get your buddy to come talk to us,' so I asked Ricky [Bennett], 'What about St. Louis?'"

Now a member of the Blues, Stevens came as advertised. Installed as the club's captain, Stevens wowed his new team only three games into the 1990–91 season. "Look at these hits," said Sutter, holding up a chart after the Blues' 4–3 win over Pittsburgh. "Scott Stevens had seven or eight hits. That's a lot for a defenseman. He provides a physical dimension to the team that we didn't have before. We talk about hits, but that doesn't even count his take-outs. Just his physical presence adds a lot."

Stevens played 78 games, producing five goals and 49 points, along with 150 penalty minutes and a plus-23. The Blues improved 10 victories and 22 points in the standings from the previous season, but in the minds of many, their chance at a Stanley Cup had been impeded by a regrettable deadline deal.

General manager Ron Caron traded forwards Geoff Courtnall, Sergio Momesso, and Cliff Ronning as well as defenseman Robert

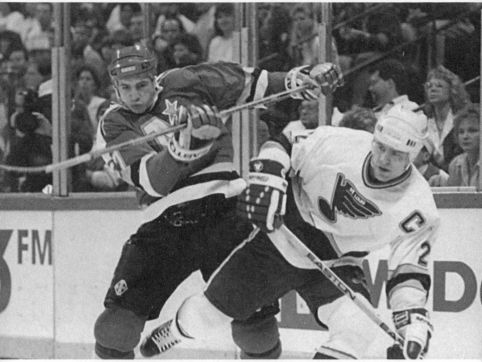

Minnesota North Stars Neal Broten (7) puts a check on St. Louis Blues Scott Stevens (2) during first period of their NHL Norris Division playoff game in St. Louis on Saturday, April 20, 1991. (AP Photo/Andre Hoekstra)

Dirk to Vancouver. In essence, the team gave away its entire second line. The fallout was a second-round playoff ouster, losing in six games to Minnesota.

The following off-season, Caron returned to the free-agent market, signing New Jersey forward Brendan Shanahan. Setting a new bar in free agency, the Blues and Shanahan reportedly agreed on a four-year, $5 million contract.

"We don't do these things with the idea of complicating other people's lives," Caron said.

But that's exactly what the Blues were doing—ruffling the NHL's feathers by driving up players' salaries. The league took

29 days to approve the Shanahan contract, seen then as a sign of its doom. The Blues then had five days to agree to compensation terms with the Devils or the case would head to an arbitrator.

"Should we fail to reach an agreement, Judge Houston shall pick one of the proposals," said Blues public relations director Susie Mathieu.

Before Judge Edward Houston's name would become villainous in St. Louis circles, the Blues were confident that the "independent" arbitrator would rule in their favor, should it go that far. Caron was offering a package of goaltender Curtis Joseph, a 24-year-old with potential but who was dealing with injuries, and center Rod Brind'Amour, a 21-year-old who had 110 points in his first two seasons. There were also two draft picks included.

New Jersey asked for Stevens, citing no need for Joseph.

"I'm not worried about the outcome," Caron said. "The risk of losing a top player is there—we knew that when we started—but hope there will be some logic in the decision."

More than two decades later, fans are still looking for the logic.

The arbitrator awarded Stevens to the Devils, giving all new meaning to the famous astronautical quote, "Houston, we have a problem!"

The backlash was immediate.

"The decision was totally fixed," Blues' star Brett Hull said emphatically. "I'll probably get sued for saying this, but I believe it. Anyone who can look at it any other way has no clue."

Remember Bennett's conversations with Plager?

"We offered more than enough…. [But] I was the one talking to [Bennett] before July 1, [and] I think the league punished us," Plager said.

The Blues took the initiative of issuing a retraction on behalf of Hull. However, after Houston reportedly called Hull "a little jerk," Hull responded, "I retract my retraction."

Stevens indicated that he would contest the ruling and didn't immediately report to New Jersey. It wasn't until the probability of sitting out an entire season became real, and the Blues moved on with the acquisition of Philadelphia defenseman Murray Baron, that the defenseman finally accepted his fate.

"Everyone knows I wanted to stay in St. Louis, but there's no way that would happen, and I was getting antsy," Stevens said. "I wanted to play hockey."

Stevens added, "We had a nice house, close to everything—the Arena, the practice rink. I'll miss it."

Not as much as the Blues missed Stevens, whose departure left the club with Jeff Brown, Paul Cavallini, and Butcher as the team's top defensemen. Not only did the Blues forfeit Stevens—they also moved on without their first-round pick in the next four drafts, the compensation still owed to Washington for signing the defenseman in the first place.

"Turn the page and keep going, that's my style," Caron said. "If you don't like something in your present situation, you improve it. That's the only way to do it.

"We feel good with our team. If we make one more trade, get another defenseman, we'll be okay. It's tough to replace [Stevens], but we'll be all right."

Stevens went to New Jersey and guided the franchise to four Stanley Cup finals, winning three, and he claimed the Conn Smythe MVP trophy in 2000. The Blues, who signed Stevens again in 1994 only to watch the Devils match the offer, qualified for the conference finals just once after he left.

After watching a real-life episode of *As the World Turns*, Blues fans are still left scratching their heads and asking themselves, "What if?"

36 Rebirth for Hall

Glenn Hall was unaware that the NHL was expanding by six teams when the newly born Blues selected the goaltender with their top overall pick in June 1967.

Before their inaugural season, the Blues held the No. 3 choice in the expansion draft. They used it on Hall who, after winning a Stanley Cup with Chicago in 1961, had been purposely left off the Blackhawks' protected list because he had planned to retire.

"When I was picked up by St. Louis, Lynn Patrick, whom I loved, came out along with [owner] Sid Salomon III and we talked about a contract," Hall said. "All of the sudden they were talking money, and we didn't make a lot in those days, so I was very interested in coming to St. Louis."

One of the reasons Hall had planned to retire was because his bones had had enough. Including his time with Detroit and Chicago, he played in a record 502 consecutive games over an eight-year period.

"I was retiring because I punished my body in order to play and I just thought, well, I had punished the body long enough," Hall said.

At age 36, Mr. Goalie decided to play again, but not without throwing up before every game.

"Yep, he had to go in the washroom and into the toilet," former teammate Terry Crisp said. "We'd say, 'Oh, he's barfing again.' And then he'd come back and away we went…. We knew we were in business."

Blues legend Bobby Plager once figured out why Hall vomited before each game.

"Because he looked around the room and saw who his defensemen were," joked Plager, counting himself with Barclay Plager, Noel Picard, Jim Roberts, and Al Arbour among the list of "unreliable" blue-liners.

Hall laughed but didn't disagree.

"He's right," the goalie acknowledged.

Hall performed well in the twilight of his career, but success didn't come without plenty of concern.

In the Blues' inaugural season, Hall steered the team to a record of 27–31–16 in 1967–68 and a seven-game win over Philadelphia in the first round of the playoffs. The club moved on to the second round against Minnesota, a battle that also went the distance after the North Stars dealt the Blues and Hall a 5–1 blow in Game 6.

"Now we're coming home for Game 7 and we were walking to the plane, and Glenn said, 'What are your plans for Game 7?'" former head coach Scotty Bowman recalled. "I said, 'What do you mean?' He said, 'Oh, I'm struggling. I don't know if I have it in me.' He said maybe I should look at putting in [backup] Seth Martin."

A rookie, Martin had played 30 games during the regular season but obviously had never made a playoff appearance.

"[Martin] never played a second in the playoffs," Bowman said. "Of course we're going to play Hall."

However, before suiting up for Game 7, Hall asked to get his vision checked when the club returned to St. Louis.

"I called the doctor and said, 'Can I bring over Glenn Hall? He wants to get his eyes looked at.'" Bowman said. "So sure enough, I drove Glenn over there, and first [the doctor] had Glenn on the table, checking his reflexes. He said, 'You've got reflexes of a 20-year-old.' Then he read the eye chart perfectly."

Still not convinced the next day, Hall approached Bowman several minutes before the puck dropped for the finale.

"Seven minutes to 8:00, Glenn came up to me and said, 'I had a tough warmup and I want you to keep your eye on me. If I haven't got it, don't hesitate to get me out of there,'" Bowman said. "Well, Glenn played into double-overtime, and I think he had 56 shots and let in one. That's how good he was."

Ron Schock's goal in double-overtime won the game 2–1 for the Blues, advancing them to the Stanley Cup final against Montreal.

Although the Blues were swept by the Canadiens, Hall was electric, winning the Conn Smythe Trophy as the series MVP. The

Goalie Glenn Hall is pinned to his net waiting to make a save on a Montreal Canadiens shot in the third period of their Stanley Cup Game on May 5, 1968. The Blues' Noel Picard (4) tries to block the puck while the Canadiens' John Ferguson (22) and Ralph Backstorm wait for the rebound. Bob Plager (5) of the Blues waits to see what happens. The Canadiens beat the Blues 3–2 in overtime. (AP Photo/Fred Waters)

award originated in 1965, and in 1968 Hall was the second player to win it as a member of the losing team. That happened only three times in the next 50 years.

Hall said that winning the Conn Smythe still "ranks high. I was honored more than I should have been probably."

Not according to his Blues teammates.

After the season, the Salomons held a celebration party and the players gathered around to watch highlights of the series against the Canadiens.

"All of the games were close and we hit some posts, so we're thinking we played so well," said former Blues defenseman Bob Plager. "But then we're sitting there watching the film and I leaned over to my brother [Barclay] and said, 'We weren't that good. Glenn saved us.'"

Hall got the backup help he was looking for the next season with the arrival of Jacques Plante. While he continued to contemplate retirement, Hall remained with the Blues for three more seasons.

In 1968–69, Hall won 19 games, posted eight shutouts and, with a goals-against average of 2.17 that year, he shared the Vezina Trophy with Plante. Hall helped the Blues to three consecutive appearances in the Stanley Cup final, although they were swept again by Montreal and Boston, respectively.

None of it would have been possible if Mr. Goalie hadn't put off retirement when the Blues came calling in the expansion draft. Hall finally called it quits after the 1970–71 season, and in 1975 he was elected to the Hockey Hall of Fame.

"He's a legend of the game," Blues goalie Brian Elliott said. "Any time you look back at old records, or old footage, he's one of the prominent guys. Playing 502 consecutive games, and probably more than half that without a mask, it's pretty special."

37 "Saved My Life"

Jacques Plante watched the shot come in. In an instant, the Blues' 41-year-old goaltender was lying flat on the ice.

It was May 3, 1970, and the Blues were facing Boston in Game 1 of the Stanley Cup final at the Arena. After being swept by Montreal in the finals during each of their first two years in the NHL, the Blues were ready to take a run at Bobby Orr and the Bruins.

Plante, the former Canadiens great who had six Stanley Cups, seven Vezina trophies, and eight NHL All-Star Game appearances on his resume, started the series in net for the Blues. But in the second period of a 1–1 game, Plante was knocked unconscious when a shot by Boston's Fred Stanfield struck him above the left eye.

Stanfield had fired a puck from the top of the circle, and it changed directions after being deflected by the Bruins' Phil Esposito. Thankfully for Plante, the blow was absorbed by his mask, which cracked upon impact.

Dr. G.L. Probstein of the Blues and trainer Tommy Woodcock tended to Plante for five minutes before he "wobbled to his feet," according to reports. He went to nearby Jewish Hospital, where he was diagnosed with a concussion.

Sporting a red welt over his eye and some discoloration in his skin, Plante would later say, "I'm convinced that the mask saved my life."

If that was the case, then Plante saved his own life, because 11 years earlier he was the first goalie to wear a mask during an NHL game.

On November 1, 1959, while playing with Montreal, Plante was struck by a shot off the stick of New York Rangers player Andy

Goalie Jacques Plante started an era for ice hockey goal tenders by first donning a mask. At left, Plante uses his face mask prior to a 1969 game in Pittsburgh. At center is Plante with out the mask, and at right, Plante wears mask in January 1960. (AP Photo)

Bathgate three minutes into the game. The puck split Plante's lip from the corner of his mouth to his nostril.

"It nearly ripped my nose off," Plante said at the time.

Plante went to the Canadiens' locker room, where he received 21 stitches for the cut.

In those days, NHL teams didn't suit up backup goaltenders. There was a "stand-in" ready to play for either club in the event of an injury, and for that game in New York, the options were either a Rangers trainer or another guy who hadn't played in two years.

Plante told Montreal coach Toe Blake that he would return to the game only if he could wear the mask that he had been using in practice. Blake originally objected but eventually gave in and, after a 21-minute delay, Plante returned to the net.

Although he was mocked for his new equipment, Plante said, "I already had four broken noses, a broken jaw, two broken cheekbones, and almost 200 stitches. I didn't care how the mask looked."

Some suggested that had Plante faltered wearing the mask, the league-wide perception might have been negative. But in his next 11 games after donning it the first time, Plante went 10–0–1 and gave up only 13 goals. That season, he led the Canadiens to their fifth straight Stanley Cup, picking up his fifth consecutive Vezina.

Eventually more goalies started to follow Plante's lead, but not all of them.

"If you wear it in practice, you get to depend on it, and then you have to wear it all the time," Minnesota's Gump Worsley said. "I've tried 'em on, and you just can't see as well. Another thing—any guy who wears a mask is scared."

To which Plante replied, "If you jumped out of a plane without a parachute, would that make you brave?"

A crumbling relationship with Blake and the need for change after Montreal was knocked out of the playoffs for the third consecutive year led to Plante's departure in 1963. He was traded to the Rangers where he played two seasons before a knee injury and his wife's illness forced him to retire.

In 1968, the Blues were looking for a backup for Glenn Hall. Blues coach Scotty Bowman, who knew Plante, successfully talked the goalie out of retirement. The Blues paid $30,000 for Plante's rights, creating a tandem with Hall that one hockey columnist called the equivalent of platooning Willie Mays and Mickey Mantle.

"Both men know that they cannot play the full 76-game schedule," Bowman said. "They are happy to share the job with each other."

Plante was glad to be back in the NHL and thrilled that it was in St. Louis.

"I remember watching the Blues on TV in the Stanley Cup final last year. I couldn't believe the fans," he said. "I still get goosepimples when the fans stand up and sing, 'When the Saints Go Marching In.'"

In 1968–69, Plante marched onto the ice for his first action in three years, posting a record of 18–12–6 with a 1.96 goals-against average. He had five of the Blues' 13 shutouts and shared the Vezina, his seventh, with Hall.

One of Plante's trademarks in St. Louis was his "victory salute," in which he raised his arms into the shape of a "V" after winning a game.

"But he wasn't a hot dog," former Blues teammate Bobby Plager said. "He backed everything up."

In 1969–70, Plante went 18–9–5 with a 2.19 GAA and five more shutouts. He was 4–1 in the playoffs before leaving in Game 1 against Boston, his last game in St. Louis.

"I'm through here. I'm convinced of it," Plante said.

Just weeks after the Blues were eliminated by the Bruins, they traded Plante to Toronto for cash. He played three more seasons in the NHL with the Maple Leafs and Bruins before wrapping up his career with Edmonton of the World Hockey Association in 1975.

Plante was inducted into the Hall of Fame in 1978 before dying of stomach cancer in 1986 at age 57. He made many saves during his illustrious career, but it was perhaps the lives he might have saved, as a result of goalies copying his mask idea, that mattered the most.

"Look what happened to Jacques Plante in the playoffs," former Toronto goalie Bruce Gamble once said. "He said it himself that the mask saved his life. I think that's fair warning to the rest of us."

38 Demitra Dies in Plane Crash

Pavol Demitra was "just a kid" playing in the Ottawa Senators' organization when Bob Plager stumbled onto him while scouting for the Blues.

"My reports were he'll play in the NHL," Plager said. "Not a role player, not a call up, but he'll play in the NHL."

Plager was right about that, but few could have predicted the career Demitra would wind up producing, finishing with 304 goals and 768 points in 847 NHL games, not to mention three appearances with Slovakia in the Olympics.

Yet it was a career, and a life, that ended much too soon when Demitra and Igor Korolev, another former Blue, were killed in a plane crash on September 7, 2011. Both Demitra and Korolev wore No. 38 in their days with the club, a number that was commemorated with a patch on the players' helmets after their passing.

Blues fans probably wouldn't have gotten to know Demitra as well as they did if not for a phone call from Plager to former coach Mike Keenan. At the time, Demitra was playing for Grand Rapids, Ottawa's minor-league affiliate.

"I phoned Mike Keenan and I said, 'The best hockey player in the American Hockey League that I've seen so far is here in Grand Rapids—Pavol Demitra,'" Plager said. "Mike said, 'He's that good?' I said, 'He's that good. He could play on our team.' Mike said, 'Well, if he's the best player in the American Hockey League and he can play in the NHL, how come he's not playing in the NHL?' which was the right question."

Plager had the answer ready to go.

"If you did your homework, [you knew] Ottawa had all of the Europeans, great skilled hockey players. [For] the position that

Pavol played, Ottawa was loaded with those players. He's good enough to play but they have the players. He just can't crack their lineup."

Ottawa's coach was Jacques Martin, a former Blues coach with whom Plager had a relationship. Martin told Plager the Senators needed a defenseman, a position in which the Blues had an abundance of talent. Keenan said he'd give Martin a call himself.

"I get a phone call and it's Mike," Plager said. "He says, 'Bob, I got your guy. We got Pavol,' Pav had never played in the NHL, so we didn't know. But I thought he was going to be good. He came in here, and we all know what a great player he was."

On November 27, 1996, the Blues sent defenseman Crister Olsson to Ottawa. After signing in March 1997, Demitra netted 22 goals and 52 points in his first season in St. Louis. He led the Blues in scoring four of the next six seasons, including a career-high 93 points in 2002–03.

Demitra's linemate and running mate off the ice was Keith Tkachuk. The two formed an inseparable bond, with Tkachuk nicknaming Demitra the "Cookie Monster."

"He's out there trying to eat up all those points, all those cookies," Tkachuk told ESPN.com in 2003.

Shy at first, Demitra eventually started dishing it out himself. Once when Tkachuk bragged to Demitra about his $11 million contract, the Slovakian replied, "In U.S., $11 million is $6 million after taxes. In Slovakia, $7 million is $7 million."

Suddenly, Tkachuk had a sparring partner.

"I liked it better when he just sat there and took it," Tkachuk joked.

Demitra told ESPN.com of his relationship with Tkachuk, "We are so close. All of a sudden, we started playing together, and we started hanging together, eating dinner together, stuff like that. We know each other very well. We got to be good friends."

Noting the Numbers

Both Demitra and Korolev wore No. 38 when they played with the Blues. But what number has been worn the most in franchise history? The No. 12 has been worn by 34 players, including current player Zach Sanford. Here is the list of players who have worn this number over the years for the Blues:

Gary Veneruzzo, 1968
Dickie Moore, 1968
Ron Stewart, 1968
Terry Crisp, 1969–72
Wayne Maki, 1970
Jaroslav Jirik, 1970
Noel Picard, 1973
Fran Huck, 1973
Gord Brooks, 1974
Bob Collyard, 1974
Jack Borotsik, 1975
Claude Larose, 1975–78
Rick Bowness, 1979
Joe Micheletti, 1980–82
Richie Hansen, 1982
Perry Anderson, 1982–85
Ron Flockhart, 1986–88

Dave Lowry, 1989
Adam Oates, 1990–92
Vitali Karamnov, 1993–95
Dale Hawerchuk, 1996
Rob Pearson, 1996–97
Chris Kenady, 1998
Derek King, 2000
Ladislav Nagy, 2001
Cory Stillman, 2001–02
Mike Keane 2002
Steve Martins, 2003–04
Lee Stempniak, 2006–09
Kevin Shattenkirk, 2011
Scott Nichol, 2012–13
Derek Roy, 2014
Jori Lehtera, 2015–17
Zach Sanford, 2019–present

But Demitra's time in St. Louis would soon end. While the team made eight straight trips to the playoffs during the right winger's stay, Demitra had just 18 goals and 33 points in 66 post-season games. After the team's exit in 2004, the player who posted the sixth-most goals in club history (204) and the fifth-most points (493) was a free agent. He signed a three-year, $13.3 million deal with Los Angeles.

"I don't want to leave [St. Louis]," Demitra said at the time. "The fans are so great here. I want to win a Cup in this city. We want to be the first guys to do it here."

There were stops in Vancouver and Minnesota before Demitra played his last NHL game after the 2009–10 season. But he was not willing to retire completely, and at age 36, he signed with Lokomotiv of Russia's Kontinental Hockey League.

"As a European player, he had certain opportunities to continue playing at a high level," said Scott Mellanby, another former linemate with the Blues. "He had some decent hockey left in him, so the opportunity for him to go and be a leader was something he wanted."

Demitra's passion, however, would lead to his passing.

Tragedy struck the hockey world when a plane transporting Lokomotiv to its next game crashed in Russia. Demitra and Korolev, who was an assistant coach for Lokomotiv, were among the 43 dead.

Korolev, who was drafted in the second round in 1992, played two seasons (1992–93 and 1993–94) with the Blues, totaling 10 goals and 43 points in 147 games.

"At first we didn't want to believe it," said a Lokomotiv official on the morning of the wreck. "But right now, there is no hope. The team is gone."

The death of Demitra, a husband and father of two, sent shock waves through St. Louis. Upon hearing the news, Tkachuk was too broken to talk but later issued a statement. "Pav was like a brother to me, and I cannot believe that he is no longer with us."

Demitra's stay in St. Louis was more than a stop in his career. "The kid," as Plager had referred to him eight years earlier, became a man with the Blues.

"[Demitra] grew up here," former general manager Larry Pleau said. "I think he really matured and grew up here, became a better person and a better player. Married, children.... You see these things happen, and he was part of your life. It's a shame when you think about the family and his wife and the kids."

39 Friends and Foes

The birth of the Blues' tag-team duo known as "Twist and Chase" began well before they came to St. Louis in 1989–90, combining for 36 fighting majors and 368 penalty minutes as rookies.

The story starts even before the two arrived together with the Peoria Rivermen in 1988–89, racking up 590 PIMs—again with only a few minor penalties scattered among the heavyweight bouts.

In 1986–87, a 17-year-old Kelly Chase and a 16-year-old Tony Twist met in training camp with the Saskatoon Blades of the Western Hockey League. And anybody who witnessed the law enforcement in St. Louis in the 1990s wouldn't be surprised that Twist and Chase got their badges long before reaching the NHL.

"You could see it developing back then," said NHL hockey legend Wendel Clark, a Saskatoon alum himself whose younger brother, Kerry, played with Twist and Chase. "You always knew something was going to happen—one would be backing the other up. It was always a 1-2 punch. In junior hockey, they had more of a role on the team. But they understood what they had to do to make the NHL, and they knew that job and took it. That's what made them—not just the toughness but how they were as people, making sure the team was together. Those guys were always a big part of holding a team together."

For as much as Twist and Chase are intertwined in St. Louis hockey lore, they only spent parts of three seasons together. But that just goes to show how many punches were packed into a small time frame.

On a collision course to be longtime teammates with the Blues, Twist and Chase were separated in their second NHL seasons. In February 1991, one month before the infamous trade with Vancouver, the Blues sent Twist and Herb Raglan, and Andy Rymsha to Quebec for tough guy Darin Kimble. Twist spent three-plus seasons with the Nordiques before former Blues coach Mike Keenan brought him back to St. Louis as a free agent in 1994. But a few months later, Iron Mike left Chase unprotected for the waiver draft, and Hartford scooped him up.

After jamming 1,005 penalty minutes into 208 games with the Blues, Chase bid a tearful farewell to the organization.

"I'm excited that Hartford wants me," Chase muttered quietly, "but leaving these guys and that city..."

Twist did not mince words when he assessed the move by the Blues.

"You know, Chaser, this club just can't get it right," Twist said. "First they got rid of me and kept you. Then they get me back and get rid of you."

Meanwhile, Chase told Keenan he "made a mistake letting me go. But I said that down the road, I'd like the chance to come back and prove that I can play."

That opportunity eventually unfolded, but for two seasons in Hartford, Chase was now the enemy rather than the longtime fan favorite. And on March 9, 1996, with 20,803 sitting ringside, it became real life when Twist and Chase squared off in the first period of a tilt between the Blues and Whalers.

Earlier in the game, Twist had fought Hartford's Mark Janssens, who stepped in because he didn't want to see Chase fight Twist. Janssens suffered a broken cheekbone.

"Keenan put Twister on the ice to settle me down because we were running around," Chase said. "He came up to me at the faceoff and said, 'You've got to stop,' and I told him where to go. I said, 'Why don't we just fight and get it over with?' He said, 'You want to fight with me?' I said, 'Listen, that clown on the bench sent you out here, so why don't we get it over with?' He couldn't believe we were going to fight. Nobody believed we were going to fight for real."

The tone of the broadcasters calling the game quickly went from joking to serious.

"I actually hit him with a left and said, 'How did that feel?'" Chase recalled. "That's when he got really mad."

Chase, however, held his own in the fight but didn't return because of a torn ligament in his left hand.

"I felt awful when he didn't show up for the second period," Twist said. "It's like fighting one of the family. I felt crummy, but that's part of the game."

But guess who had the last laugh? In St. Louis, Twist was renting Chase's house during the season.

"The rent just went up $1,000," Chase quipped.

In 1997, Twist and Chase would become teammates again. Chase, who had moved on to Toronto, was acquired in a trade with the Blues that cost former general manager Ron Caron "future considerations," which was later learned to be some of Caron's favorite wine.

"I was going to be traded somewhere, Chicago or Colorado," Chase said. "Caron called [Toronto associate GM] Mike Smith, and Mike told him, 'I'll make you a deal for future considerations.' They drank really good wine together, and Mike said to Caron, 'You owe me a case.' I used to ask Caron, 'Was it bottles or boxed?'"

Regardless, Twist and Chase were reunited and for the next two seasons they put on their boxing gloves. They combined for 50 fights in that stretch, and you would need a calculator with good batteries to add up the penalty minutes.

"We had a pretty good understanding of how to manage the game," Chase said. "We tried to make sure that guys knew not to run around and act up on the ice, and if they ever did, God,

Kelly Chase and San Jose Sharks Ronnie Stern tussle in the third period on Thursday, December 30, 1999, at the Kiel Center in St. Louis. Both received five minutes in the box for fighting. (AP Photo/Mary Butkus)

we would jump on these guys. Pavol Demitra told everybody, 'The easiest time I had playing in the NHL is when I had Twister and Chaser. We could go out there and just play. Nobody cross-checked us after the whistle, nobody rubbed their glove in our face.'

"I'll tell you what—there's nothing more appreciative than hearing that from a teammate."

Twist and Chase took on all comers. Jim Cummins. Lyle Odelein. Reid Simpson. Sam McCarthy. Bob Boughner. Sean O'Donnell. Derian Hatcher. Of their 50 fights in back-to-back years, 32 belonged to Chase (5'11", 190 lbs.) and 18 to Twist (6'1", 230).

"Most of the guys, if they wanted to get their fight in, they wanted to get it in with me," Chase said. "They didn't want to get it in with the big boy."

According to former Detroit enforcer Joey Kocur, "That still was no bargain. Chaser was never one of the bigger guys on the ice, but he had the biggest heart out there. He had to fight guys like [Bob] Probert and [Donald] Brashear, and he did a great job doing it. Tony was a huge man. Strong as a bull and a dangerous right hand. But Chaser, for what he had to do, I really respect it.

"They knew their role out there, and they did it to a T. They did everything the right way, the honest way. They didn't go out and run anyone from behind. They were there to protect their players or inject some enthusiasm into the game as needed. I really respect the job that they did."

The run ended in the summer of 1999 when, just hours after the Blues told Twist they would not be re-signing him, he was involved in a serious motorcycle accident. Twist crashed his custom-built Harley-Davidson into a car that had pulled in front of him, sending him flying into the street and later into intensive care. He suffered a broken pelvis and torn knee ligaments, but he was lucky to be alive.

"There's a long road ahead of me to play the game," Twist said. "When this is all said and done, I want to be able to walk properly. I want to lead a normal life."

Twist never played again, and Chase lasted only another season before he retired with the Blues. All these years later, Twist and Chase still live in St. Louis and remain close.

"It was great growing up with Twister," Chase said. "There's lots of stuff that happened in our lives where we had to deal with adversity the same way. It's amazing. I may not see him for a month, two months, but nothing changes how we stick together. I guess we'll always have each other's backs."

40 Jackman Captures Calder

When the subject of Barret Jackman winning the Calder Trophy as the NHL's Rookie of the Year in 2002–03 is brought up, the first question usually asked is, "Who did the Blues defenseman beat out for the award?"

When the names of Henrik Zetterberg and Rick Nash are dropped, jaws quickly follow. Zetterberg has been nearly a point-per-game player in his career with Detroit, and Nash, who ended his career as a Bruin in 2018, was the longtime face of the Columbus franchise and equally skilled.

Despite Zetterberg's 22 goals and Nash's 17 as rookies, Jackman's ability to eliminate the forwards in front of him made the stay-at-home defenseman worthy of being named the first Blue and only the ninth blue-liner in league history to lay claim to the Calder.

"I'm still in disbelief," Jackman, then 22, said at the awards ceremony in Toronto. "I just thought Zetterberg had it all wrapped up. There's not a lot exciting about a stay-at-home defenseman."

Jackman, who was the 17th overall pick in 1999 by the Blues, had only three goals and 19 points, the lowest total ever for a Calder winner. But in registering 190 penalty minutes, which was the most ever for a Rookie of the Year recipient, Jackman kept opponents on high alert.

"It usually takes a player like him a few years to get acclimated to the level of play and to get a feel for the tough play," Blues coach Joel Quenneville said. "[Jackman] got it very quickly. He was quietly being noticed and respected. He'd cross-check a guy and that guy would turn around, see who it was, and skate away. Usually, if a rookie does that to a vet, [the vet] wants the last whack. You know you'll have to deal with him."

The Blues were playing without defenseman Chris Pronger, who suited up in only five games before missing the remainder of the season due to knee and wrist surgeries. But the club paired Jackman with Al MacInnis, and the rookie didn't miss a beat, helping the Blues place second in the Central Division.

"It magnifies how much better he had to be than the other guys to win," said MacInnis, who led NHL defenseman in scoring with 68 points and was a Norris Trophy contender but lost out to Detroit's Nicklas Lidstrom. "I don't think there was another rookie who had the impact on his team that Barret had for us. We don't get 99 points if Barret doesn't have the season he had.

"He's a throwback in a lot of ways. He's a stay-at-home defenseman—a guy you love to have on your team. He's tough. He's rugged. It's hard to get under Barret's skin."

Prior to winning the award, Jackman said, "Al was pulling so hard for me, and all the guys lobbying for me. This is thanks to them, really. I think some of it comes from consistency. Right from

Defenseman Barret Jackman (5) in action during a game between the St Louis Blues and the Dallas Stars at the American Airlines Center in Dallas, Texas, on October 13, 2011. The Stars won 3–2. (Manny Flores/CSM, Cal Sport Media via AP Images)

day one, I felt comfortable and I was able to compete against the top lines."

Jackman was the only Blues player and the only NHL rookie to play in all 82 games, averaging 20 minutes, 4 seconds of ice time. His plus-23 rating was second among first-year players.

"He's the type of player that makes a coach put him on the ice," Blues assistant coach Mike Kitchen said. "I had my fingers crossed [regarding the award]. If you think about it like people in hockey do, what he did this year was phenomenal."

The Calder Trophy, named after former NHL president Frank Calder, dates back to the 1936–37 season. Other players to have their names inscribed on the trophy include Boston's Bobby Orr and Ray Bourque and the New York Rangers' Brian Leetch, among others.

At the end of his memorable night, Jackman told a reporter that he was going to "sit in a corner and examine all the names" on an award that would soon bear his name, too.

John Davidson should have known that his marriage would last when it survived the day a Blues teammate brought a horse into the couple's newly purchased house and tore up the hardwood floor.

"JD" and his newlywed, Diana, were settling into St. Louis after the Blues made the goaltender the fifth overall pick in the 1973 NHL Draft.

Shortly after trading his wedding vows, Davidson hosted a New Year's Eve party at his home, which the couple had purchased from Glen Sather, the longtime New York Rangers general manager who spent one season with the Blues as a player.

"We had 5½ acres, and there were two horses with it that Glen gave us as a wedding present," Davidson said. "[Former Blues] Floyd Thomson and Bobby Plager went out and got one of the horses, a big Tennessee Walker. Floyd got on it, went up the steps and across the patio, and tried to come into the house. But he hit his head above the door and fell off, so Bobby pulled the horse in anyway.

"The house was nothing but beautiful hardwood floor, and every time the horse went around the corner, his hoof would [scratch] the boards. It was our first year of marriage, and this didn't go over real well [with my wife]. But it was a memory…"

Davidson can look back and smile now as he closes in on his 50th wedding anniversary. Although JD's marriage with the Blues has seen two separations, he has nothing but good memories of the organization, as well.

"This is a really, really fantastic city to live in and be part of the sports community," Davidson said. "It's one of the great treasures of the United States."

Davidson, who was born in Ottawa but spent his adolescence in Calgary, might have had a hard time envisioning the career he built in the U.S. He played 10 years in the NHL, spent nearly three decades in television, and he's now with his second organization as a club executive.

As a top junior goaltender playing for the Calgary Centennials in the early 1970s, Davidson said, "All I want is to make a good living out of pro hockey. I hope somebody gives me the chance."

The Blues originally had the eighth pick in the draft, but they worked out a three-way trade with Atlanta and Montreal to get the fifth pick and take Davidson. He became the first goalie in NHL history to jump from junior hockey to the NHL in 1974, winning 13 games as a rookie and earning consideration for the league's Rookie of the Year award.

Davidson won 17 games in his second season, but with Stanley Cup winner Eddie Johnston in the fold and the Blues signing second-round draft pick Ed Staniowski, the team traded JD, along with Bill Collins, to the New York Rangers for left wingers Ted Irvine and Bert Wilson and right winger Jerry Butler.

Blues Presidents

Sidney Salomon Jr.	1967–73
Sidney Salomon III	1973–77
Emile Francis	1977–83
Harry Ornest	1983–86
Jack Quinn	1986–96
Mark Sauer	1996–2006
John Davidson	2006–12
Doug Armstrong	2013–present

"You don't get a goalie the caliber of a Davidson very often," said Rangers GM Emile Francis.

Davidson performed well in New York, winning 93 games, but after eight seasons, chronic back and knee injuries forced him to retire in 1983 at age 29.

Seamlessly, JD went into the Rangers' broadcast booth and became the preeminent TV color analyst in the NHL and became internationally known at the Olympic level. His work would later earn him the Foster Hewitt Award from the Hockey Hall of Fame.

But the emptiness of leaving the rink nightly without experiencing the emotions of wins and losses wore on Davidson, and when former MSG executive Dave Checketts bought the Blues in 2006, he asked JD to take over the hockey operations.

"During the Ranger years, I asked him a lot of questions, and we had a lot of visits about hockey and building an organization," Checketts said. "I just said, 'This is a guy who is someday going to be a general manager.' I didn't know I was going to pave the way. When it was St. Louis, I learned they drafted him, he played here—it just made a lot of sense."

Davidson's wife, Diana, agreed. She told Checketts, "Wouldn't it be a shame if John had this amazing career in hockey, these years as a player and a broadcaster…. Wouldn't it be a shame if he retired without his name being on the [Stanley] Cup?"

In June 2006, the NHL approved Checketts' purchase of the Blues, and Davidson was named president of hockey operations.

"I can't tell you how overjoyed I am at this opportunity," Davidson said.

The Blues, who finished last in the NHL the previous season, now had something they had been desperately seeking.

"He was the face of the franchise," said Bruce Affleck, a former Blues defenseman who is now a team executive. "There were no promises, it was just strictly, 'We are what we are. Come out and support us. We're going to get better.' And the fans believed him.

"It was the right move. I don't think anybody was disillusioned about the GM side of it because he had never done that. But JD was the face, and he did a good job when things were pretty bad."

Along with Larry Pleau, who stayed on as GM, Davidson traded aging veterans for draft picks, creating a young nucleus that included T.J. Oshie, Erik Johnson, Patrik Berglund, David Perron, and Alex Pietrangelo.

The Blues made the playoffs in 2009, bringing the crowds back to Scottrade Center. In 2010, Davidson's hand-picked GM successor, Doug Armstrong, took over for Pleau. Armstrong orchestrated a couple of franchise-altering moves, acquiring Jaroslav Halak, Chris Stewart, and Kevin Shattenkirk.

The Blues competed for the Presidents' Trophy in 2011–12, finishing third in the NHL standings and advancing to the second round of the postseason for the first time in a decade. After telling fans, "Come grow with us," the Blues were growing up.

After the breakout season, however, the Blues were sold to new ownership and Davidson, who had signed a four-year, $8 million contract under Checketts, was not part of their plans. Davidson agreed to a buyout of the final three years on his deal and months later accepted a position with the Columbus Blue Jackets.

"He has done a great job here, so it's certainly not about his work," said Tom Stillman, who headed the new ownership. "But we are working to get our business, our financial house, in order. That's what this is all about."

Davidson acknowledged that his hefty contract was the obstacle that led to his departure.

"I'm proud of what our group was able to accomplish, and it's not just me, it's everyone," he said. "It's no one person that makes the St. Louis Blues go. It's a collection and everybody pulls their weight and everybody does a good job. Everybody's life can be a book with chapters. This chapter here was a 10, I'll tell you."

There was no horsing around in Davidson's second stint with the Blues, and because of that, the franchise was left in better shape than the Davidson's hardwood floor.

42 "It's a Privilege"

In 1988, former defenseman Bruce Affleck created the Blues' Alumni Association with the mission of "trying to help minor hockey in St. Louis and grow the game."

An organization that began with about 16 ex-Blues has ballooned into 40-plus players, making it among the top five alumni groups in the NHL in terms of involvement and participation. The ex-players have raised more than $3 million for area youth programs and charities, not to mention their work in creating the 14 Fund, which has contributed more than $3 million since its inception in the late 1990s.

"Bruce has been a big part of that," Hall of Famer Bernie Federko said. "He's been able to keep us part of the Blues, which a lot of other teams don't have…. Because of that, we're able to raise money, and the club is very supportive of us.

"You see that with the Original Six and Canadian teams, but in a market as small as St. Louis, which you consider a small market and really a baseball market, it's amazing how lucky we've been to get the support we do from the community."

Former Blue Larry Patey is part of the alumni's six-member board, which includes Affleck, Blake Dunlop, and Terry Yake.

Patey said that the group's success "goes right back to [former Blues GM and coach] Emile Francis when we all came into town. Emile Francis' key was to sell the game. We did a lot of solicitation, a lot of PR work, whether it be golf tournaments or banquets… more or less getting to know the public."

Since then, generations of Blues fans have stories about the night they met Federko, Brendan Shanahan, Brett Hull, or Bobby Plager. These players are heroes because of the memorable goals they scored or games they won, but they were also neighbors and friends of friends.

Shanahan played for five NHL organizations, including Detroit, New Jersey, and New York. But he has said that his four seasons in St. Louis (1991–95) yielded the closest connection he had with fans.

"What struck me is just how much the city supported us and also how it just seemed really easy to connect all the people in the city," Shanahan said. "Other places I played, it seemed like there were a lot more boundaries between the athletes and the people in the city. But in St. Louis, it seemed to me that those boundaries didn't really exist."

Many former Blues, from Federko to Jamie Rivers to Reed Low, returned to the city after their careers were finished to raise their families and continued to assist with the alumni group. Sure, that happens in other NHL cities, but it's prevalent in St. Louis.

"It's one of those towns that not a lot of people know about unless they've played there," said Federko, who maintains a residence in the suburbs. "Not just hockey, but football and baseball [players]…everybody likes to hang around St. Louis. You can have your own privacy, yet you're part of the community. I think Stan the Man [Musial] is a perfect example of that. We almost become adopted children.

"The cost of living, the real estate, the school system, the values of the Midwest…. I think that's what makes everybody want to stay here. Even guys that only played a few games here have decided to stay here because their wives like it and their families like it. It's fun for us because of the number of alumni and the connections. We're very lucky."

A moving message greets guests as they enter the Blues' alumni suite in the upper level of Scottrade Center. Many occupants of the suite once wore the Blue Note on their chest, whether it was three years ago or three decades ago. They don't take their experience of playing in the NHL, particularly in St. Louis, for granted. That's the point former Blue Kelly Chase was making when he penned the inscription outside the door.

"It's a privilege," Chase wrote. "Through these doors walk the shoulders of men, men who have bled, sweated, broke bones, tore muscles, and shed tears for the right to enter this room. They enter this room with pride, yet humble. For they know that all they have, they owe to the game and the game owes them nothing. They know that God will not look at them for their trophies, medals, degrees, or diplomas, but for their scars and what they gave back. These men know you don't wish, win, or buy your way through these doors—you earn it. And when you do, you realize it's a privilege."

Given a chance to reflect on his words, Chase said, "It epitomizes what we're about in St. Louis. Once you put on a jersey, you have an obligation to give back. I think once you realize that, then you've got an ability to help a lot of people."

43 Hockey Prankster

The Blues' bus was about to pull away from its hotel in Phoenix and drive to the rink for Game 7 of the 1999 Western Conference quarterfinals. Although the club had won back-to-back games to force the winner-take-all matchup, the players were tight.

It's common for hockey fans to congregate around the visiting bus when it departs the hotel, seeking autographs or simply waving goodbye before the wheels begin to roll. That was the case on May 4, 1999, as the Blues left for their all-important battle with the Coyotes.

Only this time there was a familiar face in the crowd.

Standing on the corner, Blues defenseman Marc Bergevin was holding a sign that read ,"Go Blues, go! See you guys in Dallas." Bergevin wasn't playing because of surgery for a torn abdominal muscle but, as usual, he was keeping the mood light.

"I thought the guys would like that," Bergevin said. "They could talk about it before the game and take a little pressure off."

Later that night, with two minutes left in overtime, Blues center Pierre Turgeon deflected in a shot for a 1–0 victory over Phoenix, sending the club, as Bergevin had predicted, onto the next round against Dallas.

"He is always, always, thinking about doing something," Turgeon said. "You might think he's sitting down resting, but he's thinking about something to do. It gives the dressing room atmosphere."

In a sport where pranks are part of the daily routine, the Blues employed one of the best executioners in league history in Bergevin.

Once Bergevin dressed up in a large sumo wrestler costume, which was at the rink for in-game entertainment purposes, and danced in the locker room to the tune of "Kung Fu Fighting." His other stunts included wearing teammate Grant Fuhr's jersey along with a large Afro wig onto the ice, putting the former Blues goalie in stitches.

"The hair is not big enough," said Fuhr, the son of one African American parent. "I had more hair than that when I was young. And my tan was a lot better, too."

Then in 1999, Bill and Nancy Laurie were introduced as the new owners of the Blues. Nancy is the daughter of Bud Walton, who founded Wal-Mart with his brother Sam.

"When I heard that someone from Wal-Mart bought the team, I thought it was a guy shopping in the store," Bergevin quipped.

After the team's first practice under the Lauries, Bergevin imitated a Wal-Mart employee by putting on a blue apron and greeting those around the locker room with, "Hi, my name is Marc. Can I help you?"

Bergevin was always out to help. Perhaps his most elaborate prank came at the expense of a young defenseman named Cory Cross when the two were in Tampa Bay together.

"Marc Bergevin didn't sleep," former Blue Kelly Chase said. "He woke up one morning and he couldn't sleep. He kept looking at the clock…6:00, 6:15, 6:30. Finally, he looked over and saw that his roommate's watch was laying there. He took the kid's watch, turned it ahead, and jumped back in bed.

"Then he jumped out of bed screaming, 'Cory, Cory, you slept in! I told you to get a wake-up call!' The kid jumps up and says, 'Berg, I told them we needed an 8:45 and a 9:00 AM wake-up call.' Berg says, 'We slept through it, get up!' They got dressed, ran toward the elevators, and Marc goes, 'I forgot my contacts.'

"Berg tells the kid, 'You go downstairs and you tell them we need a cab to go to the rink in Phoenix.' And he goes, 'You make sure they hear from you at the front desk for not giving us the wake-up call.' The kid goes blasting through the lobby and says, 'I don't know why I didn't get my wake-up call. What's going on? This is ridiculous.'

"The lady is like, 'Sir, calm down. I'm so sorry. Just tell me, what time was your wake-up call?' He goes, 'I asked for an 8:45 and a 9:00 AM wakeup call and nobody called. How do you guys miss something like that?' She goes, 'Sir, it's 6:50 AM in the morning.' The kid goes, 'What?' She said, 'It's 6:50 AM in the morning.'"

Realizing he had been punked, Cross returned to his room where Bergevin was sitting in bed and watching television.

"Berg looks at the kid," Chase recalled, "and says, 'You can't teach that.'"

Former Blue Keith Tkachuk, who played with Bergevin in St. Louis briefly, said, "You had to be on your toes with that guy. I had breakfast with him one time, and he was asking the young waitress how much for the coffee and she told him. She said, 'But there's free refills,' and he said, 'Well, just give me the free refills.'"

Friends still seek their fill of Bergevin. Unfortunately, since Bergevin was hired as the GM in Montreal in May 2012, the ex-Blue has had to scale back his routine.

"Berg has a sense of humor obviously," said Rick Dudley, an NHL executive who worked with Bergevin in Chicago and has joined him in Montreal. "He's now the GM so he's tempered that a little bit, but when we get out by ourselves, he'll pull the odd prank on me or somebody else.

"Berg is always having fun with people. It's his nature and he made a lot of people smile in his life because of those little jokes. At the same time, he's a pretty intense guy. I think he understood that his sense of humor helped hockey teams along the way, so he used it very effectively during his career."

Of Bergevin's sign-holding joke in Phoenix, former Blues general manager Larry Pleau once said that because the Blues won, the team might have paid the defenseman's salary for the entire season. Bergevin made $900,000 in the 1998–99 season, and a victory against the Coyotes did eventually lead to three more home playoff games at $1 million each in revenue.

Either way, Bergevin's personality has always been, and will continue to be, priceless. If only the young Habs players could have seen him in his prime.

44 Shanahan for Pronger: Yes or No?

One morning in the Blues' offices, Mike Keenan had a yes-or-no question for his staff.

"He said, 'Would you trade Shanahan for Pronger? Just a yes or a no," Bob Plager recalled. "I said, 'Well, you know, it's…' He said, 'Yes or no—would you trade Shanahan for Pronger?'"

Keenan, of course, was referring to Brendan Shanahan, a popular power forward with the Blues who had unlimited potential, and Chris Pronger, Hartford's lanky, physical, and promising defenseman. Shanahan was the No. 2 overall pick in 1987; Pronger the No. 2 pick in 1993.

"My answer was, 'Yes,'" Plager said. "I said, 'Can I talk now?' He said, 'Yeah.' I said, 'Mike, they're going to run you out of this city.' He said, 'Don't worry about that. That's my job. Your job is answering would you trade Shanahan for Pronger.'"

Plager wasn't the only staffer quizzed by Keenan. Later, scout and former player Rick Meagher walked in and was asked the same question. After a few moments, learning how to shorten his answer to one word, Meagher responded, "Yes."

On July 27, 1995, the Blues made one of the most controversial trades in club history when they sent Shanahan to Hartford for Pronger, only 20 years old at the time of the deal. Plager was correct about the immediate reaction; fans were ready to run Keenan out of town.

At the Blues' home opener the following season, the crowd booed Keenan louder than the visiting Edmonton Oilers.

"Oh yeah, you hear it," he said. "I'll stand up for what I believe in. If I'm not good enough for this town, then so be it. I can only make judgments, along with our staff, based on my experience and what I know about the game, what I feel is best. If I'm not good enough, they can run me out of town. I guess they're starting to do that."

Keenan noted that he was mandated by Blues' ownership to trim $11.5 million from the payroll. Although it was difficult, trading Shanahan for Pronger was "the only way I could figure it out."

In the Blues' 5–3 victory over Edmonton at the home opener, Keenan said that Pronger dominated the game. He added that while coaching in Chicago, "There was a little reaction when I traded Denis Savard, but not like this because they gave Chris Chelios a chance. Chelios has become the best player in the franchise and has been for five years."

Pronger eventually established himself in St. Louis, but it didn't happen overnight.

On February 3, 1996, in a 7–3 loss to Philadelphia, Pronger was booed off the ice. Personally responsible for three Flyers' goals, he didn't receive one shift in the third period. After the game, even Keenan was critical, saying that Pronger didn't deserve the ice time.

"If I did more things right than wrong, they wouldn't boo me," Pronger said.

Following the acquisition of Wayne Gretzky, Pronger began to flourish, perhaps because there was less scrutiny on him. The 6'6",

220-lb. defenseman began to morph from a physical pushover into a ticking time bomb.

"If he can grow into his body, he'll be a great one," Keenan said.

True. Ironically, however, Keenan wouldn't be around to witness it.

In 1996–97, Pronger's second season in St. Louis, Keenan was fired in December. Pronger went on to post 11 goals and 35 points that season. Going into the next year, he was named by new coach Joel Quenneville as the youngest captain in club history at age 22.

"He's well-deserving of the captaincy," Brett Hull said. "In my 10 years here, I've never seen a guy come in and develop as he has as a player and a person. I'm so proud of him. He's the right man for the job."

Pronger's many challenges with the Blues, he said, toughened him up.

"Over the last year and a half, I've gotten more comfortable and played better," Pronger said. "Sometimes you have to battle adversity. Not everything is going to be rosy in this world. If you battle and overcome things, it'll be good. This is a little more added responsibility for my play. Hopefully I won't let the letter on my shoulder dictate how I play."

The letter did dictate him—he thrived.

In 2000, Pronger took home the Norris Trophy as the NHL's top defenseman and the Hart Trophy as the league's MVP, becoming the first blue-liner since Bobby Orr in 1972 to win that award.

"Anytime you get traded for a fan favorite it's going to be difficult, but he came in here [and] won the MVP of the league," former Blue Keith Tkachuk said. "He's a tremendous talent and one of the best defensemen, along with Al MacInnis, that I ever played with."

Over the next several years, Pronger became one of the most feared players in the league in front of the net. Injuries to his wrist and knee limited him to five games in 2002–03, but he bounced back with a 14-goal, 54-point season in 2003–04.

Pronger had made many fans forget about Shanahan.

"Who'd a thunk it?" Pronger said.

So was Plager right? Was it indeed a good trade for the Blues?

"Shanahan was a great hockey player," Plager said. "But I had watched Pronger play in his first training camp in Hartford. As an 18-year-old, he was the best defensemen on the ice in NHL games, and you'll never get a player like that, a defenseman, unless you're last in the standings.

"We told the people it will be a while, but someday Pronger could be the MVP. He could win the Norris Trophy. He's going to be our future and you can build a team around him…. It was a tough trade and it was on Mike Keenan, but it was a great trade."

Bergevin Throws Puck into Own Net

The second period had yet to begin and already Blues defenseman Marc Bergevin had a voice mail on his cell phone.

"You can't teach that," former Blues winger Geoff Courtnall relayed to Bergevin in a message while watching the game on TV. "And I told him that they clocked his fastball at 85 mph."

In Game 2 of a first-round playoff between the Blues and San Jose in 2000, Bergevin caught a puck shot by the Sharks' Gary Suter and inadvertently threw it into his own net. The Blues, who led the series one game to none at the time, lost 4–2 in Game 2.

"I thought we were going to win the game," Courtnall said. "I felt bad afterward, or I wouldn't have said anything."

The Blues lost more than the game. After winning the Presidents' Trophy during the 1999–2000 regular season with a franchise-record 114 points, the club went on to lose the series with San Jose in seven games.

"It's so disappointing," former Blues general manager Larry Pleau said. "The energy around the city was so great, then all of a sudden it stopped."

It was a season that held so much promise for the Blues, who finished with a record of 51–19–11–1, and it is still remembered today due to Bergevin's improbable mishap and a few other events.

The Blues showed up for Game 1 against the Sharks with a different look. Bergevin, Craig Conroy, and Jamie McLennan had bleached their hair blonde and looked like different versions of rocker Billy Idol, while Jamal Mayers resembled a tiger after bleaching his eyebrows in striped fashion.

"I did get a few double-takes," Mayers acknowledged.

Mayers finished with two assists, and the Blues won 5–3 over the Sharks in Game 1. The bleach-blonde Blues were in control. "But it's only one game," defenseman Chris Pronger warned. "It's a long series."

In Game 2, San Jose jumped out to an early lead, with a hand from Bergevin.

With Blues defenseman Al MacInnis in the penalty box serving a double-minor, Suter put a shot on goal from the boards.

"The puck hit me in the belly, and I grabbed it," Bergevin said. "[Mike] Ricci was behind me. [Owen] Nolan was going to the net. I didn't want to drop it or throw it in that corner, so I tried to throw it behind the net to the other side so our guys can get the puck and ice it. But the puck stuck in my glove, and I threw it.

"I honestly did not know it went in. When I saw it in the net, I knew that I did it. I guess I probably should have taken another step behind the net before I threw it."

Bergevin had to react quickly because holding onto the puck another millisecond was not an option.

"If he held it any longer, it would have been a penalty," Pleau said.

A penalty would have given the Sharks a five-on-three power play for two minutes.

"Really, there wasn't much he could do," defenseman Al MacInnis said. "When the puck comes to you like that and you grab it, you want to get rid of it as quickly as you can so you don't get a penalty. You don't want to drop it near the crease in traffic. And you don't want to give them a five-on-three. I was in the box, so put the blame on me."

Regardless of the blame, the Blues dropped Game 2 by a 4–2 decision, then they lost 2–1 in Game 3 and 3–2 in Game 4. Suddenly, the club was down three games to one, a deficit in which only 15 teams in NHL history had rallied to overcome.

One of those teams was the Blues, who did it the season before against Phoenix.

"It was a great experience going through it last year," forward Scott Young said. "This year, we have the confidence to do it again."

The Blues won 5–3 in Game 5. Then in Game 6, they claimed a 6–2 win on a hat trick by Young to even the series.

That set up Game 7 in front of 20,418 at Kiel Center, the largest crowd of the season. But a bizarre series grew even more bizarre when San Jose's Owen Nolan beat goalie Roman Turek with a shot from center ice with 10.2 seconds left in the first period.

"I don't know what happened," Turek said. "I saw it. I cannot explain it."

The Sharks rode Nolan's goal to a 3–1 win and a series upset.

"Every series has one play that's the turning point," Bergevin said. "I felt that way when [I threw the puck in the net], but I thought, *Maybe it won't be.* But it's the truth. I still feel the same way. I take the heat for that."

Pleau concluded, "Everyone's disappointed, but again, we had an excellent year. We won the Presidents' Trophy. A lot of people say that's not a big thing, but to me, it's a big thing. To win something over 82 games is a hell of an accomplishment. In the playoffs, we didn't play well and we got beat."

46 Tales from the Training Room

In four-plus decades, the number of injuries suffered by Blues players is countless. But the number of head athletic trainers responsible for getting those players healthy is just six.

Tommy Woodcock, the original Blues' trainer, was working with the Providence Reds in the American Hockey League when he received a phone call from former general manager Lynn Patrick in 1967.

"When the Blues started as an expansion team, Lynn called me and asked if I'd be interested in going to St. Louis," Woodcock said. "I said I'll go for a year and help you out, and I ended up staying 16 years."

Woodcock was followed in order by Norm Mackie, Mike Folga, Tom Nash, Ron Dubuque, and Ray Barile. Two of the six, Woodcock and Mackie, are in the Professional Hockey Athletic Trainers Society.

Many Blues fans have never heard their names, but to the hundreds of players who have passed through the training room, more so in the early days, these six men are like brothers.

"We were more or less a family," Woodcock said. "After practice, the guys all hung out together, went out to eat all the time. I remember we used to all go down to McDermott's and eat, right down the street from the Arena, by [Deaconess] hospital."

During Woodcock's days with the Blues, the club had many characters. He recalled a game in which defenseman Noel Picard was high-sticked and came into the training room for stitches. In those days, there were times when just one trainer worked the game for both teams.

"Noel said, 'Don't put your tools away yet. I'm going to send in the guy who did this to me,'" Woodcock said.

On another night, the Blues lost an overtime game to Los Angeles, and goaltender Glenn Hall wasn't happy after giving up the game-winning goal.

"Glenn came storming into the dressing room and was mad and everything," Woodcock recalled. "I said, 'Glenn, what's wrong?' He said, 'I feel sorry for that kid who scored the goal.' I said, 'Why?' He said, 'Well, he's going to go home and tell everybody that he scored against the great Glenn Hall and they're not going to believe him.'"

Woodcock worked during many financially unstable years for the Blues, including the late 1970s when the Salomon family was trying to sell the club and again in the early 1980s when Ralston Purina abandoned the franchise.

"We used to have to steal sticks from the home team," he said. "We had to steal sticks because we didn't have any money."

Woodcock left the Blues for Hartford in 1983, passing the torch to Mackie, who was the first hire of owner Harry Ornest.

Mackie, who had 15 years in the NHL when he came to the club, was an old-school trainer, the type who would recommend duct tape for a broken bone.

When Mark Hunter arrived in St. Louis, he told teammate Jim Pavese, "I've got to see Normie. My knee hurts when I move it this way."

Pavese replied, "Don't bother. Normie's just going to say, 'Then don't move it that way.'"

In 1989, Mackie, who was battling Parkinson's disease, ended his run as the Blues' trainer after six seasons and was named director of alumni services.

Folga, the next in line, showed his respect for his predecessor by putting a sign on the trainer's door: "The Norm Mackie Office."

The door to that office, however, continued to swing for a few years before Barile was hired in 1995. Folga was fired in the early 1990s, and his replacement, Dubuque, was let go after less than six months on the job.

Barile has been the Blues' trainer for the past two decades, eclipsing the tenure of Woodcock, with whom Barile had a preexisting relationship.

"As a kid, I went to the Providence College hockey school," Barile said. "They roomed me with Tommy Woodcock's son, and I met Tommy as a kid [when] he was a trainer for the Blues, not knowing I would have his position some day. Woody is phenomenal. I consider him a good friend and kind of a mentor."

Woodcock and Barile have traded stories about how the training room, although still a sacred area, has changed.

"The old-school players were a lot different," Barile said. "Those guys back then, they did a lot more together. The athletes have changed over time, and it's seen more as a business today, dollars and cents. Now you need to take care of your body because your body is what makes you money. Not that those guys didn't, but it was more of a college atmosphere when Tommy was working with the team."

Years ago, a player having a beer before the game wasn't out of the question, and after the game it was a certainty.

"Yeah, that's for sure," Woodcock said.

But the beverage of choice is different these days.

"Now it's protein shakes," Barile said.

Before, there was a smoking lounge for players, some of whom puffed between periods. That's not the case any longer.

"Alexander Khavanov is the last player that I can remember that was a smoker," Barile said. Khavanov's final season with the Blues was 2003–04. "He would pull a dart in between periods, and he'd be the first one out of the locker room after the game to go have a smoke. That's how the game has changed."

Another change has been the team's response to concussions. In the old days, they were called "bell-ringers," and players continued to play through them.

"It's unbelievable," Woodcock said. "Now they're out 10 days, at least."

Some players these days, like former Blue David Perron, sat out 13 months.

"They didn't treat concussions the way we do now," Barile said. "Now we hold them out and err on the side of caution. One time in Calgary we had a player get concussed, and he wanted to go back out. We had to hide his helmet and gloves so he couldn't play."

The list of stories goes on and on, but the number of trainers who can tell them in St. Louis is limited to just a select few.

"It's been a short list of trainers," Barile said. "We've got a couple of them in the Hall of Fame, so that gives me something to live up to."

47 Take a Ride on an Olympia

Longtime Red Wings fan Premal Thaker, a native of Detroit, had always wanted to take a spin on the ice-resurfacing machine. But in a hockey-crazed city, she figured her chances of ever being a passenger on a Zamboni—or an Olympia, as used by some rinks—were slim.

When Thaker became engaged to her husband and thought that she would be moving to Pittsburgh, she began wondering how she could fulfill her dream at the Penguins' arena. Instead of settling in Pittsburgh, however, the couple settled in St. Louis.

"I've been trying to find [an opportunity], and it's really hard, especially in cities where hockey is one of the die-hard teams," Thaker said. "I didn't even think about how I would go about it. Some teams do have ways for fans to get on, and other teams you have to go through an auction or know somebody."

Frank Zamboni invented the world's first self-propelled ice-making machine in 1949. While many people refer to all ice-resurfacing machines as Zambonis, the Olympia, which is operated by the Schlupp family, is another popular brand. In fact, that's the brand used by the Blues.

For decades, the machines have been used in the NHL to "clean" the ice during intermission breaks. But the idea of hockey fans taking a seat on one and waving to the crowd as it laps around the rink is new in St. Louis.

"It's only been the last three years or so," said Jim Schmuke, who has been behind the steering wheel of the Blues' ice machine since 1989. "People are fascinated by the machine and what it does. It kind of baffles me sometimes, but I guess because I've done it so long, it's just old hat for us."

The Blues have a longstanding charity called the 14 Fund, which is now called "Blues for Kids." The money raised for the charity contributes to programs that positively impact the health and wellness of youth in St. Louis.

Bruce Affleck, the Blues' president of business operations, recently came across the concept of the Zamboni/Olympia rides and thought it would be a enjoyable experience for fans and a great way to raise resources for the 14 Fund. The club charges $500 for a package that includes two tickets to the game and one Zamboni ride.

"I saw a list of the [Chicago] White Sox game experiences," Affleck said. "They sell everything from taking the balls and scorecard out to the umpire, going out with the rake crew every three innings, taking the tarp out…. And they make a lot of good money at it. So we instituted riding the Zamboni, sitting on the bench before the game—different things like that—for the 14 Fund."

Thaker, however, claimed her ticket after winning an auction. The Blues had donated the package to the St. Louis Ovarian Cancer Awareness group, which then auctioned off the item, and Thaker, a doctor, had the highest bid.

"I wasn't even at the auction," she said. "I was on my honeymoon in Italy. One of my patients bid on the Zamboni ride for me. She emailed me and said, 'You won!' Being on my honeymoon, it was a wonderful way to celebrate."

The day finally came during the 2012–13 season during a game against the Chicago Blackhawks. Thaker climbed up a ladder to her chair and locked in her seat belt. Then it was time for the ride of her life.

"For me it was a dream come true," she said. "I actually had my parents [fly in from Florida] to watch me on the Zamboni because my dad is a huge hockey fan. I offered him the ride and he said, 'No, no, it's your chance.'"

Schmuke said that once fans get on the Blues' Olympia, they ask tons of questions.

"People want to know how long we've driven or what the machine does, stuff like that," Schmuke said. "It's tough because people want to talk to you but there's a lot of noise. A couple of times they'll be real soft-spoken and you kind of lean over and pretty soon you're not paying attention to what you're doing out there. All of a sudden, whoa, there's the boards."

While the machines are driving on ice, they don't slide as much as one might think.

"They have studded tires, so you're okay out there. You're kind of safe," Schmuke said. "It's funny because when we have bad weather here in St. Louis, all of a sudden everybody is asking me what's the secret to driving in the ice and the snow. I'm like, 'Well, studded tires is one thing that would help you.'"

Thaker became curious about Schmuke's career, too.

"It's interesting. I don't know how you get into being a Zamboni driver," she said. "I told him it was a great way to participate in the sport."

The preparation for becoming an ice-machine operator has changed over the years.

"Now there are schools you can go to and not just learn to drive, but you learn the basics of making ice, troubleshooting, stuff like that," Schmuke said. "But when I learned, the guy that drove the machine at the Old Arena, he pretty much pulled it up to the entrance of the ice and said, 'This switch does this, this switch does that.' He pointed to all of the knobs and levers and said, 'Okay, go do it.'"

Intermissions last approximately 17 minutes, and with two machines these days, the job of resurfacing the ice can be done in about seven minutes.

"It's not extremely fast, but they make those laps a lot quicker than you think," Thaker said. "You see all the fans and you get to see how big the ice really is because you're never really on the ice otherwise. So it's your chance to see what the hockey players really see. The way they skate back and forth so quick, you don't really appreciate how large the rink is until you're actually driving on it and seeing it. It's quite impressive."

Schmuke said he's heard stories of fans in other cities getting caught up in the moment.

"I think it was in Colorado, somebody actually unbuckled their seat belt and got on top of the machine and was standing up there like they were surfing," he said. "Naturally the driver pulled over to the exit and took them off."

No surfing for Thaker.

"She was well-behaved," Schmuke said.

But Thaker did admit to being a little overzealous.

"The [passenger] on the other Zamboni, she must have been a teenager because she wasn't waving," Thaker said. "She just sat there very stoically, and here I am waving to fans. I'm thinking I'm a lot older than her, but I'm acting like I'm a 2-year-old. I was like, if you're going to be on there, you might as well wave to the fans. It's something I've always wanted to do, and it really was a lot of fun."

48 Russian Invasion

Many NHL fans think of Detroit as the NHL team that first tapped into the Russian market for talent.

In the late 1980s and early 1990s, Detroit drafted Vladimir Konstantinov, Sergei Fedorov, and Vyacheslav Kozlov. But it wasn't until the mid-1990s, under Scott Bowman, when the Red Wings gained notoriety for putting five Russians on the ice at once, earning the nickname the "Red Army."

"Probably the team that started it first was Winnipeg with general manager Mike Smith," Detroit general manager Ken Holland said. "Unfortunately they were in the same division as the Edmonton Oilers, and they could never get by."

In 1989, Winnipeg drafted Russians Evgeny Davydov and Sergei Kharin, and in 1991 the Jets added four more Russian players. At the time, taking Russians in the NHL draft was a risk because of the Cold War. Teams would essentially be wasting picks if the player decided not to come to North America, or if the Russian hockey federation demanded hefty transfer fees.

But in 1991, the Iron Curtain was removed, the Soviet Union and Czechoslovakia fell, and NHL teams immediately began trying to pry players out of the Eastern Bloc. The next year, 11 of the first 21 picks in the draft were from either Russia or the former nation of Czechoslovakia, including No. 1 pick Roman Hamrlik by Tampa Bay and No. 2 Alexei Yashin by Ottawa.

In that draft, Winnipeg took nine Russians.

"Two-thirds of the way through the first round, fans were booing the picks because there were so many Europeans and Russians," Smith said. "All of a sudden the entire league realized there were players in Europe capable of playing here."

The Blues and general manager Ron Caron were not to be excluded from the new trend. Caron, on the advice of head scout Ted Hampson, used the club's first three draft picks on Russian players. They took Igor Korolev with pick No. 38 overall, Vitali Karamnov No. 62, and Vitali Prokhorov No. 64. Those were the notable ones, but the team also grabbed Igor Bouldin No. 180 and Yuri Gunko No. 230 in the same draft.

In all, five of the Blues' 12 selections in the 1992 draft were Russians.

"We accomplished what we tried to do," Hampson said. "I hope it's what we want."

There was much hype surrounding the new Blues. Korolev, 21, was a "major prize," according to Caron.

"He could play on the Blues' top line," the GM said.

Karamnov, 23, was a left winger whom Caron envisioned playing alongside superstar Brett Hull.

Prokhorov, 25, was another left winger who was considered feisty.

"I've been told by other GMs that Karamnov and Prokorov will score 60 goals for the Blues next year," Caron said. "That's 60 more than our picks last year. They're good for 30 goals each."

To find out, the Blues first had to get them to North America. That proved to be no problem, signing each of the Russians in time for the 1992 training camp. The challenge was getting them acclimated to their surroundings and learning a new language.

First-year coach Bob Plager joked that the only two English words the three Russians knew were "per diem."

"We told them forecheck, backcheck, and then paycheck," Plager joked.

Okay, so he was half-joking.

"We said that all the time—they could spend it," former Blues enforcer Kelly Chase said. "They just weren't accustomed to walking in a store and having choices. When they got over here, they didn't know what was going on. They were completely clueless."

On the ice, the Blues were hoping for a different story, and if one preseason game was any indicator, fans were going to be thrilled. Placed on a line together to ease the transition, the three Russians dazzled the crowd in a 4–2 exhibition win over Minnesota in September 1992. Although they didn't score in the game, the trio had several "scintillating" offensive rushes, according to the game story in the *Post-Dispatch*.

But those nights were few and far between. In their first season, the Russians combined for eight goals and 25 assists in 84 games. Korolev netted four goals and 23 assists in 74 games, Prokhorov had four goals and one assist in 26 games, and Karamnov mustered one assist in seven games.

"Funny, in Brett's case, he knew right away," Chase said. "He goes, 'The little one is the only one that can play.' He was talking about Korolev. [Hull and Korolev] played together a little bit, and it didn't work.

"Then the coaches would put the three of them together and sometimes they would look like the Russian national team—whirling, twirling, the whole works. But then you had other times there would be a giveaway, the puck is in our net and they were minus-3, and you didn't dare put him on the ice. But I think that in fairness to them, there was a lot expected of them because of what had gone on in other places. It didn't work out great."

Korolev had the longest NHL career. After being claimed in the waiver draft in January 1995, he went on to play 795 games with Winnipeg, Phoenix, Toronto, and Chicago. Karamnov lasted only 92 games and Prokhorov 83 before each returned to Europe.

After retiring from the NHL in 2004 and spending seven more seasons playing in Russia, Korolev accepted a position as an assistant coach with the Lokomotiv of the Kontinental Hockey League.

He was killed in the 2011 plane crash that took the lives of 40-plus members of the organization that were traveling to an away game.

Following the disaster, the Blues held a pregame ceremony honoring Korolev. Regardless of how the Russian experiment transpired in St. Louis, Chase remembered the three Russians during their days here as friendly. He recalled being invited out by Korolev, Prokhorov, and Karamnov during a Blues road trip to Los Angeles.

"They were saying thanks for helping with the shopping and getting around St. Louis," Chase said. "We went to a Russian restaurant in L.A. the night before a game, and they closed the back end. We were in there eating authentic Russian food, caviar, Vodka, more Vodka, and more Vodka. [Korolev] was the one who spoke the best English, and he comes to me and tries to tell me, 'You can't say to the coaches that we were out all night.' I'm saying to him, 'I was with you. No kidding. You don't have to tell me that.' I laughed. I loved it that they included me. But they were concerned that I might say something. I'm like, 'Hey boys, I'm the last guy who will ever say something.'"

49 Golf Getaway

It was billed as a team-bonding experience, but for defenseman Erik Johnson, the Blues' players-only golf getaway at the Lake of the Ozarks in September 2008 ultimately led to his departure.

Johnson, the face of the franchise after being drafted No. 1 overall by the Blues in 2006, was injured in what he insisted was a "freak incident" at The Club at Porto Cima. While attempting to stop his golf cart and step out to hit his next shot, the 6'4", 225-lb.

Johnson got his foot stuck between the accelerator and brake, twisting his right knee.

"I just yelled," Johnson said. According to Johnson, he had to tell himself, "It's just a freak incident, and it's tough to deal with, but hopefully it's nothing."

The screech of the tires, followed by Johnson's screech, could probably be heard 2½ hours away in St. Louis, where Blues fans looked at Johnson as their reward for a last-place record in 2005–06, giving them the top overall pick for the first time in team history.

Meanwhile, hundreds of miles away in Traverse City, Michigan, the Blues brass had gathered for the NHL rookie tournament, which happens the week before NHL players report to camp. Club president John Davidson got the call about Johnson's accident.

"When I first heard it, it didn't sound like it was anything serious," Davidson said. "And then it got worse and worse and worse."

The first MRI was inconclusive because of swelling in Johnson's knee, but the knee wasn't nearly as huffy and puffy as Davidson, who wanted answers. Was the injury really caused by a golf cart accident, or was there more to the story?

An anonymous source told the *St. Louis Post-Dispatch* that players were "goofing around" on the course that day. A report in the newspaper documented that a golf cart was wrecked by the Blues, an incident that players acknowledged and took responsibility for afterward, reimbursing the course for the damage.

"The [wrecked] golf cart had nothing to do with me being hurt," Johnson said. "We apologized for [the damage], but as far as my injury goes, there's no correlation with that at all."

But Johnson could do nothing to quiet the rumors. And as speculation grew, the defenseman grew more defensive.

"First off, I can understand why people would think [it's a lie] just because how weird the accident was," he said. "But it really

The Top Draft Picks of 2006

The Blues had the No. 1 overall pick in the 2006 draft and selected defenseman Erik Johnson. Here are the top five picks in the 2006 NHL Draft:

1. Erik Johnson
Position: Defenseman
Team: U.S. National Development Program
Drafted by: Blues
Note: Traded to the Colorado Avalanche in 2011

2. Jordan Staal
Position: Center
Team: Peterborough Petes (Ontario Hockey League)
Drafted by: Pittsburgh Penguins
Note: Won a Stanley Cup with Penguins in 2009, traded to Carolina in 2012

3. Jonathan Toews
Position: Center
Team: University of North Dakota (NCAA)
Drafted by: Chicago Blackhawks
Note: Won a Stanley Cup with Chicago in 2010, 2013, and 2015

4. Nicklas Backstrom
Position: Center
Team: Brynas IF (Sweden)
Drafted by: Washington Capitals
Note: Rookie of the Year finalist in 2007–08

5. Phil Kessel
Position: Right wing
Team: University of Minnesota
Drafted by: Boston Bruins
Note: Winner of the Bill Masterton Trophy for perseverance in 2006–07, traded to Toronto in 2009

bothers me when people make assumptions, people who have no clue about the situation. The only guys who know were the guys that were with me, and they didn't even know until we got back and my knee was hurting. I played the next three or four holes of the round.

"It really bothers me when I hear things that are just so stupid. Don't assume things until you have the facts. The facts are what we said. People can have their thoughts, but what's happened, happened. We've said how it happened, and there's no reason for people to make anything up."

Unfortunately, you couldn't make up the final MRI results—Johnson had a torn knee ligament and would miss the entire season.

The Minnesota native had surgery in November 2008 and was recovered in time to begin his second full season in the NHL in 2009–10. He scored 10 goals and had 39 points in 79 games, but concerns arose about whether Johnson would ever live up to the hype of being the No. 1 overall pick.

On February 18, 2011, when Johnson landed in St. Louis after a game in Buffalo, he learned from Blues general manager Doug Armstrong that he had been dealt to Colorado, along with forward Jay McClement, in exchange for Avalanche forward Chris Stewart and defenseman Kevin Shattenkirk. Draft picks were also swapped.

"I was obviously not expecting this," Johnson wrote in a text message to the *Post-Dispatch* upon hearing news of the trade at 2:40 AM.

In the end, Johnson's lost year of development, spent recovering from the freak knee injury, was the turning point. Not being on the ice cost him valuable time on what is a steep learning curve.

"The only thing I'd say that was unfortunate was the knee injury," Davidson said after the trade. "Anybody at that young age, it can't be helpful."

Johnson was quick to get revenge on the Blues, however, as the Blues and Avalanche met in St. Louis just four days after the trade.

Late in the game, he scored to give the Avs a 3–2 lead in a game they would win 4–3.

"I want to make them regret trading Erik Johnson," Johnson said. "There's no doubt about that, and I say that with the utmost respect in the world…. I respect Doug Armstrong. I respect John Davidson, everybody in this city. At the end of the day, I want them to be kicking themselves for trading me. I definitely want [Armstrong] at the end of the day saying, 'Why did I trade Erik Johnson?'"

50 One-Hit Wonder

Wayne Babych had racked up 43 goals before selection time for the 1981 NHL All-Star Game, but the Blues' right winger was not voted onto the roster by the Professional Hockey Writers' Association, and head coach Pat Quinn failed to add him.

"Whether I was chosen or not, I still want to score 50 goals," Babych said. "I think that's a target everyone would dream of reaching, and this is my chance."

Babych had scored exactly 50 goals in back-to-back years with the Portland Winterhawks, leading the goal-challenged Blues to select him with the third overall pick in the 1978 NHL Draft. Starting out on the "Kid Line" with Bernie Federko and Brian Sutter, Babych responded with 27 goals in 67 games as a rookie and, despite a shoulder separation in his second season, he had 26 goals in 59 games.

No player in the 13-year existence of the franchise had reached the 50-goal plateau. But in just his third season, at age 22, Babych was poised to become the first Blue to score 50 goals in a season.

Head coach Red Berenson adjusted his lines in 1980–81, moving Babych with Jorgen Pettersson and Blake Dunlop, and the chemistry was evident early.

"I remember Babs always said, 'Feed me! Feed me!'" Pettersson said. "He was joking, but he'd be in the slot and we'd feed him. He had a great shot."

Babych had 26 goals by the 37th game of the season. He scored a goal in eight consecutive games from December 23 to January 10, including a hat trick on December 30 against Toronto.

"Wayne picked up a lot of his goals by going to the net," Dunlop said. "He was so strong that he picked up some rebounds and things in front of the net. But that certainly wasn't the only way he scored. He had a good shot."

The Blues' record for goals in a single-season was 43, set by Chuck Lefley in 1975–76. Babych reached that number by the All-Star Game, and after initially being left off the roster, he was a last-minute replacement for injured New York Islander Bryan Trottier. Babych even contributed a goal in the Clarence Campbell Conference's 4–1 win over the Prince of Wales, but by that point, the winger was more concerned about his 50 goals as a Blue.

It came on March 12, 1981, with the team trailing Montreal 4–2. Babych beat Canadiens goalie Richard Sevigny with a shot from about 25'.

"I had the puck on our blue line, and I made a rink-wide pass over to Wayne," Pettersson said. "It was a big thing. Not too many had done it then."

Montreal's Maurice "Rocket" Richard was the first NHL player to record 50 goals in a single season, doing so in 50 games in 1944–45. In the history of the NHL, only 24 players—some multiple times—had accomplished the feat prior to the 1980–81 season.

"You just go game by game, and you do your best," Babych said. "I'd get into the hole or the slot area, and everything was put on the table for me. They were feeding me. Blake and Jorgen were very good with the puck."

Babych established the Blues' new scoring record with 54 goals, including an NHL-best 40 even-strength goals. His 96 points were second behind Federko's 104 points, also in 1980–81.

The Blues signed Babych to a new four-year, $400,000 contract, featuring a $125,000 signing bonus. Unfortunately, he would never live up to it, as his goal-scoring numbers went from 54 to 19, 16, and 13 before he left St. Louis.

In 1981–82, Babych suffered a torn rotator cuff when a linesman yanked him back while he was punching Winnipeg's Jimmy Mann during a preseason fight. Babych missed almost 30 games.

"He never played quite as aggressively after that," Dunlop said. "Babs was never a great stickhandler. Jorgen and I had to carry the puck for him, and he had to get himself open. He needed the extra room to get the extra time to shoot the puck. When he couldn't play aggressively anymore, he didn't have the room he needed."

After Babych's production fell to 13 goals in 70 games in 1983–84, a change of scenery was welcomed by both sides. Babych was made available in the waiver draft, and Pittsburgh took a chance on the former 50-goal scorer.

"I scored 54 goals, and [the Blues] expected that year after year," Babych said. "How many can you score when you're hurt? I was hurt for three years. I couldn't do what I was capable of doing."

In his first season with the Penguins, playing with Mario Lemieux and Warren Young, Babych scored 20 goals in 65 games, the most he would net during the remainder of his career. He was traded to Quebec and later Hartford, where he finished his playing days with his brother, David.

In 1989–90, Babych watched his single-season scoring record be obliterated by the Blues' Brett Hull.

"He's a good hockey player," Babych said. "I know he's going to score 50. The way he's going, he should score 70. But don't put that pressure on him."

Hull finished with 72 goals that season, reaching 50 in 16 fewer games than Babych. Hull, who eclipsed 50 goals five times as a Blue, set the new franchise record of 86 goals in 1990–91. The only other player in club history to reach the 50-goal plateau was Brendan Shanahan with 51 in 1992–93 and 52 in 1993–94.

51 Go to OB Clark's after a Game

In the 1980s, the Blues practiced at Brentwood Ice Arena in suburban St. Louis. And down the street at 1619 South Brentwood was OB Clark's, a pub run by brothers Joe and Jimmy O'Brien.

"After practice, we used to get a lot of players to come down," Jimmy said. "They'd grab lunch and it was pretty relaxed back then, so they'd have a couple of beers. That's how my brother and I got to know some of the players."

What began as a pit stop for Kelly Chase, Brett Hull, Brendan Shanahan, and company over the years is a must-stop today for Blues fans before and after games. And when the Blues won the Stanley Cup in 2019, it was the first place they took the trophy upon landing in St. Louis. The next day, players stood on the bar's balcony overlooking a sea of fans chanting, "Let's go Blues!"

While it's the most popular hockey bar in St. Louis these days, the traffic hasn't stopped former and current players from skating in unannounced. It's nothing to see Chase and Alexander Steen sipping on a cold one.

"It's just been our spot," Chase said. "They take care of you. It's a sense of security. I just started dragging guys in there, and it's just kind of evolved into what it is now—a hockey bar where guys hang out. They're like family. There's nothing they won't do to take care of you."

In 1996, Joel Quenneville became head coach of the Blues and moved to St. Louis six months ahead of his family. The O'Briens provided Quenneville with several TVs and a scratch pad to take notes on the NHL games.

"[Quenneville] stayed at the hotel nearby, at the Rez Inn," Jimmy said, "so he used to come in every off night he had and watch hockey games and scout other teams, and that's how we became close with Joel."

The former head coach of the Chicago Blackhawks, who led his team to the Stanley Cup in 2010, 2013, and 2015, Quenneville still stops by OB Clark's when he's in St. Louis.

"I like the camaraderie when we get to see the O'Brien boys," Quenneville said. "I used to stop in there for a pop, and I still get in there once or twice. It's just a nice place to hang out, talk hockey, watch all the games that are on, and visit with a lot of friends from over the years."

In 2000, OB Clark's changed addresses, sliding down the block to 1921 South Brentwood, but it kept the same clientele. In a trade with Phoenix, the Blues acquired power forward Keith Tkachuk, who became a regular at the pub.

"It's pretty much the only place I would go out to after a game on the way home," Tkachuk said. "Just a great place to wind down. Nobody bothers you. You go in, just relax. Jimmy and Joe are very good at what they do. They're great friends of mine."

Like all close friends, though, the O'Briens and Tkachuk are constantly taking jabs at one another.

"In 2006, we were all getting ready to go down to Game 1 of the Cardinals World Series," Jimmy said. "[Tkachuk] was talking about how he was dreading going to the Halloween party that was Monday night at Dougie Weight's house. He didn't know what he was going to wear, and he wasn't a fan of dressing up.

"He asked us for a couple of suggestions. I don't believe he had scored a goal yet, and I think they were 10 games into the season. I told him that he should dig into his closet and see if he could find an old jersey and maybe go as a goal scorer."

Not to be outdone, Tkachuk replied, "I've got to make sure that Jimmy is not an NHL general manager because the way he talks sometimes, he thinks he can do it all."

The O'Briens never set out to have NHL coaches such as Quenneville on speed dial or attend baseball games with 500-goal scorers.

"In all honesty, I think one of the reasons we have become good friends with a lot of those guys is because we treat them just like normal people," Jimmy O'Brien said. "That's how I think they prefer to be treated. They come in here and fans are respectful enough to them. They're in here all the time, so nobody gets too excited when they're here."

One time, however, a patron did cross the blue line.

"During the lockout of 2004–05, there was a fan who was questioning the toughness of Tkachuk and Chase," Jimmy O'Brien said. "He kept jabbing them and poking them in the side. They didn't pay much attention to him, but he kept pestering, telling them that neither one of them was that tough. Finally they told him if he jabbed them one more time that he was going to get it. He persisted on, so Chaser turned around and gave him a two-handed shove. [The guy] slid across the floor, hit the rug, and the guy's prosthetic leg fell off.

"Chaser left all disgusted. He called me back on the phone and said, 'Please tell me that guy that I just pushed did not have a prosthetic leg.' I told him that he did and he was still trying to strap it back on."

The visit by the Stanley Cup in 2019 isn't the only time it has been to OB Clarks, and the World Series trophy for that matter.

In 2006, former Blue Doug Weight won it with Carolina and returned home to St. Louis with it. Another time, Kirkwood youth hockey supporter and ex-Blues staffer Jamie Kompon brought the Cup home after winning with Los Angeles.

"Jamie played on our Thursday night beer league team for 8–10 years," Jimmy said. "When he had a chance, he brought it back through St. Louis and celebrated it with his former beer league team. Had it in here for like two hours. It makes us feel kind of special that they are going to take time to come to your place."

Jimmy and Joe O'Brien have also had the Cardinals' 2006 World Series Trophy in the house.

"By the time my son was six months old, he had sat in the Stanley Cup and held the World Series Trophy," Jimmy said.

Not a bad run for a couple of guys who happened to own a bar next to the practice rink.

"You try not to take it for granted, but it's special," Jimmy said. "We've built up a lot of good relationships with a lot of good people, and it is kind of surreal sometimes."

52 Pronger's Heart Stops

The NHL playoffs offer many heart-stopping moments for fans. But in Game 2 of the 1998 Western Conference semifinals, the Blues' Chris Pronger survived a serious one. A shot by the Red Wings' Dmitri Mironov hit Pronger just to the left of his heart, causing it to stop beating briefly. He lay unconscious for about 20–30 seconds.

"[Pronger] took a slap shot really high off the chest," John Davidson, who was the color analyst covering the game, described on the TV broadcast. "Boom, the left side of his chest, near his heart. You don't know if it's a rib problem or something more serious than that. He started to skate toward the bench…and then he kind of went down…just collapsed. Immediately you could see that he needed help, and he got a lot of help."

The crowd of 19,983 at Joe Louis Arena, cheering on Detroit's 4–1 lead in the third period, grew silent. Blues team physician Aaron Birenbaum and trainer Ray Barile rushed onto the ice. Pronger's parents, Jim and Elia, who were watching Chris play on Mother's Day, headed down from their seats to learn what had happened to their 23-year-old son.

"He was turning purple," Blues forward Geoff Courtnall said. "The doctors were massaging his heart. He looked scared. It just gave you such a sick feeling. You felt so helpless."

Pronger's No. 44 jersey had been cut down the middle by the medical personnel tending to him. He had a welt on his rib cage where the puck had hit.

"It's just frightening to see a man buckle like that," forward Blair Atcheynum said. "His eyes rolled back in his head. You don't know what happened."

Pronger's heartbeat became "thready, or weak," according to Barile, who said the defenseman regained consciousness after a short lapse. Pronger was fitted with a cervical collar, guarding against any further damage. But he wasn't heading to the penalty box for slashing earlier in the sequence. Instead, he was on his way to nearby Henry Ford Hospital by ambulance for observation.

"Where's Chris?" Elia Pronger asked as she made her way to ice level. "Where's my Chris?"

Pronger had told Courtnall to tell his parents that he was fine.

"At the end, he was talking to me," Courtnall said. "He was asking me what happened and asking how much time was left in the game…. They were trying to get him out of there, but he kept saying, 'No, no, wait.' He wanted to get up and play. Amazingly, I finally had to pull his hand off me so they could take him."

Birenbaum said that Pronger's heart did stop briefly, but its rhythm quickly returned to normal. This is what's known as "cardiac arrhythmia."

"It's not a common thing," Birenbaum said. "But when anyone is hit on the chest wall over the heart, it certainly can cause arrhythmia. The potential was there for it to be more serious. Fortunately it didn't happen. He recovered very quickly from it. It was a very brief incident."

Without Pronger, the game continued, and Detroit added two more goals for a 6–1 victory, evening up the best-of-seven series at 1–1.

"[The injury] took the life out of both teams," Red Wings captain Steve Yzerman said. "The game can be really brutal at times. You know these things happen, but it's difficult to play when someone gets hurts like that."

Pronger was released from the hospital on Monday, the day after the incident, and he returned to St. Louis where Game 3 would be played Tuesday.

When asked if Pronger could be available, Blues coach Joel Quenneville replied, "It's way too premature to guess on something like that."

Pronger was pragmatic.

"I'd like to play, but I have to hear what the doctors say about the tests," he said.

The loss of Pronger, who led all NHL defensemen with a plus-47 rating, would have been devastating to the Blues.

"He's a competitor, a warrior, but we have to make sure his health is taken care of," Barile said. "We want to make sure Chris Pronger the person is okay."

About one hour before the 6:30 PM faceoff, Pronger received word that he had checked out okay and could suit up for Game 3. The crowd of 20,621 gave him a loud ovation when he hit the ice.

"It's nice to be appreciated," Pronger said.

His ability to play just two days after his heart stopped was made even more impressive when the playoff game went into double-overtime.

"I felt good," Pronger said. "Actually I felt better in the fifth period than I did in the fourth. It must have been the IV I was on."

But in the second OT, former Blue Brendan Shanahan scored for a 3–2 Detroit victory.

"It was a tough day for us, a tough game to lose," Pronger said.

The Red Wings eventually captured the series four games to two. Fortunately for Pronger, there were brighter days ahead.

53 Perfect Attendance

Tom Calhoun had a serious case of the flu, and outside the Old Arena, a blizzard was dropping out of the sky. Otherwise, on that night in the late 1980s, Calhoun was glad to be at work as an underpaid substitute public-address announcer for the Blues.

"I remember going back between the first and second period and losing my lunch really bad," he said. "I told myself, 'I'm going to try and get through the next period.' I didn't feel a whole lot better, but I made it through the game."

More than two decades later, Calhoun still hasn't missed a night of work, famously calling out the names of Blues players for close to 1,500 consecutive games, including the 2019 Stanley Cup final. It doesn't earn the attention of a Brett Hull goal-scoring streak, but those around the rink are familiar with and admire what Calhoun notes as his own personal "Ironman" streak.

A local radio personality, Calhoun never set out to be the Blues' PA announcer. In January 1987, he was asked to fill in after Charlie Hodges, the person who previously held the position, left for a job with Bud Sports, a TV production company.

Blues vice president Susie Mathieu, play-by-play voice Dan Kelly, and fellow broadcaster Ron Jacober suggested Calhoun's name to the club.

"I kind of volunteered to finish out the season," Calhoun said. "They didn't really pay much in those days. Those were the Harry Ornest days, and they were still counting paperclips. I said, 'Yeah, I'll do it as a favor for the rest of the season.'"

The Blues bumped up the pay the following season, "and I've been at every game since," he said.

When Calhoun says every game, he means it.

"Preseason, postseason, exhibition games, touring Russian teams that came through St. Louis way back when, two [Blues] games in Sweden," Calhoun counted.

In 2009, the Blues opened the regular season with two games against Detroit in Sweden in what the NHL dubbed the "Premier Games." Regardless of where they were or what they were called, the second of the two games was technically considered a home game. So if Calhoun missed it, technically the streak was over.

"At that time, the Detroit [PA announcer], Budd Lynch, either couldn't go or wasn't up to going," he said. "So the people from the league office called and said, 'We'd like you to go over and do those two games. Would you be interested?'"

Calhoun made the trip and worked the two games, continuing the streak. It was well before Sweden when Calhoun realized something special was brewing.

"About 400 or 500 games into it, I said, 'Boy, that would be really neat if I could continue this for a while,'" Calhoun said. "To me, it was just like showing up for work. You've got a job to do, you go do it. But then after a while, I thought this is a pretty special 'Ironman' streak. I should try to keep it going. I've been lucky. I've been healthy and there haven't been too many big conflicts, and when there have been my family has been understanding about it."

Like the time when Calhoun received an invitation to his nephew's wedding, and the nuptials were on the same day as a Blues game.

"When I told my nephew, who is a huge Blues fan by the way, that I was going to have to miss a game to come to his wedding, he said, 'Don't you dare. You can come to the reception, but don't break your streak by coming to the wedding,'" Calhoun said. "I've missed some school concerts and plays and things like that, but really no major events, like a funeral. I've been pretty lucky."

Calhoun's career has spanned from Brian Sutter, now in his early sixties, to Vladimir Tarasenko, in his late twenties.

"I've gone from the days when having a Russian or Eastern European in the league was a rarity to now it being commonplace and almost celebrated that we have so many people from foreign countries in our league," he said.

But there's a catch. The European names can be hard to pronounce.

"I think Maxim Afinogenov is probably at the top of the list," Calhoun said. "That's a dandy. The first time I saw that, I thought, *What in the world is this?*"

His favorite name to belt out was ex-Blue Keith Tkachuk, who arrived in March 2001 in a trade with Phoenix.

"I remember when he first came here, the very first game he suited up for the Blues, I went into the locker room before the game and introduced myself," Calhoun said. "I said, 'I've got a treatment I want to do on your name. I'm going to have some fun with it, but I want to make sure it's okay with you before I do it.'

He said, 'You've been doing this for a long time. Whatever you do with it is great.'

"I remember that first time he scored a goal, I announced it, 'KEEEITH KAAACHUCK!' That's the name that I've had the most fun with, and it seems to be the one that sticks with everybody."

Even more so than Hull.

"You know, as great a player as Brett was, he's got a one-syllable first name and a one-syllable last name, so you can't do a whole lot with it," Calhoun said. "But it was a lot of fun calling every goal that Brett Hull scored in a Blues' uniform at home. I can say that. That's one of my favorite things to say."

And there are more memories to create because Calhoun doesn't have any plans of stopping the streak.

"As long as my health holds up, I enjoy doing this so much. If people still enjoy what I do, I'll do it until I fall down," he said. "It's just something I think is a big part of my personality, my life, and if people continue to enjoy it, I'll keep doing it."

54 Hometown Hero: Pat Maroon

In one year's time, St. Louisan Pat Maroon went from a hometown discount to a hometown hero.

Maroon grew up playing ice hockey and roller hockey in St. Louis, and was among the first wave of players from the city to make it to the NHL when Philadelphia selected him in the sixth round (No. 161 overall) of the 2007 draft.

Maroon would play nearly 400 games over nine seasons with Edmonton, Anaheim, and New Jersey before becoming an unrestricted free agent in 2018. The 30-year-old had a few opportunities on the open market, and one of those options would be playing for the club he grew up watching.

On July 9, Maroon signed a one-year, $1.75 million contract with the Blues, whose arena is about a 20-minute drive from the suburb in which he was raised. It was less money than the 6'3" forward was being offered by others, but this would allow him to perhaps re-establish himself in the NHL and play in front of his nine-year-old son, Anthony.

"It came down to, if I was going to take a one-year deal, what team was going to help me prolong my career and I felt like the St. Louis Blues had my best interest," Maroon said at the time. "I left some things on the table, but it's a life-changing thing for me and I think this is the team that's going to get my game where it needs to be and put me in the right direction for the next five years."

Maroon couldn't have known then how life-changing the experience would be.

But before scoring the game-winning goal in double-overtime of the Western Conference semifinals against Dallas and later hoisting the Stanley Cup, the road less traveled by professional athletes was quite bumpy. He had no goals in his first 15 games and just three in 32 games before the Blues made him a healthy scratch January 5.

"Patty obviously hasn't produced like he's wanted to and like we've wanted him to," Blues coach Craig Berube said in January. "I think he's been playing pretty good hockey the last 10 games, but production is just not there."

The Blues were scheduled to give away a Maroon "Big Rig" bobblehead on January 8 and there was a chance that Maroon could be scratched on that night. But he remained in the lineup, and despite the swirling speculation about his future, he stayed positive.

"It comes down to just playing good hockey," Maroon said. "I've got to be better, we all know that. [But] good things happen to people that work hard and believe in themselves. I still believe in myself. I'm a good hockey player and I still believe I can get to where I need to be and be an everyday NHL player."

The Blues might have wanted to trade Maroon, but he had a full no-trade clause that turned into a modified clause, in which he could veto deals to a list of eight teams. It was perhaps the only reason they didn't move him, and by the time the Blues had some leverage, the club found some traction on its season.

They won 11 straight games and, by late February, Maroon had landed on a line with veteran Tyler Bozak and rookie Robert Thomas. He scored six of his 10 goals in the final 15 games of the regular season and the trio was arguably the Blues' best in the first round of the playoffs against Winnipeg.

Before the series started, Maroon gained some inspiration after the passing of his grandfather, Ernest Ferrara. The 94-year-old was among Maroon's biggest fans, keeping his grandson's bobblehead on a dresser at his senior living community, along with a No. 7 Blues' T-shirt.

"He really enjoyed watching me play," Maroon said.

But on the day the Blues were flying to Winnipeg, Ferrara died from complications following surgery on a broken left femur. Maroon got the news as he was wrapping up practice and heading to the airport.

Teammate Alexander Steen offered to drive Maroon to the hospital and general manager Doug Armstrong gave him the option of spending the afternoon with his family and traveling commercially later that night. But Maroon wanted to go to the hospital by himself and told the club that he would be on time for a chartered flight that was taking off in about two hours.

"It was tough, a bit of a blow for sure to him," Berube said. "But he wanted to come."

First, however, Maroon walked to the hospital room where his grandpa's deceased body still lay, leaned over the World War II veteran, and gave him a kiss.

"It was tough," he said. "I told him I loved him. Hopefully he heard me."

Maroon stayed for about an hour, and then his uncle, Rob Ferrara, told him that it was time to head to the plane.

"'Grandpa would want you to go,'" Ferrara said. There's nothing you can do here for any of us. Go with your team; they need you. Just play your [butt] off and score one for Grandpa... just get him a goal!' When he walked out, he was totally upset. Very emotional, and I said, 'Hey, make him proud!'"

Maroon went to Winnipeg with the Blues, and with the team tied 1–1 late in the period of Game 1 against the Jets, that moment came. He didn't score a goal, but he set up the game-winner by Bozak with 2:07 left in regulation.

Back in St. Louis, about 15 members of the Maroon and Ferrara families had gathered at Rob's home and erupted when the goal went in.

"We were screaming, all of us," Rob Ferrara said. "I just kept rewinding it and watching it again. A couple of people texted me, 'Divine intervention.' You could have written a better script if he scored the goal, but he made a good play."

It was early April and Maroon asked his uncle if they could delay the funeral until after the season, to which his uncle responded: 'Wait? I'm expecting you to be playing into June.'"

A couple of days later, Maroon returned to St. Louis and attended his grandpa's services, and as it turned out, his uncle was right. The Blues did play into June and they may not have if not for Maroon, who scored the series-clinching goal against Dallas in Game 7 of the conference semifinals.

There was a good omen that day. The date of Game 7 was May 7, and the Blues were handing out a rally towel with Maroon's No. 7 jersey. His mother, Patti Maroon, received a text message early in the morning, wondering if that would be an omen.

Well, with the Blues and Stars tied 1–1 after the first over-time, Maroon left the locker room with his teammates and told them to "dream big." Six minutes into the second OT, he would work a play with Thomas that wound up in the back of the net, ending a string of 48 straight saves by goalie Ben Bishop, another St. Louisan.

"Thomas made a great move and hit the post, and then it hit Bishop's back," Maroon said. "It was a loose puck and just make sure you get it in. If I miss that, I'd be on the other side of it, not the hero, a lot of boos. You play street hockey with your brothers, or you're in the basement, and you dream of those moments. To score a goal like that, I'll never forget that moment."

Neither will his parents, Patti and Phil, who have season tickets and were watching from those seats in Section 112.

"The fact that Pat scored, I couldn't have written the story better myself," Patti said.

And neither will Maroon's son, Anthony, who was a big reason why he came home to play.

"I was looking at [a souvenir game program] and all I heard was everybody scream," Anthony said. "My friend turns around and says, 'It's your dad!' I just started crying."

"I saw my son and I pointed to him, and he was crying," Maroon said.

In that moment, Maroon became a hometown hero, and that status was only solidified when the Blues won the Stanley Cup and he was part of the parade down Market Street that ended at The Arch.

"I love proving people wrong, and Craig Berube gave me a second chance and gave me some life," Maroon said. "He really revamped my season and got my confidence back to where I needed to be. My back has been against the wall my whole career and nothing has been given to me, but I always knew I had it."

55 Do I Look Nervous?

When the Blues would inform Jordan Binnington every year that he was being re-assigned to the minors, the goaltender would always give the club an incredulous look.

Normally this wouldn't be surprising coming from a competitive prospect like Binnington, who was a third-round draft pick in 2011. Except in this case, he was wearing that disbelief in face-to-face meetings with Marty Brodeur, the all-time winningest goalie in NHL history, who was the Blues' assistant general manager at the time.

"I think I cut 'Binner' like five or six times," Brodeur said. "Like, 'All right, that's enough buddy, you're going to Chicago… sorry!' When you get to that age [24 or 25], you move on to the next guy. But he never accepted not to be the top prospect, like he didn't believe it, even though that's what was going on, and I think that was to his benefit."

People throw around the word 'perseverance' like popcorn, but that doesn't even begin to describe the rise to prominence of Binnington. He began the 2018–19 season fourth on the Blues' depth chart and ended the season hoisting the Stanley Cup after a 4–1 victory over Boston, in which he delivered one of the most incredible Game 7 performances in NHL history, particularly by a rookie.

If not for Binnington's 12 first-period saves, and 32 in a row, including a highlight-reel leg kick that kept the Bruins' Joakim Nordstrom from scoring, the Blues would not have ended their 52-year championship drought. Then again, they never would have been in that position if not for a season that seemed to come out of nowhere.

"I think 'Binner' really set the tone for us early [in Game 7]," Blues center Tyler Bozak said. "They came out really hard. They got a lot of good scoring chances, and he shut the door. He made incredible saves and gave us the confidence that he was dialed in, like he was all year."

When Binnington was brought into the organization eight years earlier, the Blues had a goalie tandem of Jaroslav Halak and Brian Elliott, who won the William Jennings Trophy for allowing the fewest goals in the NHL in 2011–12. They were grooming Jake Allen and meanwhile made moves for Brodeur, Anders Nilsson, Pheonix Copley, and Carter Hutton. In Binnington's first five years as a pro, he played 13 minutes of one game in the league.

"We got drafted together in 2011, and he's been one of my best friends since then," former Blues defenseman Joel Edmundson said. "It wasn't an easy process for him. There were definitely some dark days. You're bouncing around in the ECHL and AHL, and it's not easy on the body or the mind.

"But he wanted to make a push to make the NHL and I think he really dialed it in and became a professional. I knew he had it in him the whole time, I saw it in him, but just the way he did it is remarkable. He doesn't really care what anyone else thinks, he's just going to do it his way, and it paid off."

In 2017, the Blues asked Binnington to play in the lower-level ECHL because the club had moved 2014 fourth-round pick Ville Husso ahead of him on the depth chart and they only had room for one of them in the AHL. But he wouldn't go, forcing the team to go to Plan B, loaning him to the Providence Bruins, Boston's AHL affiliate.

Already holding hard feelings toward the organization for not giving him an opportunity, Binnington now had more incentive because of the internal doubters. He went to Providence and posted a record of 17–9 with 2.05 goals-against average and a .926 save percentage.

"I, for sure, used it as motivation, people not believing in me… it kind of fueled me," Binnington said. "It's how you handle it and I think I handled this one well. I stayed humble, I stayed quiet, and just did what I could to be prepared for the opportunity. I believe confidence comes from preparation."

In 2018, the Blues began a new AHL affiliation in San Antonio, where Binnington was the backup to Husso. He outplayed Husso, however, so when Chad Johnson was placed on waivers and claimed by Anaheim, he was brought up to back up Allen.

But Binnington only saw mop-up duty the first nine times he dressed with the Blues, not getting his first NHL start until January 7 in Philadelphia. Confirming that preparation breeds confidence, he made 25 saves for a 3–0 shutout over the Flyers.

"It feels good, for sure," Binnington said that night. "I was definitely excited to finally get the call. It was a long road, and I'm happy where I'm at right now, and I'm hoping to get some more action and be part of the solution on the rise with the Blues."

Binnington was more than a "part" of the solution.

By late February, he was solidified as the Blues' starting goalie, running his record to 15–2–1 with a 2–0 victory over Nashville on February 26. It was his fifth shutout in those 18 games, making him just the second goalie in the modern era (1943–44) to blank his opponent five times in 18 decisions.

"I mean listen, nobody expected that," Brodeur said. "He had that chip on his shoulder, and he just kind of plowed through all the adversity that got in front of him, and that's why he's successful. You look at the stats—they're not just amazing, they're unbelievable. It's well-deserved on his part."

After that win over Nashville, Binnington, now being referred to as Jordan "Winnington," did a postgame interview that would prompt a memorable response. Asked by reporters if he felt nervous in tight games, he deadpanned: "Do I look nervous?"

The answer, of course, was no.

Jordan Binnington stretches to make a save against the Bruins' Joakim Nordstrom in the third period of Game 7 of the Stanley Cup Final.
(AP Photo/Charles Krupa)

There were concerns about how Binnington would handle his first NHL postseason, but he quickly put those to rest.

In the Western Conference quarterfinals against Winnipeg, with Jets fans directing chants of "You look nervous!" at Binnington, he won three games at Bell MTS Place. In the conference semifinals against Dallas, he seemed to lose his cool, whacking the stick of Stars goalie Ben Bishop while heading off the ice in Game 4, but then responded with wins in Games 6 and 7 of that series. And in the conference final, he moved on quickly from the "hand-pass" loss to San Jose in Game 3.

"He's done a good job of just ignoring all of that," Blues coach Craig Berube said. "Anytime you have success, and I talk about it with all of our team, you've got to keep yourself like even-keel. It's very important because you're going to have ups and downs, not only throughout the year, but your whole career. He's responded really well through that. Again, for me, it's about his head, and he's keeping himself pretty even-keeled."

Binnington finished the playoffs with a record of 16–10, including a mark of 8–2 after losses. He became the first rookie in NHL history to win all 16 of his team's games in the postseason.

"It wasn't like a surprise to me," Binnington said. "I felt good about the man I was becoming along this process. I'm continuing to learn as I go. I'm just taking it in."

Binnington, who finished second in the Calder Trophy voting as the NHL's Rookie of the Year, finalized a two-year, $8.8 million contract extension after the season. He'll be back as the Blues' starting goalie, adding new chapters to a story that's still hard to believe.

"One of the things we always say, and we even say it to the prospects, 'Everyone's path looks different and there's no right path and there's no wrong path,'" Blues goalie coach David Alexander said. "There's some goalies who will play 400–500 junior and American League games combined before they make it. Everyone is different and Jordan falls into that, too. His story is unique and, you know what, it probably didn't unfold how he would envision it when he was 18. But what matters most is your sticktoitiveness and your resiliency and that's all you can really control. You figure out what works for you and away you go. He figured out what worked for him. He earned it, and every one of us is very proud of him."

56 St. Louis Scribe Publishes Plus-Minus Stat

Before the NHL began keeping track of every statistic imaginable, former Blues beatwriter Gary Mueller kept a notebook of his own numbers.

Self-described as "very stat oriented," Mueller's interest in one particular stat, and the decision to print it in the *St. Louis Post-Dispatch*, would eventually put him in hot water with the NHL's hierarchy.

"It was back in the dark ages," said Mueller. "At that time, the league sent out stats every Monday, and they arrived by mail. But I had my little pad. I'd have the players' names, even strength goals for, even strength goals against. Then I'd run the little table in the paper."

The official scorer for the Blues when Mueller covered the club was Eddie Olsen. One night Mueller asked Olsen if he could glance at the scorer's sheet that was turned in to the league after every game. Olsen obliged and Mueller noticed a nugget right away.

"I said, 'You keep track of who's on the ice for every goal?' They said, 'Of course.' I said, 'That's interesting.' But nobody seemed to think that it was something to let everybody know. The plus-minus stat always existed, probably going back to the Original Six teams in the league. Someone once said that I invented it, and that's definitely not true. But nobody to my knowledge had ever published it. That's where I got started with it."

The plus-minus system gives a player a plus when he's on the ice for one of his team's even-strength goals and a minus when he's on the ice for a goal against. Then these totals are combined. For example, if a Blues player has been on the ice for five of his team's even-strength goals and three of the opponent's even-strength goals, then he's a plus-2.

Today, the statistic is as common as wins and losses. It's published on the NHL's official website and used by teams across the league to measure a player's individual success. The stat is often included in standard contracts, triggering a higher salary if certain plus-minus levels are reached.

But it wasn't always that way, as Mueller can attest. As soon as he began printing the statistic, including a plus-minus table in the *Post-Dispatch* and using the numbers in feature stories, Mueller received a notice from the NHL.

"Where it got notoriety was the fact that as soon as I published it, everybody said, 'You can't publish that—that's not official,'" Mueller recalled. "I said, 'Why not? It's on the score sheet.'

"I got a letter from the president of the National Hockey League, Clarence Campbell, telling me to 'cease and desist'—don't publish it."

Of course, reporters are much like children. "Once they told me, 'You can't do that,' that made it for sure I would do it," Mueller said. "It was kind of a neat statistic that was different than most other sports. But it was top secret."

Keeping track of the plus-minus statistic wasn't always easy for Mueller.

"Some of the press notes they handed out included who was on the ice for each goal," he said. "The home games, I was fine. I would double-check with Eddie. But the road games, it was just what I saw with my own eyes, and you know how that goes. I always knew I was a little inaccurate.

"It got to the point where I'd ask the Blues players, 'Who was on for that goal?' It was kind of comical. Once in a while, I'd walk into the dressing room after a game and they'd come up to me and say, 'Now, you know that I was going off [the ice] when that goal was scored.' Noel Picard was one. No matter when a goal was scored, he'd swear he was coming off. Every once in a while, somebody threatened to steal my notebook."

Not everyone was opposed to Mueller's work, however.

"When [Blues general manager] Emile Francis came in, he thought it was a great idea," Mueller said. "But he said, 'Never tell anybody I did this, but if you're ever missing a game or you want to know who was on the ice for a specific goal, just let me know and I'll get it for you.' He was always supportive."

Mueller has a story to back up his belief that he didn't invent the plus-minus system. In 1968, pre-dating the reporter's coverage of the team, former Blues player Red Berenson scored a franchise-record six goals in an 8–0 victory over the Philadelphia Flyers.

"The night that he scored six, somebody said, 'Red, you had a good plus-minus rating for a change,' just to tease him. So the term existed. I'm not kidding myself. I don't think because I put the table in the *Post-Dispatch* about seven or eight times a season that it caused the league to make it public. But at the same time, it was the only time I'd seen it published anywhere. Whether somebody decided it was a good idea because of what they saw in the *Post-Dispatch*, I don't know. I think that's kind of far-fetched. But why it suddenly became a major statistic, I don't know."

Mueller laughed when told that NHL players today still contest whether they were on the ice for a goal against.

"Some things never change," Mueller laughed.

57 Voice of the Blues

The Blues would have constructed a Chinese restaurant in St. Louis if that's what it would have taken to bring broadcaster Dan Kelly to town.

The Blues broke into the NHL in 1967 without a full-time radio announcer, putting well-respected but part-time announcers Jack Buck and Jay Randolph behind the microphone.

"We had some great announcers that did a few games here and there, but the owners of the team, especially the father, Sidney Salomon Jr., wanted to really get someone," former Blues coach Scotty Bowman recalled. "He wanted a 'Voice of the Blues.' He asked, 'Who's the best play-by-play man in the NHL?'"

Initially, the Salomons reached out to broadcaster Danny Gallivan, who at the time was working for *Hockey Night in Canada* and the Montreal Canadiens. Gallivan declined the Blues' overture, but before hanging up the phone, he made a recommendation.

"Gallivan said to Salomon, 'There is a young guy that comes in from Ottawa. He's like the host but he's an excellent play-by-play man,'" Bowman said. "Salomon then said to me, 'Have you heard of a guy named Dan Kelly?' I said, 'Oh sure.'"

Prior to coming to St. Louis, Bowman had been coaching a pro team in Ottawa, and Kelly had called some of the team's games. He was climbing the NHL ranks, finding intermission work on *Hockey Night in Canada*, and it was only a matter of time before he would land a permanent position.

Kelly obliged the Blues' request for a tape, and Salomon Jr. was impressed. He offered the job right away, but Kelly was also considering an opportunity with the Minnesota North Stars.

"The first year of the NHL expansion, I had a couple of chances to go to a team, but I decided to see what happened," Dan Kelly said at the time. "Scotty Bowman, who was then in St. Louis, and other people with the Blues asked whether I'd be interested in coming there. I didn't give them an answer. I sort of hemmed and hawed for a lot of the summer."

Salomon ordered Bowman to get Kelly back on the phone.

"Dan said, 'Yeah, I'm coming to St. Louis. I talked to my wife, Fran, and we're excited,'" Bowman said. "Then just off the cuff he said, 'Are there any good Chinese restaurants in St. Louis?' I said, 'I'm sure there must be.'

"So I told Salomon that Dan was all set. He said, 'What else did he say?' I mentioned that he wondered if there were any good Chinese restaurants. He said, 'Are you serious? You phone him back and you tell him that if there isn't a good Chinese restaurant in St. Louis, I will build one.'"

The Blues took a shot and scored, similar to the signature call that was created by legendary NHL announcer Foster Hewitt and popularized in St. Louis by Kelly.

"One night, I was sitting with my wife in our cottage near Ottawa, and she said to me, 'I don't know what's so hard about the decision. You've always wanted to do play-by-play for a club in the NHL,'" Kelly said. "She was right. And that was the chance. What kind of move did it turn out to be for me!"

Kelly called many sporting events during his illustrious career, but hockey was "by far and away his favorite," said son John Kelly, and the Blues were by far his greatest passion. Dan Kelly should have known that his time in St. Louis would be special soon after he arrived in October 1968.

"One of his first games was the night [Red] Berenson scored six goals," John Kelly said. "I remember our family was still in Ottawa, and we woke up the next day and it was all over the radio."

Many more memorable calls were on the way, as the expansion Blues went to the Stanley Cup final in Kelly's first two seasons. The club was swept by Montreal in 1969 and Boston in 1970, but in defeat, Kelly broadcast arguably the most famous goal in hockey history.

"Bobby Orr...behind the net to Sanderson to OOOORR! BOBBY OOOORR SCORES!" Kelly described. "And the Boston Bruins have won the Stanley Cup!"

Kelly never called a Cup for the Blues, but in a career that spanned two decades, he witnessed the brawl in Philadelphia and the Monday Night Miracle, he covered Bobby Plager and Bernie Federko, and he called every event between.

In fact, Kelly delivered the account of Federko's first point in the NHL and, on March 19, 1988, he called the 1,000[th] point of Federko's career.

"Hrkac in across the line, left it for Federko, back to Hrkac, to Mark Hunter, he scores. And Bernie Federko will get an assist for point No. 1,000. Tony Hrkac raced over and got the puck as a souvenir. He'll get an assist, and that is point No. 1,000 for Bernie Federko."

Federko gave the puck to Kelly, and the memento still remains at the family's home. It is inscribed, "Thanks Dan, you've called them all. Hopefully many more."

"It meant a lot to me to give it to Dan," Federko said. "He was the biggest hockey supporter we ever had. He was the Blues. He lived and died with the Blues."

Not every night was blissful for the organization, however.

"He was doing a game one night, and it was after the first period and he gave himself a pep talk," John Kelly said. "He said, 'This team is terrible and I was terrible in the first period, and I'm going right down the drain with them.'"

On occasion, Kelly had to build up the Blues for the radio audience.

"We were not a great team by any means with all the ownership changes," Federko said. "Dan Kelly made our games exciting all the time, and a lot of times they weren't. Dan sold the game like no one else did in St. Louis."

Kelly had opportunities to leave the Blues over the years. Hurt by the fact that the Salomons had to sell the club, Kelly watched weeds grow over the parking lot at the Arena in the 1980s when the Blues nearly moved to Saskatoon.

"He could have gone to Chicago," John Kelly said. "At one time he was talking very seriously with the Wirtz family, but he decided in the long run that he wanted to stay in St. Louis. I don't know in particular why he didn't want to go. He was very loyal to the Blues in very tough times over a span of maybe 10 years."

Meanwhile, Kelly continued to make a name for himself at the national level. In addition to being in the CBS booth, he broadcast games for CTV in Canada, where he had the assignment for the 1987 Canada Cup.

Seventeen years after the call on Orr's goal, Kelly turned in another keepsake.

"Hawerchuk wins it, and here's Lemieux poking it to center. Lemieux ahead to Gretzky, has Murphy with him on a two-on-one. To Lemieux. In on goal. He shoots! He scores! Mario Lemieux, with 1:26 remaining!"

John Kelly said that one goal epitomized his father's style.

"He had an ability to build up the call of the goal in a crescendo-like fashion," Kelly said. "If you listen to the call, the faceoff began in the Canadian end and they moved up the ice. You could hear the excitement in his voice grow every second. It just got louder, more authoritative, and I think that goal to me summed up why he was a great hockey broadcaster."

John and his younger brother followed in their father's footsteps, becoming NHL broadcasters. John has spent a majority of his career with the Blues and is reminded by fans every day about his dad's impact.

"It was obviously a great honor to carry on what he did," he said. "The one thing that he always tried to impress upon me was that it is a great privilege to [call games], and the players and the game are the reasons why we're here—not to be the show. Let the players and the game be the show. I've always tried to abide by that, to be very well prepared and respectful of people."

Although they hung out together in the booth for hundreds of games, Dan and John shared the Blues' microphone only once.

"When he was sick, he went to Philadelphia and I was there," John said. "It was probably his last game on the road. He was quite ill at the time and had to walk up about 15 flights of stairs to the old pressbox at the Spectrum. He would go up two or three flights and stop and rest.

"Why did he feel it was important to do that game? He didn't have to do that game. He had a contract, but he was very sick. It was just his love of hockey, and he just wanted to carry on as long as he could."

Dan Kelly died in 1989 after a bout with lung cancer. A banner with a cloverleaf and his name hangs in the rafters at Scottrade Center. His spirit and his voice, through vintage Blues' highlights, remain a local treasure.

"He was a competitive guy. He wanted to do so well when he worked," said John Davidson, who worked with Kelly both as a player and a broadcaster. "I remember when we had the dinner for him here when he was in the hospital, and he couldn't make the dinner. The place was packed. Not long after that, he passed away. The people lined the streets at the funeral. That was really something. They cared about him here."

58 "It's a Real Barnburner"

Walter Lawrence "Gus" Kyle wasn't a professional broadcaster, but in 16 seasons as the Blues' color analyst on KMOX, that mattered little to those listening.

Perhaps that's because Kyle, the unlikeliest of candidates to be seated next to famed play-by-play man Dan Kelly, was a fan himself. And his off-the-cuff and grammar-challenged delivery was well-received.

"I never made any bones about it," Kyle said. "I pulled and cheered for the Blues."

Born in 1923 in Dysart, Saskatchewan, Kyle served five years with the Royal Canadian Mounted Police (RCMP). He signed up for a second stint, but New York Rangers general manager Frank Boucher bought him out of that deal and sent the defenseman to the team's minor-league affiliate in Regina, Saskatchewan.

"We were getting big money in the RCMP in those years," Kyle said. "One dollar and 25 cents a day."

But the move paid off for Kyle, who showed enough talent with the Regina Capitals that he was called up to the Rangers in 1949. In his first year, Kyle finished a few votes behind Boston's Jack Gelineau as the NHL's top rookie. Kyle played 203 games in the NHL before finishing his career in the Western Hockey League.

Kyle then moved behind the bench, and in 1962 he accepted a job as the head coach of the Syracuse Braves, who played in the Eastern Professional Hockey Association. When the EPHA ceased operations that season, the Braves joined the Central Hockey League in St. Louis and Kyle followed.

The Braves, who were the minor-league affiliate of the Chicago Blackhawks, played at the Arena. Kyle coached the Braves through the 1963–64 season, then he moved into broadcasting with the team, and in 1966 he began working in insurance. He had that in common with Sid Salomon Jr. when the two met by chance one day, and when Salomon gained ownership of the Blues in 1967, he hired Kyle as director of ticket sales.

In the Blues' inaugural season, Salomon requested that Kyle "temporarily" join the broadcast with Jack Buck and Jay Randolph.

"The little I know about hockey, Kyle taught me," Buck once said. "But he used to make me stiffen. He'd say, 'Minnesota are at Toronto.' and 'The Canadiens is winning.'"

A short time later, Kyle and Kelly were partnered up and, perhaps because of their opposite styles, they were a perfect fit.

Once Kelly said, "Gus, it's overtime. What do you suppose the coach is saying?"

Kyle replied, "'Fellas, the next goal is a big one.'"

Fans will remember Kyle's catchphrase in describing a tight game: "It's a real barnburner," he would say. That popular slogan stemmed from his days on the Saskatchewan prairie.

"There was nothing for miles and miles but farms and no fire departments," Kyle said. "When a barn would occasionally catch on fire, it was an exciting event."

Gary Mueller, a former Blues' beatwriter for the *St. Louis Post-Dispatch*, remembers when the barnburner line became quite literal.

"One night, someone in Buffalo gave him a 'barn' made out of cardboard," Mueller said. "Gus proceeded to set the barn on fire, and he almost destroyed the KMOX broadcast booth."

Kyle loved his job.

"Every hockey man, if he's honest, would admit that he's had an ambition to coach or manage in the big leagues," he said. "But I don't envy coaches anymore. After seeing the pressure under which they work, I wouldn't want one of those jobs, even at $50,000 a year. I am beginning to realize that I have just about the best job in the world. This sure beats riding a horse in the RCMP."

Kyle never forgot about selling Blues' tickets either, and he was just as good at that.

"Gus obviously sold the high seats very well in the Arena," the Blues' Bruce Affleck said. "People still come up and say that he told them, 'That's where the scouts sit.'"

In 1983, Kyle's days with the organization were dwindling after the Blues brought in broadcaster Ron Oakes to handle the play-by-play duties when Kelly was away working for USA, a cable-television network. Kyle was the color man for a few games, but that arrangement lasted only until the end of the season.

Blues fans revolted.

"I wanted to put out a release because everywhere I went—service stations, restaurants, taverns—people were asking me why I wasn't doing the games," Kyle said. "A nun wrote to me and tried to explain why she'd gotten interested in hockey because of my comments. I can see why they would write Dan. He's the best in the business. We're two different personalities on the air. He's very precise, and I'm not. I just say what I feel, and those comments went home to roost with people. But I can't put my thumb on why people are so kind to me in letters and phone calls. You just try to be yourself and if it hits home, fine."

Others, however, could put their thumb on it.

"The hockey area really missed something when a guy like Gus left the scene," said Blues former coach and player Red Berenson. "You never knew what he was going to say. He knew the game, and he knew the players, so he could say it the way it was in his broadcasts."

Ken Wilson, who later followed Kyle in the Blues' booth, added, "He didn't sound like a broadcaster. He sounded like an old-time hockey guy who weaved in fabulous stories. They were earthy. He was rough and gruff. He was entertaining and humorous. You could feel the game when he was talking, and it was a great contrast with Dan."

Kyle, who had one heart attack in 1983 and another in 1991, died of heart-related problems on November 17, 1996. Some suggested that his heart was broken by the Blues.

59 KMOX and the Blues

When their son finally achieved his goal of making it to the NHL, Nick and Natalie Federko were ecstatic that he would be playing in St. Louis.

The seventh overall pick in the 1976 draft, Bernie Federko probably would have enjoyed a Hall of Fame career wherever he landed. Because he joined the Blues, however, the family was able to hear his games on the radio back home in Saskatoon, Saskatchewan, Canada.

The club's longtime former affiliate, KMOX (1120 AM) in St. Louis, was a 50,000-watt station whose signal covered most of the United States east of the Rockies and much of Canada.

"My folks got KMOX in Saskatoon and could listen to all the games," Federko said. "They listened to Dan Kelly call all the games, and that was really special."

Not only did Blues games come in loud and clear on KMOX for much of the last half century, the broadcasters were some of the best in the business: Kelly; his sons, John and Dan Kelly; Gus Kyle; Jack Buck; Jay Randolph; Ron Jacober; Ken Wilson; Chris Kerber; and Kelly Chase, among others.

"KMOX has always been a special sports station," Wilson said. "I think when you have that kind of reach, it's wonderful for the club obviously. And if you look at some of the folks who have done play-by-play in St. Louis on KMOX, there are some pretty talented folks who had some long runs. St. Louis certainly can't complain about the quality of the sportscasters they've had."

"St. Louis has such an amazing history of not just good broadcasters, but great ones," Kerber added. "When you get an opportunity to sit in that booth and do the games, history can't be lost on you. It's your job to do everything you can to maintain that standard that was set before you. You go in there and you have to make sure that you're respectful of what Dan Kelly brought to the St. Louis Blues, that you know the importance of what Ken Wilson meant to Blues fans. It's your job to make sure that you carry on what the people before you did. That's a humbling and important characteristic of being a play-by-play broadcaster in St. Louis."

The Blues had a couple stints on KMOX. The first run lasted from 1967–85, a period that was highlighted by the presence of the elder Kelly.

Frank Absher, a St. Louis media historian and former employee of the station, worked side by side with Kelly and remembers the passion he brought to the job.

"Dan Kelly was under contract with the CBC [Canadian Broadcasting Corporation], and while he was working at KMOX, he would leave every Monday and do a game of the week for CBC," Absher said. "Every week, the newsroom at KMOX would get a collect call around 1:00 am from Dan Kelly in the middle of Canada, asking us what the hockey scores were that night. And a lot of times while he was in Canada, he would go watch the kids in the farm system play."

Absher recalled that one year KMOX needed a broadcaster to fill in on the St. Louis Cardinal baseball games and tapped Kelly.

"Dan was a fish out of water," Absher said. "At one point, Jack [Buck] noted that the pitch had just hit the outside corner. Dan said, 'I have no idea how you can tell sitting all the way up here that that ball hit the outside corner.' Buck's response was, 'I have no idea how you can tell sitting all the way up in the arena press box

Notable Calls from the Voices of the Blues

Dan Kelly on Red Berenson's sixth goal against Philadelphia on
November 7, 1968:

> "Van Impe lost it to Berenson. Berenson has a break. One man back. Here
> he comes. A shot...he scores! Red Berenson has tied the record with
> six goals in one game! He gets a great ovation from this crowd at the
> Philadelphia Spectrum. Six goals in one hockey game, tying the record."

Ken Wilson on the fight between Detroit's Tim Cheveldae and the
Blues' Curtis Joseph on January 23, 1993:

> "Here comes Cheveldae! He'll be thrown out of the game. Now Joseph
> gets into it.... Curtis Joseph grabs Cheveldae, and the two goalies go at
> it. Joseph with three great rights to Cheveldae! For those of you watching
> [the goalie fight] on television, we'll try to update you on everyone else."

Dan Kelly on Wayne Babych's 50th goal of the season on March 12,
1981:

> "[Bill] Stewart for St. Louis, on left wing to [Jorgen] Pettersson, right
> wing pass to Babych...he breaks in. Babych in on goal, he shoots, he
> scores! Babych gets his 50th of the year, cuts the Montreal lead to 4–2.
> And Wayne Babych is the first Blues' scorer in history to score 50 goals."

Ron Jacober on Brett Hull's 500th career goal on December 22, 1996:

> "Ahead to [Stephane] Matteau to [Pierre] Turgeon to Hull. Hull shoots, he
> scores. There it is! There it is! No. 500 for Brett Hull, No. 500! The 25th
> man in National Hockey League history to score 500 goals, and the first
> father-son combination in the history of the game. Brett Hull, No. 500, a
> standing ovation here at Kiel."

John Kelly on Brett Hull's 86th goal of the season on March 31, 1991:

> "Here's Paul Cavallini, ahead to Hull, he's in alone, a shot...he scores!
> Brett Hull, No. 86!"

Dan Kelly on Brian Sutter's 300th career goal on March 17, 1988:

> "Now Minnesota tries to center, but Herbie Raglan knocks it down to
> [Rick] Meagher at center. Here's Meagher, leaves it for Sutter, he shoots,
> he scores! Brian Sutter gets No. 300, and the Blues take a 2–1 lead. Brian

Sutter becomes only the second player in Blues' history to get 300 goals, and it couldn't happen to a better guy and a more fierce competitor."

Dan Kelly on Mike Crombeen's double-overtime goal in the Blues' 4–3 playoff win over Pittsburgh on April 14, 1981:

"Now [Mike] Zuke wins the faceoff to [Joe] Micheletti to [Rick] Lapointe. Lapointe in across the line in the Pittsburgh zone. He tries to center one, Zuke gets it back to the goal, in front to Crombeen, he scores! Mike Crombeen! And the Blues win the series! Mike Crombeen has just scored for St. Louis!"

Dan Kelly on Doug Wickenheiser's Monday Night Miracle goal in a 6–5 win over Calgary on March 12, 1986:

"[Rick] Wamsley to his knees, sets it up for [Rob] Ramage. Ramage into center ice to [Bernie] Federko. Federko stole it from [Paul] Reinhart, breaking in, to [Mark] Hunter. Hunter shooting, rebound, Wickenheiser scores! Wickenheiser to win it for St. Louis and force a seventh game Wednesday in Calgary!"

Ken Wilson on Hull's first period hat trick on Easter Sunday on April 16, 1995:

"[Steve] Yzerman can't clear, knocked down by [Brendan] Shanahan at the blue line. He's straight away. He's got [Steve] Duchesne nearside, gives him the puck. Now to Hull, Hull circles back by the blue line. Blues have a two-man advantage, nearside to Duchesne to Hull, one-timer, he scores! Hat trick, hat trick! Oh baby! Brett Hull! A first-period hat trick and they go bananas here at Kiel Center. It is hat day, and hats are flying through the air. Brett Hull as pure a hat trick as you'll see, three goals in the first period. Oh baby, it's 3–1 Blues!"

Chris Kerber on the Blues' Stanley Cup win on June 12, 2019:

"A team that was in last place on January 3rd, the players on the bench are bouncing up. History will be made tonight in Boston. Fifteen seconds to go as Schenn blocks a puck to the corner. Ten seconds remaining. Get up St. Louis! Get on your feet. Raise 'em high. Five seconds to go. And the time winds down. They did it! It's over! The game is over! The series is over! The wait is over! And the St Louis Blues are the Stanley Cup champions for the first time in franchise history!"

how the puck bounces off the post and into the net.' They loved each other and had a real camaraderie in what they did."

But in 1985, the Blues left KMOX, signing a five-year deal with KXOK (630 AM). There were reports that KMOX was losing more than $100,000 to broadcast the games. Under Blues owner Harry Ornest, the club signed a five-year deal with KXOK, but the change did not go over well with fans and the move didn't last long.

"The hockey club ended up getting a lot of complaints from listeners in Canada, who could no longer listen to the Blues," Absher said.

The KXOK experiment flopped and, after only two seasons, KMOX executive Robert Hyland worked out the team's return to its original home in 1987. Legions of fans outside St. Louis were able to hear the Blues again, including a college student at Miami University in Ohio.

"When Curtis Joseph and Felix Potvin were battling it out in the playoffs, I was listening to those games in my dorm room on KMOX," said Kerber, who several years later would take over the Blues' play-by-play job. "We had enough people from St. Louis to get together and listen to the games."

One long-standing dilemma for the Blues on KMOX, however, had been playing second-fiddle to the Cardinals. Often when there were scheduling conflicts, the Blues would get bumped.

In May 2000, the team elected to go where it would be top priority, moving to KTRS (550 AM). Despite devoted, quality coverage of the club at KTRS, fans once again complained, citing the station's weak signal.

In 2007, after the NHL lockout and amid the Blues' poor performance, new ownership was trying to reconnect with fans and decided to move back to KMOX. Club chairman Dave Checketts insisted that the change was necessary "when you are trying to rebuild an audience and bring people back."

The third run, however, lasted just more than a decade, as the Blues made the switch to WXOS 101.1 FM in 2019. Fittingly, their final game on KMOX, ending a stretch of 43 years on their longtime affiliate in the franchise's 52-year existence, was a Stanley Cup clincher.

60 Oh Baby

One of the first times that Blues broadcaster Ken Wilson uttered the words, "Oh baby," he didn't even realize it. And when his wife, Marlene, mentioned that he should use it more often, maybe even as a catchphrase, he balked.

"I just said it a few different times, without ever thinking," Wilson said. "It was just natural like you say 'holy cow' or 'wow' whenever something unusual or exciting happens. Then my wife heard it in the game, and she said it was kind of cool. I said 'What?' She said 'oh baby' was cool.

"She said, 'Why don't you use that more often?' I said, 'Well, I don't believe in made-up things. I just want to react naturally.' She said, 'Well, I think you ought to use it.' I said, 'Nope.' But I tried it, and it seemed to be a nice exclamation point. Then people started talking about it all the time."

That's when "Oh baby!" was born.

During a 20-year career in the Blues' broadcast booth, Wilson became a fan favorite in St. Louis, where his energized descriptions of slick goals and highlight-reel saves earned as much recognition as the plays themselves.

Like his signature call, Wilson's career with the franchise almost never took off. He was broadcasting Chicago Blackhawks and Cincinnati Reds games in the early 1980s when he accepted a three-year contract from a new TV venture called Sports Time Cable Network, a project of Anheuser-Busch. He would continue working Reds games but added college basketball and the Blues, calling his first St. Louis hockey game on October 11, 1984.

It turned out that Wilson would split the play-by-play duties with the legendary Dan Kelly on Sports Time and KPLR, a local TV affiliate in St. Louis, during alternating periods. That might not have been the role that Wilson envisioned, but he had no complaints with the arrangement.

"Dan was well-established there and did some national stuff," said Wilson. "He didn't owe me a thing. He was good to work with, and he was very generous. I always appreciated the fact he was very good to me and very fair when other people in that position might not have been so kind."

After one season, Sports Time dissolved in 1985. They still owed Wilson two years on his contract, however, and there was at least some thought by the brewery folks that they would buy him out of the deal.

"One guy wanted to pay me to go away," Wilson said. "Then some other guys said, 'If we've got this guy Wilson, and we're paying him, why don't we make him work?' I thought that was a novel approach."

Wilson's duties expanded to cover a variety of events for an operation called Bud Sports, and he eventually became the voice of the Blues. It was a memorable era in the franchise's history, highlighted by strong squads, the goal-scoring prowess of Brett Hull, the defiance of Mike Keenan, and one night a fight between goaltenders Curtis Joseph and Tim Cheveldae.

"We were in the playoffs every season—every single season," Wilson said. "We never won a Stanley Cup, but we always had competitive teams. We had some interesting coaches, if not sensational coaches. It was really a wonderful time. I was lucky, just lucky, to be there at that time."

Hull scored a franchise-record 527 goals with the Blues before leaving in 1998. "I must have called every one of his NHL goals until he went to Dallas and Detroit. Recently, I discovered that I called his first NHL goal. It was in a playoff game with Calgary, and I called it. Little did I know that I would then call four zillion more of his goals."

If you were a fan of Hull, you probably weren't a fan of Keenan. But Wilson had a different take on Iron Mike behind the scenes.

"I found him really interesting, really enjoyed spending time with him, getting to see a side that the fans never saw," Wilson said. "He's the kind of guy when somebody says, 'Who'd you like to go to dinner with?' you might go with Bill Clinton. I always thought Mike Keenan would be that kind of guy because you knew he was really intelligent. I must tell you I never had dinner with Mike Keenan, but he'd be the kind of guy who would say some really interesting things."

In 1993, Wilson would witness something interesting—a brawl between the Blues and Red Wings that led to one of his most famous calls.

"It was back in the era when you could have four or five fights going on at one time, which was always fun to try to describe," Wilson said. "I always tried to make the fights be as exciting as I could possibly make them, especially on radio. I was always rooting for the Blues' players, and if there was a fight I was always involved in it in my mind. My blood felt it. Then when you've got two goalies fighting, that was like a once-in-a-lifetime thing.

"So you're looking at a lot of things. 'Oh, this starts it. Oh, we've got a fight over here, another one over here, and...here comes Cheveldae!' I'm not expecting it.... Why would I think I'm going to see a goalie come in my vision? I was just a fan reacting to it."

And that's what made Wilson's enthusiasm seem genuine, particularly with his different level of voice inflections when he belted out, "Oh baby!"

"It jumped when you had an exciting goal," Wilson said. "The ones that got guttural were even more exceptional. Something that was really like 'Wow!' Again, I never thought about it—it just sort of happened."

In 2004, Wilson left the Blues in a messy split and moved to Hawaii. He worked as president of the West Coast Baseball League and called MLB games for the Seattle Mariners. He has also spent time hanging out at his son's amateur hockey games in Portland, Oregon.

"After a couple of years, people asked me what I did for a living," Wilson said. "I said that I had been a sportscaster. Finally somebody found out I had been a hockey broadcaster, and they got excited that I was a real hockey broadcaster. Then they discovered some [videos] on YouTube. So now I have some youth hockey players in Oregon coming up to me all excited, saying, 'Geez, I found this great fight you called.' It has brought my NHL days back to me."

61 A Coup for Coach Q

With either positive words of encouragement or a sternly delivered sermon, former Blues coach Joel Quenneville always had a few words for his players during intermissions. The one time that Coach Q chose to be silent in the locker room may have been his biggest coup ever.

The Blues were trailing Toronto 4–0 when they went into the locker room after the second period on November 29, 2000.

"Usually you go in and talk to the team, giving them a couple of things to work on or think about going into the next period," Quenneville said. "We just went right out."

The strategy appeared not to be a good one when, less than three minutes into the third period, Toronto enforcer Tie Domi scored his second goal of the game for a 5–0 Maple Leaf lead. Game over, right?

The largest comeback in Blues history was just beginning. What the coach lacked in words at the intermission the players made up for in goals, netting five in the final 15 minutes, 9 seconds of regulation and picking up the clincher in overtime for a 6–5 stunner.

"All of a sudden, it was one, it was two, it was three, it was four and then five," Quenneville said. "It was incredible."

In hockey parlance, Quenneville gave the Blues the proverbial jolt when he replaced starting goalie Roman Turek after Domi handed the Maple Leafs a five-spot. In came backup Brent Johnson, a rookie who had to assume his appearance was for mop-up duty.

But earlier in the 2000–01 season, the Blues had rallied from a 4–0 deficit against the Los Angeles Kings, eventually skating off the ice with a 4–4 tie. And at least one player had that night in mind when the Blues fell behind in Toronto.

"We knew we came back in L.A.," forward Jochen Hecht said. "Why not again?"

Although Quenneville had kept to himself during the intermission, the players did not. They kept talking.

"We went in after the second period and said, 'Work as hard as we can. Things will go our way. We just have to shoot and work hard. It'll work out.'" Hecht said. "It was 5–0 with 15 minutes left. We just wanted to get out of our bad game and play well. It was unreal."

The rally began when Blues defenseman Chris Pronger ripped a slap shot past Toronto goalie and ex-Blue Curtis Joseph at 4:51

of the third period. A Maple Leafs' penalty then put the offense on the power play, and 2:02 after Pronger scored, Alexander Khavanov converted the man-advantage for a 5–2 deficit. Another power-play goal, this one from Al MacInnis 1:44 later, cut the score to 5–3.

"It's never over," Khavanov said. "You can be losing in blackjack and win $1,000 in one hand. That's the game…. If you let your heads hang and think, 'Oh, we're done,' then it ain't going to happen. The game is 60 minutes, and we have to play all 60."

With only 11 of those 60 minutes remaining, the Blues still weren't sitting pretty. Then with 5:40 left in regulation, Michal Handzus put a backhanded shot by Joseph for a 5–4 game, providing what seemed at the time to be an interesting finish.

But in the final minute, with Johnson pulled for an extra attacker, the defenseman Khavanov jumped up in the play, grabbed an unclaimed puck, and put it behind Joseph for his second goal of the game, completely erasing all the work the Maple Leafs had done.

"I'm standing here right now saying, 'How in the hell did that happen?'" Toronto coach Pat Quinn would say after the game. "It seemed like everything they shot went into the net."

The comeback wasn't official, however, until 18 seconds into overtime, when Hecht took a pass from teammate Pavol Demitra in front of the net and sealed the score.

"I just shot it," Hecht said. "It was bouncing a little bit, and I just got it there. To score a goal like that, the game-winner, that's great."

Now Quenneville was truly at a loss for words.

"Crazy, unbelievable…. I've never seen anything like that," he said. "Unbelievable."

The coach left St. Louis and went on to win three Stanley Cups with the Chicago Blackhawks. But somewhere in his home, he has a picture of the Blues celebrating their improbable win over the Maple Leafs in the hockey mecca.

"That game really stood out," Quenneville said, "especially being in Toronto."

62 Pleau Forced to Trade Pronger

Blues general manager Larry Pleau received the order from ownership—trade defenseman Chris Pronger.

Bill and Nancy Laurie, who had owned the Blues since 1999, were in the midst of selling the club following the lockout-canceled season of 2004–05. Pronger made $9 million in 2003–04, and as a restricted free agent when hockey returned, he had a $7 million qualifying offer even after a 24 percent rollback in salaries.

Game Plan, the Boston-based broker hired to help sell the Blues, advised the Lauries that ridding the roster of hefty contracts could attract potential buyers. That strategy would be debated, but undebatable was the horrific timing of trading the former MVP and Norris Trophy winner.

"It wasn't a great time to be trying to trade Chris, that's for sure," Pleau said. "The cap ceiling was going to be $39 million, and all these teams, they weren't looking to add big payroll. I talked to every team about a trade, and it's not that they weren't interested in him. They just weren't interested in a guy who was on a qualifier at $7 million and was going to be unrestricted in a year. You know what it's like trying to trade a guy like that? It's difficult."

But Pleau had his orders, so he attended the 2005 NHL entry draft in Ottawa looking to make a deal. As many as three clubs stayed in contact with the Blues' GM, but one backed out of the

Pronger Sweepstakes on July 29 and another on July 30, the day of the draft.

On August 2, at approximately 10:00 PM, the Blues finally came to an agreement, trading Pronger to Edmonton for a package of three Oilers defensemen—Eric Brewer, Doug Lynch, and Jeff Woywitka. Brewer was a bona fide NHL player and a member of Canada's 2002 gold medal team at the Olympics, but the other two had never played in the league and were marginal prospects.

"You're wishing you had done better than that, but the market wasn't what you would have hoped it would be at that time," Pleau said.

For once, Blues fans agreed with Pleau, but it was because they also believed the trio of players he received for Pronger was underwhelming, and Pleau became the public scapegoat. Truth be told, Pleau had been the one behind the scenes, pleading with the Blues—and in particular Dick Thomas, the Lauries' attorney who had been hired as the team's point man—not to make the trade.

In fact, it was Pleau who had to convince the organization to even make Pronger the qualifying offer of $7 million so that the Blues could retain his rights and get something for him in a trade. If not for that, Pronger would have become an unrestricted free agent and could leave with no compensation.

"It bugs me that the truth has not been told about what [Pleau] had to do to go about his business," said former Blues President John Davidson, who came aboard after the trade. "If it weren't for Larry Pleau, Chris Pronger would have walked away as a free agent for nothing in return. Nobody understands that. And the trade that he made, that's the best trade that was there."

In the end, Pleau knew that he had no choice but to make the deal, and he also realized that he would face the backlash alone.

"That's why you get paid the big bucks," Pleau said. "You're always paid to take the hit."

Pronger, 30, who had overcome many personal obstacles in St. Louis after he was acquired in 1995 for fan favorite Brendan Shanahan, left the Blues after nine seasons.

"Well, it's obviously something that was a difficult decision for [the Blues]," Pronger said. "Not knowing the future and what I was going to do next year as an unrestricted free agent and not being able to give me the long-term deal that had been asked about, it was a difficult decision, I'm sure."

Pronger went to Edmonton, where he signed a five-year, $31.3 million extension.

Now that Pronger was off the Blues' payroll, Game Plan insisted that a sale was more feasible.

"Our experience tells us every buyer of a team wants to have as much flexibility and opportunity to do things their way," Game Plan founder Robert Caporale said.

But the eventual sale to SCP Worldwide, led by chairman Dave Checketts, would not take place for another 10 months, and when it did, the incoming ownership group was none too pleased about the departure of Pronger.

"Bill [Laurie] thought he was doing the best thing to not commit the organization to long-term expensive contracts," Checketts said. "He thought that would make the franchise more desirable. I would have rather had the franchise with Chris Pronger, but it wasn't in my hands."

Making matters more unsettling for St. Louis was that Pronger led Edmonton to the Stanley Cup final in his first season there. Only a 3–1 victory by Carolina in Game 7 prevented the ex-Blue from hoisting the Cup less than a year after the trade.

Pronger was quickly an ex-Oiler, as well. Despite signing a five-year extension, the lanky defenseman asked the team for a trade, citing personal reasons. Reportedly his wife, Lauren, a St. Louisan, disliked living in Edmonton.

Pronger moved to Anaheim, and the Blues moved on, as well, but the results were contrasting. Pronger won a Cup with the Ducks while the Blues celebrated making the playoffs just once, in 2009, with the players they received from Edmonton.

Brewer held the title of the Blues' captain from 2008–2011 but never won the hearts of the fans. Woywitka played 152 games but was never more than a fill-in. Lynch, meanwhile, never suited up for St. Louis.

63 How Swede It Is!

On a 10-hour flight from St. Louis to Sweden in 2009, former Blues head coach Andy Murray paced the aisle before finally settling into his seat for some shut-eye.

"Coach, coach, coach," repeated veteran Keith Tkachuk while simultaneously tapping Murray on the shoulder.

A startled Murray wiggled momentarily, finally awakening and fixating his pupils on the oversized left winger.

"What time is it?" joked Tkachuk, who cracked a smile as the Blues' bench boss realized he had been snookered by the player's prank.

Just three years earlier, the Blues had finished 30th in the NHL standings, meaning their appearances on the big stage were few and far between. But the buzz in the air—literally in the air—was tangible as the team made the flight to Stockholm to participate in the league's Premier Games against rival Detroit.

What time was it? It was prime time!

Expectations were high for the Blues in 2009–10 after they posted the NHL's best record in the second half of the 2008–09 season. They squeezed into the No. 6 seed in the Western Conference, earning the franchise's first playoff berth since 2004. Vancouver swept the Blues in the first round, but the postseason experience was thought to be a building block for the team's young roster.

In addition, the Blues were returning defenseman Erik Johnson, who missed the previous season rehabbing a torn knee ligament, and forward Paul Kariya, who was limited to 11 games the year before because of an injury that was eventually diagnosed as torn labrums in each hip.

"Most of the experts picked us to finish 30th in the league last season, and that was before we lost Erik Johnson, Paul Kariya," Murray said. "Now the expectations are different. We are being challenged in a different way. I like the expectations that people have for us. We set a standard last year, and that's good. If the fans are expecting more from us, why should we as individuals, and as an organization, expect anything less from ourselves?"

In Sweden, the Blues' fans wanted some face time with Murray before the club began its two-game set against the Red Wings.

While Blues players were getting familiar with their surroundings at the Globe in Stockholm, Blues public-relations director Mike Caruso was preparing Murray for what he told the head coach would be an intimate conversation with European fans. In reality, it was a group of Blues season-ticket holders who made the trip from St. Louis. The setup made for an interesting scene when the multilingual Murray stepped in front of the crowd of about 100, situated in the lower bowl of the arena.

"I told Andy there was a group of people from Sweden he was supposed to address," Caruso said. "He said, 'Great, I speak Swedish.' So we go up there, he had a microphone on, and we were filming it. He starts speaking Swedish to these people, and you could hear a pin drop because they were like, 'What's he saying?'

He looks at me and says, 'They're not answering. Should I keep going?' I said, 'Yeah, keep going.' He starts saying some more and then turns to me again. I'm busting out laughing. I said, 'They're from St. Louis.' He got real red."

The punching bag for two pranks, Murray was perhaps as eager as anyone to see the Red Wings. After two exhibition games, the puck dropped on October 2, 2009, against Nick Lidstrom and company.

In the first game, Detroit was the home team officially and legitimately, with a huge following in Sweden because of the eight hometown heroes on their roster, including Lidstrom, Henrik Zetterberg, Niklas Kronwall, and Tomas Holmstrom. The Blues countered with two: Alex Steen and Patrik Berglund.

But it was the small section of Blues' fans cheering the outcome of the opener, with Kariya accounting for two goals in his return to the lineup. The club fell behind 3–1 in the second period, but Kariya's second of the game, with 2:24 left in the middle frame, gave the Blues the game-winning goal in a 4–3 victory.

"There's no 'give up' in this team, that's for sure," Kariya said.

It would take less than 24 hours to see more support for Kariya's assessment of the Blues. After falling behind 2–0, and later 3–2, the Blues netted three unanswered goals for a 5–3 triumph over Detroit in Game 2.

Tkachuk had two of the team's five goals and seven of its 38 hits.

"Makes [the flight] better," he said. "And it keeps Murray off my back for another 24 hours."

How Swede it was to open a promising season with a two-game sweep, starting 2–0 for the first time since the 1994–95 season.

"You can talk about team-building," Murray said. "You can go out for meals, you can do scavenger hunts. But the best type of team-builder is seeing one player sacrifice for the other. Nobody in that room wanted to let down the guy sitting beside them."

When the Blues arrived back at their team hotel in downtown Stockholm, their cheering section, which had swelled to a couple hundred, met them in the lobby.

"When we got off the bus, one of the employees said, 'There's a lot of people in here,'" Johnson said. "It was awesome. Obviously we won two big games, but it seemed like we won something a lot more with the fans doing that."

When Blues President John Davidson entered the hotel, chants of "J-D! J-D!" reverberated through the crowd.

"It was like being part of the Olympics," Davidson said. "It was an emotional experience for us. That was totally unexpected.

"It was a big stage, and our players got big-stage experience, which is hard to come by. If you come home 0–2, it certainly wouldn't have been enthusiastic for us. But sometimes that's what sports are. If you want to move up in your master plan, you've got to do these things…so we did it."

Unfortunately, the Blues couldn't build on the momentum they created in Sweden. The club traveled the 4,600 air miles back to St. Louis and went winless in its next three games. Murray's team finished 40–32–10 for 90 points that season, falling five points short of the final playoff spot in the Western Conference.

64 Mental Case

You don't get dubbed with nicknames like "crazy" and "mental case" for no reason, and Steve Durbano did plenty to deserve those nicknames.

One incident on February 21, 1979, in his second stint with the Blues, will be remembered for many "moons."

The New York Rangers made Durbano the No. 13 overall pick in 1971, but he never suited up for a game with the Rangers. He was traded to St. Louis in May 1972 for future considerations.

The Blues should have known what kind of wild ride it would be when, in his first season in 1972–73, Durbano set a club record for minor penalties in a period (5), penalty minutes in a period (26), penalty minutes in a season (231), and game misconducts (10).

"You didn't know what he was going to do," former teammate Bruce Affleck said.

There were gems like the night Durbano was sent to the penalty box, took off a skate, and threw it over the glass toward the referee. When the official realized what Durbano had done, the belligerent Blue claimed that he was tossing it to the team's trainer for re-sharpening.

"The ref kicked him out," Affleck recalled. "Durbano said, 'All I wanted was my skate sharpened.'"

Another time Durbano left the rink in the first period of a game against the Rangers, upset with Blues coach Jean-Guy Talbot and mad about his ice time? He was showered and gone before his teammates came in the locker room for the first intermission.

"He never said a word to anyone," Talbot said.

Durbano was hit with a two-week suspension, but after six days, he showed remorse for his actions and, after a vote of his teammates, was allowed to return to the club.

During his second season, the Blues traded Durbano to Pittsburgh, along with fellow enforcer Bob Kelly and defenseman Ab DeMarco, in exchange for Bryan Watson, Greg Polis, and the Penguins' second-round pick in 1974.

But Durbano's escapades were far from over.

In September 1974, Durbano was suspended for two games after swinging his stick and nearly taking the head off the Kansas

City Scouts' Gary Coulter. Did we mention it was a preseason game?

While Durbano gave Pittsburgh the courtesy of not walking out during a game, he did leave the rink in the middle of two practices. Once again, his antics grew old and Durbano was traded to the Scouts in January 1976. Between the two stops that year, he set an NHL record for a defenseman with 370 penalty minutes.

By 1977, Durbano found himself playing in the World Hockey Association with the Birmingham Bulls. One legendary story while Durbano played in the WHA occurred when he plucked the toupee off Winnipeg's Bobby Hull and tossed it into the crowd.

But in August 1978, hockey's bad boy had returned to the NHL and the Blues, signing as a free agent. While he would only wear the Blue Note for another 13 games, he made sure that he got in one more signature moment before his tumultuous retirement.

It came in 1979 at Madison Square Garden against the club that drafted him.

The Blues' Brian Sutter had just scored his third goal of the game. While the team celebrated, Durbano swung his stick at the Rangers' Nick Fotiu. It took several moments to calm the situation. When that finally happened, Durbano skated cross-ice and went after Fotiu again, engaging in a fight.

The announcer broadcasting the game belted out, "It's Durbano…. He's been suspended in the National Hockey League, suspended in every league he's played in."

As the bout was broken up, Durbano zoomed toward the door that leaves the ice. In his last strides, Durbano turned himself so that he was skating backward and mocked like he was mooning the crowd, although he was polite enough to keep his pants on.

"He got ejected, and they opened the Zamboni doors," former teammate Larry Patey said, noting that the game was shown on national TV. "He starts going toward the door, and I don't know if he just got over the blue line or what, but he bent over and just spread his cheeks."

Added Affleck, "He mooned the crowd at Madison Square Garden. We were just howling. Typical Steve Durbano."

Durbano received 45 penalty minutes, was suspended five games, and fined $450. In his career, he racked up 1,127 penalty minutes in 220 games, or an average of 5.1 minutes per game.

"If I just went on talent alone, I never would have made the NHL," Durbano once said.

In 1983, after his retirement, Durbano was arrested and charged with drug trafficking and was sentenced to seven years in prison. In the mid-1990s, he was charged with running a prostitution ring, and he was also arrested for shoplifting.

Durbano died in 2002 of liver cancer at age 50.

65 Shorthanded Success

In 1975–76, the Blues' penalty-killing unit wanted more than to just keep the opposition off the scoreboard. Chuck Lefley, Derek Sanderson, Red Berenson, Larry Patey, and the rest of the PK group wanted to score themselves.

"Scoring a shorthanded goal gives the team a lift," Lefley said. "We've been picking our spots and making the most of them."

Through the first 17 games of the season, the Blues' PK had already netted 10 shorthanded goals. Lefley had six of those, followed by Sanderson with two, and Berenson and Bob Plager with one apiece.

"Chuck should get 15 and could be the first man ever to score 20," Sanderson said. "I'll probably score eight."

The Blues didn't quite reach those lofty projections, but Lefley finished with eight "shorties," which set a new single-season team record, and Sanderson chipped in six. The club's total, which was four short of Boston's NHL record at the time, did establish a franchise record that still stands today.

The Blues scored a total of 249 goals in 1975–76, meaning the 21 by the penalty-kill accounted for 8.4 percent of the offense. It opened a whole new door for the Blues, who at one point in the season had more goals from their PK unit than their power-play unit.

"They get the puck and hang on to it until somebody gets into the open," said former Blues coach Garry Young. "Lefley has to be one of the fastest guys in the league. He gets himself open."

Lefley and Sanderson had tremendous chemistry.

"With Lefley's great speed, all I have to do is send him on his way," Sanderson said. "They're real backbreakers, and the other team has to be conscious of it. They start thinking negatively and keeping an eye on the penalty-killers. They may even sacrifice a forward and put another defenseman back there, and that's to our advantage."

Patey contributed just one of the Blues' 21 shorthanded goals in 1975–76, but he took notes that paid off later.

"In those days, penalty killing was dump it in, ice the puck, back up, and be a four-man defensive team," Patey said. "It seemed like that year we really tried to be much more aggressive, [to] do something before they got into our end, try to cause havoc, and I think it worked better than just giving them possession and letting them walk right in."

In the late 1970s the Blues scored fewer shorthanded goals, but they were still successful as a unit. In 1979–80, with new faces such as Mike Crombeen, Ralph Klassen, Hartland Monahan, and Mike Zuke, the team led the NHL in killing penalties at 84.8 percent.

"A lot has to do with our goaltending back in those days," Patey said. "Mike Liut had some big years, and every time the goalie plays a little better, it makes everybody on the team better, including the penalty killers."

In 1980–81, the Blues were back up again with 16 shorthanded goals. Patey had half of those, tying Lefley's single-season club record. He would finish his career in St. Louis with 23, which is the most of any Blue in history.

"A record like this means a lot to me," Patey said. "One of the reasons our team is having success is because everyone is made to feel important."

Berenson, Patey's former teammate who had taken over as coach of the Blues, preached that.

"The beauty of Patey's [single-season] record is that not only does he lead in shorthanded goals, but the team is also one of the best in the league at killing penalties," Berenson said. "It's like a car. If you've got a million-dollar engine but you get a flat tire, you aren't going to win any races. All the parts of the car have to be working together. It's the same way with a hockey club. All the parts have to be working together or you're not going to win a thing."

66 Stastny Suits Up for Blues

Yan Stastny was 11 years old when his father, Peter, carried the Slovakian flag at the opening ceremonies of the 1994 Olympics in Lillehammer, Norway.

"What an emotional moment it was," Yan said. "I remember sitting on the floor, 6' from the TV, glued to it. I could see tears in his eyes. I get chills down my spine just thinking about it."

Peter Stastny was a trailblazer in the sport before wrapping up his sensational career in St. Louis in the mid-1990s.

In 1980, Peter and his brother, Anton, defected from Czechoslovakia at a tournament in Austria. They signed as free agents with the NHL's Quebec Nordiques, and a year later their third brother, Marian, joined them to create the third-ever trio of brothers in the league.

By the 1990s, Peter had built a Hall of Fame–caliber resume, posting more than 1,200 points. But in 1993 when the former Czechoslovakia split into the Czech Republic and Slovakia, Peter put his NHL career on hold, potentially for good. He returned home to help pave the way for the Slovakian national team to play in the Olympics.

"I always say I'm Slovak," Peter Stastny said. "Slovakia always suffered from an identity crisis. Czechoslovakia was really two countries. The Czechs were stronger. There were twice as many Czechs as Slovaks. They dominated everything—all the political, economic, and cultural institutions."

Despite the odds, Stastny had the Slovaks ready for the 1994 Winter Games. The club went 3–0–1 in a pre-tournament to advance to the 12-team Olympics, which Stastny called "huge, huge…. Everyone was going crazy."

In the medal round, Slovakia suffered an overtime loss to the Russians, a game that Stastny labeled "the most disappointing loss I've ever experienced," but the country finished sixth overall with a record of 4–2–2 and he tied for second in scoring.

Having been released by the New Jersey Devils at the end of his contract in 1993, it could have been the last of Stastny's playing days. But rejuvenated at age 37, the player who had posted 100-plus points seven times and was a six-time All-Star signed a free-agent contract with the Blues.

The club agreed to pay him $200,000 for the remainder of the 1993–94 season.

"After 13 seasons, this is a refreshing break," Stastny said after joining the Blues. "To help Slovakia win, there is always so much excitement, motivation, inspiration. Now this is just perfect. I feel like newborn, young, and looking forward to being back in the big leagues."

Some people around the NHL scratched their head about the Blues' signing of Stastny, who in his last season with New Jersey had 17 goals and 40 points in 62 games, all career lows. After joining the Blues, however, he netted five goals and 15 points in his first 14 games, including a nine-game point streak.

"He's still at the top of his game," said former Blues center Craig Janney. "Everyone who watched the Olympics saw where he brought that Slovakian team. He's one of the greats, and he's still producing."

Stastny centered a line that had Brett Hull at right wing.

"I think it's kind of neat," Hull said. "He's got what, 1,200 points in the league. He works hard. There are a lot of kids half his age who don't work as hard."

Stastny certainly wasn't a kid.

"I played against Brett's dad, Bobby, when he was with Winnipeg," he said. "And I played against Petr Nedved's dad, Jaroslav, back in the Czechoslovakian league."

Petr Nedved remembered watching Stastny play in the Canada Cup on television.

"Every time [Stastny] touched the puck, the [Czech] announcer didn't mention his name," Nedved said. "They didn't want to give him any publicity because he had defected."

Stastny still remembers vividly the difficulty of choosing whether or not to defect.

"It was very hard to leave," he said. "There were so many things to consider that the more you thought about it, the more you didn't want to leave. But [government officials] threatened my career and my dreams, and I cannot think of anything more damaging. I was actually forced to make the decision. I knew it would hurt a lot of people close to me."

But in 1998, Stastny was able to repay his loved ones, inviting them to Toronto for his Hockey Hall of Fame induction. He played 23 games with the Blues, wrapping up a career in which he finished with 450 goals and 1,239 points in 977 games.

"I'm so thankful that we are able to share this all together," Stastny said. "This is a very unique and special event in anybody's life, and if your family can be here and share it with you, all by itself, that's a gift."

Stastny's audience included wife, Darina; daughter, Katarina; and sons, Yan and Paul, who were both drafted in the NHL. Yan followed in his dad's footsteps, playing for the Blues and competing for Team USA at the World Championships. Paul played for the Blues and also competed for Team USA at the Olympics.

Paul was only eight when his dad carried the Slovokian flag in Norway in 1994.

"I guess I didn't know too much about his history and how big it was until I matured and I could grasp things," Paul said. "I was probably thinking that a lot of people made it. But as I got older, I realized how hard it is, and what a special moment it is to be able to represent your country in the Olympics. I realize more what my dad did on the international stage. It's something we didn't talk about too much, but I couldn't be more proud of him, and I feel lucky just to be his son, and learn from him all of the experiences he's been through in his career."

After retiring in 1995, Stastny remained with the Blues as a consultant and kept his family in St. Louis.

"They're very blessed that they can grow up in this kind of environment," he said. "I'm blazing new trails, I guess. St. Louis is a great city, something special. This is the place for me. Things turned out better than I ever thought."

67 Salomons

The destination was the Golden Strand hotel in Miami Beach.

Every year after the Blues' season concluded, owners Sid Salomon Jr. and his son, Sid Salomon III, flew the players to their Florida hotel for some postseason unwinding.

"They'd take the whole team—wives, babysitters, kids, the whole thing," former Blues defenseman Bruce Affleck said. "We chartered a plane and went down and took over the hotel for six or seven days. The other [NHL] owners hated it."

If the Salomons were known for something other than bringing the Blues into existence in 1967, it was catering to those who were responsible for the product on the ice. Their generosity lured many big-name players to St. Louis, which their counterparts around the league saw as a huge advantage.

"Those Blues keep getting and getting," Toronto general manager George "Punch" Imlach griped at the time. "They get so much in the way of bonuses and other side benefits that the rest of the players in the league are on the verge of staging a protest march because they are not included in the loot.

"I understand that when a player with the Blues gets the hat trick, the management gives him a $750 watch. And I hear that if somebody scores the winning goal on the Blues, he gets a luxury cruise on the Riviera."

It was all part of the Salomons' plan to make St. Louis a destination, forming the expansion franchise into one that could compete quickly and catch the attention of a town not all that familiar with hockey.

"The Blues were Sid III's dream," said his father, Sid Jr. "He talked me into it when I really wasn't very enthused. St. Louis has hockey today for just one reason—Sid's persistence.

"Sid doesn't do it for the money. He could make three or four times as much in the insurance business."

The elder Salomon was an executive with Sidney Salomon Jr. and Associates Inc., a local branch of sorts for Crown Life Insurance Co. in Regina, Saskatchewan. Once the family was awarded the club, the younger Salomon jumped into the day-to-day operations, becoming the Blues' No. 1 follower, which eventually became his downfall.

"He flew to Palm Springs, California, and listened to Dan Kelly's play-by-play account of our game in Boston on the telephone," former coach Scotty Bowman remembered. "Then he went to Los Angeles and Oakland to watch games. He's really some fan."

The Salomons' watch over the Blues gained support when the club advanced to the Stanley Cup final in each of the first three seasons, playing in front of a packed house at the newly refurbished Arena. Seating expanded from 8,900 to more than 14,000 after the 1968 final.

"I think I'm doing a good job," Sid III said, "and I know that if I weren't, my dad would kick me out of here."

His support started at the top.

"He could make it on his own in this league," Sid Jr. said. "I can introduce you to an owner in the NHL who came to me and asked if Sid might be available. If he were, he said, he'd give him a five-year contract at $100,000 to run his team."

Meanwhile, Sid III was throwing the Blues' money around, bringing goaltender Jacques Plante to St. Louis.

"Today I make $35,000, which is $15,000 more than I ever earned in my best year in Montreal," Plante said. "To tell you the truth, I never dreamed of getting a salary like this. With other teams, there is a wall between the owners and players. That is not true here. They are not interested in us just as hockey players, but as human beings. So we put [out] extra for them."

When Red Berenson tied the NHL record with six goals in a game in 1968, the Salomons presented him with a 1969 station wagon, license plate "RB-6666."

"In New York or Montreal, all you'd get would be a handshake," Berenson said.

The Salomons also introduced a room for the players' wives to gather before and after games.

"For a new team and ownership," former Blue Terry Crisp said, "they were pioneers in treating players and their families with class, dignity, and respect."

While other owners complained, Sid III said, "It's just good business."

But soon Sid III was making it too much of his business.

"He liked the limelight. He liked the fact that he was running a hockey team. He thought he knew more about hockey than Al Arbour and the rest of them," Affleck said. "I remember one time we were in Washington and [Sid III] is running down by the locker room, telling the coach that this guy should be benched. He's been around hockey for six or seven years, and here he's telling the coach who to play. He got too involved."

Sid III was involved in the firing of Bowman and Arbour, as the Blues' played musical chairs with their coaches.

"He'd change his mind overnight," Arbour said. "We were wondering what was going on. He was sick at the time. We didn't know that."

The Salomons' health and finances took a turn for the worse.

Sid Jr. was on the verge of back-to-back heart attacks, while Sid III had a relapse with Hodgkin's disease.

The Owners of the Blues

Sidney Salomon Jr. and Sidney Salomon III	1966–77
Ralston Purina	1977–83
Harry Ornest	1983–86
Mike Shanahan Sr.	1986–91
Kiel Center Partners	1991–99
Bill and Nancy Laurie	1999–2006
Dave Checketts and SCP Worldwide	2006–12
Tom Stillman	2012–present

A 26-year run with Crown Insurance ended, and Salomon Jr. lost a wrongful termination suit. The City of St. Louis planned to sue the Blues over delinquent taxes, and former player Jim McCrimmon sued over unpaid wages. Meanwhile, attendance was in massive decline.

"We knew they were hurting," said Hall of Famer Bernie Federko, who was playing with the Blues' minor-league affiliate at the time. "In Kansas City, everything was left over. We used the underwear, for crying out loud, the passed-down underwear from the Blues' team here. We had to cross out the number that was on the back of our underwear and put our own number on it. It was that bad."

The debt had grown too high.

"They say we got [the franchise] for $2 million, a bargain," Sid III said. "But remember this—we spent another $8 million for our building and improvements. That's a big investment. We don't know if we'll be able to compete well enough in the future to make it pay off."

On January 31, 1977, when it became clear that making the following month's payroll might not happen, the Blues dismissed numerous employees.

"The financial burden of The Arena forced the Blues to consolidate efforts of various departments, necessitating reduction of various office personnel," the Salomons said in a statement.

The Salomons attempted to gain approval from the NHL to relocate the Blues, but that might have been done as a ploy to gain leverage against the city rather than any real intention to move the team. However, when a potential deal fell apart with Fred Kummer, president of a company headquartered in St. Louis, the team's future in the city was indeed in jeopardy.

"The darkest day in the history of the team," club attorney Jim Cullen said when the agreement unraveled. "What we need now to save the team and the franchise for St. Louis is a prayer, a minor miracle, some emergence of civic pride of some potential buyer."

68 Ralston Purina

A chance encounter between Blues general manager Emile Francis and R. Hal Dean from Ralston Purina, a pet food company based in St. Louis, might have saved the Blues from moving.

"We were both in the men's room at the stadium during a Cardinals game," Francis said. "Dean comes up to me and asks me how we're making out at The Arena. I told him that if something didn't happen in the next month, we'd be in trouble. That's when he said the franchise would never leave St. Louis."

After months of uncertainty concerning the Blues' stability in the city, Ralston Purina stepped up and purchased the Blues. On July 27, 1977, the company reached a tentative agreement with the Salomons to relieve them of their insurmountable debt and relieve Blues' fans of their worst fear.

"Ralston Purina wouldn't have entered the hockey business if we weren't convinced that, unless we bought the team, the Blues would have left St. Louis," Dean said.

The sale price was announced at $4 million, and Ralston also solved the Salomons' financial issues with The Arena. The family owed a mortgage of $5.4 million, but three St. Louis businessmen were able to work out a lease of the building and rent it to Ralston.

"Ralston Purina is a serious business concern; we are not fat cats," Dean insisted. "We are in a very competitive business, and we're used to driving hard to succeed. And that's the way we're going to run this hockey team. It's going to be a very business-like business. We expect hockey to pay its own way."

That remained to be seen. But initially, news of the purchase by the local company jump-started the fan base again.

"The phone calls have been unbelievable," Blues official Dennis Ball said. "I'd say a lot of the new people are interested, and the old regulars have been calling to say they're happy. The response has been great."

While Ralston had inherited many problems, the club's new owners inherited Francis, a strong-minded, front-office executive.

"We have no hockey experts at Ralston Purina, and we aren't going to become hockey experts," Dean said. "In Emile Francis, we have a president and general manager who is the best in the business. He will run the club, and he will run it well."

The Blues endured a couple of difficult seasons in the beginning under Ralston. However, thanks to the drafting of Francis—who added Brian Sutter, Bernie Federko, and Mike Liut—the franchise enjoyed a resurgence. In 1980–81, the Blues finished first in their division with 107 points.

Meanwhile at Ralston, Dean was forced into retirement. With his replacement, William Stiritz, at the helm, the company was more focused on making a profit. Although the Blues were selling out their games at the Checkerdome, Ralston lacked television revenue. Plus its five-year tax write-off of losses of player salaries ended in the early 1980s.

On January 12, 1983, the St. Louis–based company stunned the city when it announced that it had reached a purchase agreement to sell the Blues to Batoni-Hunter Enterprises Ltd., which had plans to relocate the team to Saskatoon, Saskatchewan, Canada.

"We feel our company has gone far beyond its normal call of duty in prolonging the life of the Blues in St. Louis," Stiritz said. "The National Hockey League has stated that their preference is for a franchise to remain in an existing location if a qualified buyer is available. During our ownership of the franchise, we have had discussions with individuals and groups looking toward finding permanent St. Louis ownership for the Blues. We have received no firm offers from local interests to assume the liabilities of the operation."

Peter Batoni and Bill Hunter had made an offer, believed to be about $11.5 million, to buy the Blues and put them in a new 18,000-seat, $45-million arena in Saskatoon. They had even chosen a name—the Saska Tunes—in which they could have kept the Blue Note logo.

"They'll be buying geography books all over North America to find out where Saskatoon is located," Hunter said.

Hunter was right about one thing—no one knew the whereabouts of Saskatoon.

An outdoor pep rally on January 22, 1983, just days after Ralston's announcement, drew many loyal fans waving placards and bumper stickers that read, "Where the hell is Saskatoon?"

Blues radio analyst Gus Kyle had been a college roommate of Hunter, who was now trying to steal his team.

"I can't believe he did that to me," Kyle said. "I can tell you this, I'm not going to return his Christmas card this year."

The Saskatoon bid would need two-thirds support from the 21 NHL owners to gain approval, and those in St. Louis weren't the only ones objecting.

"I wouldn't let them move that team one inch," Toronto Harold Ballard said. "They'll never get it from me.

"What's that dog food company in St. Louis think it's doing anyway? That team deserves to remain in St. Louis because of the support the fans of St. Louis have shown over the years. Surely there are enough civic-minded people in St. Louis to throw in a dollar apiece and keep the team. Where's that 'Spirit of St. Louis?'"

Anheuser-Busch, which owned the St. Louis baseball Cardinals, looked into the situation.

"As corporate citizens of St. Louis, Anheuser-Busch felt an obligation to take a look at the St. Louis Blues franchise," the company said in a statement. "They did so and could not justify the acquisition financially."

The possibility of the Blues having a new home for the 1983–84 season increased as the vote went to the NHL Board of Governors on May 18, 1983, in New York.

"It won't be easy, but it's going to get done," Hunter said. "They may not want us in, but we're coming in. No question about that. For all the critics who said we couldn't bring the Blues to Saskatoon—drop dead!"

The players were resigned to the relocation.

"It felt pretty close," former Blues defenseman Bruce Affleck remembered. "You were sitting there going, 'Okay, maybe this is going to happen.' It was pretty scary."

But at the NHL meeting in New York, the board voted 15–3 to reject the Saskatoon deal. Ralston sued for $60 million, and the league counter-sued for $78 million.

"The NHL has always fought its battles in court, and we are prepared to do so again should that action come up," NHL president John Ziegler said.

Ralston essentially ceased operations of the team. In fact, it would not authorize any of its hockey operations personnel to participate in the amateur draft on June 8, 1983, at the Montreal Forum. The Blues' three-minute period to pick a player came and went each time without a selection.

"The St. Louis table was empty," said Hunter, who was in Montreal in case the league allowed him to draft for the Blues. "It was sad."

Less than a week later, at a meeting in Chicago, the NHL stripped Ralston of the franchise, assuming all player contracts while it searched for an owner.

"If a serious-minded group in St. Louis came forward, the league probably would prefer to keep the team in St. Louis," Francis said. "When we went through all this before, in 1977, it looked as if no one was going to come forward, but Ralston Purina did at the last minute. I'm not assuming that isn't going to happen again. I don't know of any group out there, waiting to jump in."

After the NHL's takeover, a St. Louis lawyer representing Beverly Hills, California, businessman Harry Ornest flew to New York to meet with league officials about making an offer.

69 Harry Ornest

Harry Ornest wanted to own an NHL franchise since he could remember, and in 1983 the Blues were in desperate need of an owner. Desperate, in fact, was an understatement.

For the second time in a half-dozen years, the Blues were changing hands, and this time the possibility of relocating had loomed extremely large. It took a vote of the NHL's Board of

Governors to block a move to Saskatoon, but the team wasn't out of the woods yet. The league had seized control of the Blues' operations from Ralston Purina, which had abandoned the club after its ill-fated relocation bid.

An Edmonton native who had made a fortune in vending machines, Ornest was a businessman living in Beverly Hills, California. A religious reader of newspapers, he came across a headline in the *Los Angeles Times* one morning proclaiming that the Blues had been on the brink of heading to Saskatoon.

"I said, 'What the hell is going on here?'" Ornest recalled. "We used to call Saskatoon 'Saskabush.'"

All joking side, Ornest expressed serious interest in the Blues, and on July 21, 1983, he exited a Chicago hotel with approval from the NHL's Board of Governors to purchase the club. After securing a few local investors from a group named Civic Progress, Ornest paid $12 million for the Blues. He also bought The Arena for $4.7 million.

"I started wanting to be an [NHL] owner at the age of six, and it's taken me 54 years to get this far," said Ornest. "I didn't do it unblinkingly."

Ornest had a plan, and as long as the plan involved remaining in St. Louis, Blues fans were ecstatic. Former St. Louis mayor Vincent Schoemehl initially viewed Ornest as "Harry the Great, the savior who came in and made it possible to keep major-league hockey here."

But that moniker would not stick with Ornest throughout his three-year reign. With Ralston losing $3 million in 1982–83, Ornest's blueprint for the team required major cost-cutting moves. And by the end, despite keeping the Blues in St. Louis, spending $3 million to renovate The Arena, and putting a competitive team on the ice, Ornest developed a reputation as a cheapskate.

"[Ornest] senses a business opportunity as well as anyone," said Jack Quinn, who was brought into the Blues' organization after running Ornest's minor-league baseball team in Vancouver, British Columbia. "The league had nobody else. He used that leverage to his business advantage. He knew how long he'd be in it and what he wanted out of it.

"What we wanted to do was prove that St. Louis would be capable of supporting major league hockey. People just didn't understand [that] our job was to put the Blues back on the road to fiscal soundness. We just tried to live within limits. There was a statement by the previous ownership that hockey could not survive here. I think we demonstrated it could."

Quinn hired Ron Caron as general manager, and Caron hired Jacques Demers as head coach. The Blues, relieved that they were no longer headed to Saskatoon, quickly became a formidable NHL opponent again. The Blues were in first place in their division by Ornest's second season, and while selling new season tickets proved to be a tough task, attendance stayed steady at 11,000 fans.

"The most satisfying thing is that we've created credibility in the NHL and in the community," Ornest said. "We're proud of what we've accomplished in such a short time."

The accomplishments on the ice were even more impressive considering the corners that were being cut behind the scenes.

Flights home from Montreal and Hartford consumed most of the day, as Ornest saved money with routes that zigzagged around the country. The penny-pinching pattern continued and eventually it would become public with personnel moves that didn't please the fans.

The Blues traded both Mike Liut and Joe Mullen for budgetary reasons. After back-to-back 40-goal seasons, Mullen wanted $250,000 a year and Ornest balked. The team dealt Mullen, along with Terry Johnson and Rik Wilson, to Calgary for Eddy Beers, Gino Cavallini, and Charlie Bourgeois.

"We don't make trades for expediency's sake or for financial gain," Ornest contended. "We make trades with one objective—to improve the quality of our club for today and tomorrow. As for Mullen, Joey was a terrific asset to the Blues, but in the past two years we were knocked out of the playoffs by Minnesota. We felt we needed more balance on the forward lines and more size to help us in the playoffs. And we got it."

In a matchup that must have been cued up by the hockey gods, the Blues met Mullen and the Flames in the Campbell Conference final in 1986.

"I'd love to stick it to Harry," Mullen said. "I didn't like some of the things he said last summer. Then I hear one of the reasons they traded me was because I couldn't score in the playoffs."

Mullen scored a goal in nine straight playoff games for Calgary that season, and after scoring in Game 2 against the Blues, he nearly sent the Flames to the Stanley Cup final in overtime of Game 6 but his shot rang off the post.

The Blues won Game 6 by the score of 6–5 in OT, a game better known as the Monday Night Miracle. However, the Flames blew out the candles on the series with a 2–1 win in Game 7.

Several Blues from that squad confirmed that after the Game 7 loss, Ornest canceled the team's charter trip back to St. Louis. Players were forced to find their own commercial flights home.

The "cheapskate" label was muttered once again.

At one point during his tenure, Ornest responded to the label by saying, "If being a 'cheapskate' means that my team goes first-class, like it does; that I meet my payroll, which I do; that our payroll is among the top 10 among NHL teams, which it is; that we're competitive, which we are; that I spent a fortune refurbishing The Arena, which I did; that the same people I started with are still with me, which they are; and I run a business wary of waste, which I do—then I am a cheapskate in the illustrious company of IBM, Monsanto, CBS, and other Fortune 500 companies who don't hesitate to review their businesses from the standpoint of waste, cost returns, and success."

In 1986, the Blues turned a $300,000 profit, according to Ornest, their first in 14 years. But by then, he had made more enemies than friends.

After once raving about Demers, Ornest failed to provide him with a formal contract extension, and when the head coach bolted for Detroit, Ornest sued the Red Wings for compensation.

Still bickering with Schoemehl over tax issues, Ornest fielded an offer to sell the Blues to a group in Hamilton, Ontario, and he planted a story in a Seattle paper that the team would move there. But in the end, Ornest never pulled the relocation trigger.

Instead, Ornest sold the team to local businessman Mike Shanahan for $19 million and The Arena to the city for $15 million. In only three years, he pocketed an estimated profit of $30 million.

"He was a businessman," former Blue Bob Plager said. "He was out to make a dollar no matter what. But he was a smart man. He rode in on a white horse, and he was god for a while. Then he started doing all of those things and ticked everybody off.

"When my brother Barclay was the assistant coach here, I'd say, 'That Ornest!' My brother would say, 'Hey, no matter what you think of him, he saved the hockey team in St. Louis.' I'd say, 'Well, you're right, but....'"

70 Mike Shanahan

When Mike Shanahan arrived on the Blues' scene in 1986, outgoing owner Harry Ornest was jealous of the reception Shanahan received from fans.

"He resented the reception I got when I took over, being a St. Louis guy," Shanahan recalled. "He'd say, 'If they'd treated me like they treated you....'"

On December 13, 1986, Shanahan, who was the head of Engineered Support Systems in St. Louis, completed his purchase of the Blues. He held only a 12 percent controlling interest, and in his group were many of the same key figures from Civic Progress. Nonetheless, the spotlight was quickly focused on the club's new 46-year-old chairman.

"Mike just had that certain charisma that certain people have. People just fell in love with Mike Shanahan," Blues CFO and former player Bruce Affleck said. "Mike has that Irish heritage that came out every once in a while when he got upset. He got St. Louis to buy in both corporately and with the blue-collar guy. It was a great mix."

The list of investors still included Anheuser-Busch but also featured Boatman's, Centerre, and Mercantile banks, along with Emerson Electric, McDonnell Douglas, and Monsanto.

After multiple threats of relocating under previous ownership, this St. Louis–based group obviously wasn't taking the team anywhere. And that was good news.

"Under Harry Ornest and before, we have always felt a threat that the team could leave town...that chapter in the history of the Blues is closed," St. Louis mayor Vincent Schoemehl said.

Shanahan had been a Blues fan who even owned season tickets at one time. But he gave them up after a game in 1981 when he had a run-in with another fan who was shouting obscenities.

"I complained to management, but nothing happened," Shanahan recalled. "I just gave the unused tickets back to Ralston Purina, or whoever was managing The Arena at the time. I didn't even ask for a refund. I just walked away. That was the end of it."

But in 1986, at the urging of Schoemehl, Shanahan returned to The Arena—this time as owner of the Blues.

"I went home and talked to my wife about it," said Shanahan, who was on the board of directors for approximately a dozen companies in St. Louis. "She said, 'You're into so many things already, how are you going to do this? Really, what do you know about this?' I said, 'Well, he's not asking me to go out and skate with the players.'"

Shanahan was a talented athlete growing up in the St. Louis suburb of University City, but his success came in soccer, winning back-to-back NCAA championships at St. Louis University in 1959–60. Now he had a goal of taking the Blues to that level.

Shanahan elevated Jack Quinn to team president and promoted general manager Ron Caron to Vice President.

After nearly advancing to its first Stanley Cup final since 1970 in Ornest's final year ownership, it was a different era under Shanahan and Co.

Caron traded for Brett Hull, and when Hull produced, the Blues rewarded him with a four-year contract worth more than $5 million. They followed with a similar deal for free-agent defenseman Scott Stevens, showing the club's purse strings had loosened significantly.

"They've made my job very simple," Caron said at the time. "They let me do what I want, but carefully."

The Blues were thriving on the ice and at the box office. In 1990–91, the club finished the regular season with 47 victories and

105 points, placing second in the Norris Division. The number of season-ticket holders reached 12,000, and near-sellouts of 17,000-plus crowds were plentiful. Relying solely on ticket revenue, the team showed consistent profit.

However, because of the ownership group's lopsided lease agreement with the City of St. Louis, which collected the revenue from parking and concessions, staying status quo was a risky business considering that the size of NHL player contracts was on the rise.

Shanahan, who was on the hook for any potential losses, saw his relationship with Schoemehl disintegrate over the lease issue.

"I don't see how a team can survive with a lease like we have for The Arena," Shanahan said. "And unfortunately, I am not in a position where I can build a new arena and bankroll a team."

In 1989, Shanahan had reached a tentative agreement to sell his control of the Blues to Anheuser-Busch, which wanted to build a new arena across the street from Busch Stadium. But Schoemehl blocked Anheuser-Busch's idea and the brewery chose not to purchase the club.

In 1990, Shanahan thwarted a "hostile" bid by a group of out-of-town investors to buy control of the Blues.

But in 1991, the Kiel Center Partners, a newly formed group of 23 area businessman, many of them who were in Shanahan's ownership group, engaged in talks to buy the team. The group was making plans to build a new 18,000-seat downtown arena, estimated at $85 million.

Shanahan had always believed that the Blues and the building in which they played needed to be under the umbrella of one ownership group. He also strongly believed that the club needed a new building.

"We had to have a new arena for hockey to survive here," Shanahan said. "The old Arena, it was just in bad, bad shape. It was a great building to watch game, but the infrastructure was bad, the concourses were horrible, the restrooms were deplorable, and we just needed to be out of there."

In the summer of 1991, with arena plans taking off, Shanahan agreed to sell his controlling interest and turn over the day-to-day operations of the Blues to Kiel Center Partners. He was asked to remain on as chairman and continue to serve as the team's representative to the NHL Board of Governors. But now Shanahan was part of a three-man board that included Mark Sauer, the head of Kiel Center Partners, and Andy Craig, chairman of Boatman's.

"It was an agreement," Shanahan said. "They wanted me to stay until a new arena got built. For all intents and purposes, it was business as usual."

Publicly, the partners stood behind Shanahan.

"He'll have a lot of autonomy," Sauer insisted. "His track record is very successful, and we want to give him as much autonomy as he desires."

The Shanahan era was not over—yet.

71 Kiel Center Partners

While Mike Shanahan's popularity was the reason for his success as owner of the Blues, it would eventually lead to his demise.

On June 20, 1991, Shanahan sold his controlling interest in the club to Kiel Center Partners, but he stayed on as the team's chairman and remained the engaging figure he had been during his own five-year reign.

Two years into his new role, Shanahan continued to attend Blues' public practices at Brentwood Ice Arena and chat with fans.

"Saturdays are especially fun," he said. "On Saturday you see more younger children here, and they're happy to be here to get a chance to see their heroes. At the games, you don't get this close. You're watching from a distance. This is a chance to get to know them. They are our customers. You get feedback on the kind of job you're doing."

Apparently, Shanahan was doing a good job.

On March 18, 1994, Kiel Center Partners gave Shanahan a two-year contract extension, even though the new arena was scheduled to open in time for the 1994–95 season (which was delayed by a NHL lockout) and his agreement stated that he would step away when the arena was complete.

"I'm very happy," Shanahan said at the time. "Now we can continue trying to build a team to win the Stanley Cup."

But less than 14 months later, on June 16, 1995, Shanahan was fired during a lunch with the group's Andy Craig.

"Mike was getting so much favorable press, and deservedly so," former Blues president Jack Quinn said. "I think that [Kiel Centers Partners] said he's getting too much…. They wanted him out. The way they did it, Andy Craig took him to lunch and showed him next year's executive page [of the media guide], and he wasn't on it."

Shanahan had finally lost his battle.

"Mike was not a favorite of August Busch III, or of Chuck Knight from Emerson, who kind of ran Kiel Center Partners," said the Blues' Bruce Affleck. "[Shanahan] was a local boy who made good, not a blue blood, and there was a little animosity going both ways. And then they ousted him. No love lost there."

Shanahan claimed years later that he wasn't fired. In the lunch with Craig, Shanahan has said, he was told that Kiel Center Partners were bringing in former St. Louis Cardinals baseball executive Jerry Ritter and they "needed to find a place for him."

"I said, 'Well, what do you want to do?'" Shanahan said. "Andy said, 'Well, he would be chairman of the Blues.' I said, 'Well, then I'm out.' He said, 'No, no, no, we want you to stay as president or vice chairman.' I said, 'I don't want to do that.' He said, 'Well, he can't work for you. He's a big executive at Anheuser-Busch, and he could not possibly be perceived as working for you.'

"I thought they kind of handled it poorly. You want Jerry Ritter to run the thing, he runs it. You don't need me. I'll just move on because I've got other things to do. Really, the fun had gone out of it by then. It was probably good timing. The hand-off could have been made a lot smoother, but that's life."

Kiel Center Partners, who promoted Quinn, would soon find out that the challenges ahead were daunting. An arena that was originally projected to cost $85 million had climbed to $170 million.

"I didn't think we needed to build a $170 million arena," Shanahan said. "The revenue streams just weren't there to support that kind of a building. With the new salaries in hockey, it just wasn't going to work. You would have had a better chance of looking out the window and seeing God than you would making a profit with those circumstances. I don't think I could have done it—and they didn't, obviously."

Ticket sales dipped 18 percent during a two-year time frame, and in its first full season, Kiel Center lost about $7 million in 1995–96. The Blues had brought in Mike Keenan, and he was in the process of wearing out his welcome with fans.

"The trust built over 30 years between the St. Louis Blues and our fans is being strained. And that's absolutely unacceptable," Ritter said. On December 19, 1996, Ritter fired Keenan and Quinn, who was replaced by Mark Sauer.

A month later, Kiel Center Partners had its second "cash call," pumping a total of $32 million into the Blues at that point to cover their losses. By December 1998, under the new name Clark Enterprises, the group had sunk a total of $70 million into the operation to keep it afloat.

Ritter cited several reasons for going back to investors for more money, including operating costs of the Blues and Kiel Center, the debt service ($10 million), and deferred compensation for players no longer on the roster ($5 million for 12 players).

It all proved to be too costly so on December 30, 1998, Clark Enterprises announced that it had hired Goldman Sachs to explore options about potentially selling the Blues.

"We simply have large, ongoing losses that we must address," Ritter said.

Shanahan maintained that he would not have been able to overcome the Blues' financial woes, but others disagreed.

"I don't think you could have gotten more than two or three guys in the entire area who were able to do what Mike Shanahan did for this club," one anonymous investor said. "He was always doing something for the players. Things were always done in the right order, and things start with the players because they are the team."

In 1999, Clark Enterprises struck a deal with Bill and Nancy Laurie, a couple from Columbia, Missouri, to buy the Blues and the arena lease.

72 Bill and Nancy Laurie

If the Blues needed an ownership group that could absorb significant losses until the team turned around, they hit the jackpot in 1999 when Bill and Nancy Laurie stepped up and bought the club.

Nancy was the daughter of Bud Walton, one of the founders of Wal-Mart. Nancy and Bill married in 1974, and the couple had a net worth of $1.3 billion, according to *Forbes* magazine.

On September 6, 1999, the Lauries paid $100 million for the Blues and the lease to Kiel Center. The seller, Clark Enterprises (formerly Kiel Center Partners), claimed to have bled $70 million in the final years of its ownership.

No one could continue down that financial free fall, but the Lauries were buying a club that had made 20 consecutive playoff appearances and played in an arena that was just five years old. The Lauries also possessed the resources to make the Blues a Stanley Cup contender.

"This is a good franchise and organization," Bill Laurie said. "I'm not sure how easy it will be to attain. We'll have to be patient. We're patient people."

Bill Laurie played college basketball at Memphis State and participated in the 1973 NCAA Championship Game, in which his team lost to UCLA at the Arena in St. Louis. He coached basketball at Christian Brothers College in Memphis (1978–83) and at Rock Bridge High School in Columbia. Along with Nancy, they were boosters for the University of Missouri athletic department.

"They're very passionate in their love for sports," said Mark Sauer, who was part of Clark Enterprises and remained president of the Blues after the Lauries took control.

Bill jumped wholeheartedly into his new role as an NHL owner. On his second day on the job, he addressed the Blues' players on the ice, promising his support.

"His speech really means a lot to all the guys in the organization," Blues winger Geoff Courtnall said at the time. "The last three years we lost out to the team that won the Stanley Cup—Detroit twice and Dallas. Those teams went out and added [players] at the trade deadline that made a difference."

The Blues had a payroll in the neighborhood of $32 million under third-year general manager Larry Pleau, but that number was about to get a boost.

"You don't necessarily have to go out and get carried away with your bank account to have a good franchise and a good organization, but I'm comfortable that we'll acquire players to get us where we want to be," Laurie said.

While certainly enthused, Blues fans couldn't help but wonder about Laurie's intentions. Five months earlier, he had reached a deal to buy the NBA's Denver Nuggets and the NHL's Colorado Avalanche, along with the Pepsi Center, for $400 million. But shortly after the agreement was made, the package was instead sold to businessman Donald Sturm for $461 million. (Eventually, Sturm's deal fell through and Stan Kroenke, Bill Laurie's brother-in-law who was married to Ann Walton, the daughter of Bud Walton, bought the Nuggets, Avalanche, and the arena for $450 million.)

Was Laurie more interested in the NBA? The prevailing thought was that he only bought the Blues and the lease to the St. Louis arena because he needed a home for his future basketball team. If he acquired one, how would he treat the Blues? That speculation became reality just 16 days after he closed the deal on the hockey team.

On September 23, 1999, the Lauries announced a deal to buy the NBA's Vancouver Grizzlies for approximately $200 million.

Laurie held a press conference and downplayed Vancouver's concerns about relocation.

"This is just our first day as NBA owners, and it is much too soon to settle on long-term plans or focus on the future," he said.

The deal still needed the approval of the NBA's Board of Governors, and when the finance committee wasn't convinced that Laurie would give the Grizzlies five more years to try to make it work in Vancouver, the deal was dissolved.

"Everything revolved around getting the team to St. Louis," Laurie said. "I'm concerned about the fans of St. Louis. They deserve an NBA franchise. And I'm going to do whatever I can to accomplish that."

Laurie was unsuccessful in doing so, but to his credit, he didn't dispose of the Blues right away. The couple owned the club for six more seasons and carried a payroll never before seen in St. Louis, reaching $60 million.

As Laurie had promised, the Blues injected new blood into the team at the trade deadline, acquiring Keith Tkachuk from Phoenix in March 2001. Unfortunately, they lost in the Western Conference quarterfinals to Kroenke's Colorado Avalanche.

At one point, the Blues had three players on the roster making more than $9 million: Tkachuk, Doug Weight, and Chris Pronger.

"They wanted to win, and you felt bad that we couldn't win enough," general manager Larry Pleau said. "When we lost to Vancouver [in 2003], when that team went down [in seven games after leading the series 3–1], that was the end of it. That was the end of the line."

The Lauries lost a combined $60 million in 2002–03 and 2003–04. Despite the lockout the following year, which would bring about a salary cap and a new financial structure, the couple wanted out of the business.

"Who could blame them?" Pleau said. "They had the money to do it. But it doesn't matter how much money you have—you lose enough, you get fed up after a while."

In 2006, a year after the lockout ended, the Lauries sold the Blues to Dave Checketts who headed up a group from New York. The sale stretched out over many months, during which the Lauries elected to trim the payroll to attract buyers. That decision led to the trade of Pronger, leaving a bad taste among Blues' fans as the Laurie era ended.

But many people insist on looking at the Lauries' reign as a whole.

"Unfortunately they decided to sell and things changed a bit, but they were great owners," Tkachuk said. "I don't know why they get a bad rap. They came in, saved the franchise, put money into it, and kept it going. It was a tough ending, but when I was there, they were nothing but great to all the players. They would do anything to win. There were no excuses."

73 Dave Checketts and SCP Worldwide

When Sports Capital Partners surfaced as the probable owners of the Blues, there was a bit of skepticism about the New York–based business. However, when chairman Dave Checketts indicated that the group wanted to keep the Blues in St. Louis and followed up by promising a Stanley Cup parade for the city…well, many fans were on board.

"I will guarantee you in the near-distant future we're going to be carrying a giant silver cup down Market Street," Checketts said.

SCP bought the Blues in 2006 during a time when Bill Laurie was ready to sell and there weren't many other legitimate offers. The group, which paid $150 million, restored faith in the organization by hiring John Davidson as club president and reconnecting with franchise icon Brett Hull.

Checketts' staff also thought outside the box. Who could forget Free Food Day, an annual event in which fans gobbled up free hot dogs and popcorn at a Blues' home game? Or how about the season-ticket promotion in 2010–11 when a select few ticket holders were charged 50 percent up front and only had to pay the other half if the Blues made the playoffs? The team fell 10 points shy of a postseason position that year.

In his six seasons heading up the ownership group, Checketts made some strides with the franchise. But he made too many promises that he couldn't keep, and after running the Blues on a shoestring budget for six years, he was forced to sell in 2012.

The end came crashing down when TowerBrook Capital Partners, a private-equity firm that owned a 75 percent stake in the Blues, decided to divest its interest. After Checketts' search for new investors came up short and he ran out of extensions on his bank loans, he had no choice but to put the Blues in the hands of minority owner Tom Stillman, who led a group of St. Louis–based investors, for approximately $130 million.

"Tom went out and raised a lot of local money," Checketts said. "It's a hard time to find buyers for clubs, particularly clubs that have shown a propensity to lose a fair amount of money."

Checketts claimed that he lost more than $100 million while owning the Blues.

"His game plan on how he did business was wrong," former Blues player and current chief operating officer Bruce Affleck said. "He had a great public persona, but if people really knew the story, they'd question it. Running it the way they did, and how much they spent—they didn't have the money to do that—was just ridiculous."

Checketts and Stillman had an icy relationship throughout their business relationship, triggered by Checketts animosity over his inability to raise corporate support locally while Stillman was able to do so.

When the sale was final and the Blues were in Stillman's possession, Checketts said, "Tom and I do have one thing in common, and that is that we both love the Blues and are both very hopeful that this is the club that can finally break through that barrier and bring the Stanley Cup to St. Louis. Of course I have regrets, but I'm not going to get into them because the way I think about it, we did our very best. We can be criticized for not spending more, I guess. But holy smokes, we put our whole heart and soul and our money into this deal."

74 Tom Stillman

When Tom Stillman was finally able to step to the podium and address Blues' fans as the team's new owner, his first words were that he wasn't really the "owner."

That was true, in part, because Stillman actually headed up a large group of St. Louis–based investors. But that's not what he meant.

"We see ourselves more as stewards of the Blues than owners," Stillman said. "An important element in Blues' history is its legacy, and more than anything else, that legacy is made up of the players who have worn the Blue Note—the players who have won games and lost games and played their hearts out over the last 44 years. As owners, I see us as guardians of the legacy that these men have created. We are going to make sure that we are respectful of that legacy and that we enhance our connections to it, to the alumni, and to Blues' history."

Perhaps few ownership groups in NHL history have been faced with such a difficult challenge as Stillman's investors, being wrapped up in a four-month league lockout shortly after taking over in May 2012. But the group, which came up with the marketing campaign "Long Live the Note," stuck to its blueprint and in 2019 brought home the franchise's first Stanley Cup.

In hindsight, Stillman's competitiveness in the business world should have been a signal of the Blues' coming success. In the 1980s, the former hockey player at Middlebury College in Vermont, took over a dilapidated beer distributorship in St. Louis and Riverfront Distributing became Summit Distributing. Specializing in Miller products, the company beat the odds, holding its own against the locally-run "King of Beers," Anheuser-Busch, over the next three decades.

"I learned by trial and error, but it gave me a lot of experience in trying to turn around a business," Stillman said.

One of Stillman's long-time friends is Steve Maritz, CEO of Maritz Inc., who has been so impressed with Stillman's business acumen that he became an investor in the Blues' ownership group.

"He survived the challenges of being a Miller distributor in St. Louis, and he succeeded," Maritz said. "Tom knows what he's doing, works hard, and gets the job done."

Another investor is former U.S. Senator John Danforth, who is Stillman's father-in-law. Danforth is admittedly not a hardcore hockey fan, but he saw the Blues as a St. Louis institution and believed that his son-in-law was the right man to lead the franchise.

"He is very dedicated," Danforth said. "He's very into getting from Point A to Point B. I was asked by somebody about his focus. I said, 'Well, he's a turkey hunter.' He builds the blinds, wakes up at about 4:00 am, and goes out and turkey hunts. He is just very,

very persistent. That was clear from the way he was so persistent in bringing [the acquisition of the Blues] to reality."

After becoming a minority owner of the Blues in 2007, Stillman beat long odds to gain majority control of the club. He had two offers rejected by previous owner Dave Checketts but stayed the course, continuing to put together a who's who list of investors. The group also includes Donn Lux, CEO of Luxco; Andy Taylor, CEO of Enterprise Holdings Inc., and his wife; Jerald Kent, CEO of Suddenlink Communications, and others.

"Tom is putting together a group of distinguished people from St. Louis," NHL commissioner Gary Bettman said. "And if it all comes together, we think fans of the Blues have reason to be very comfortable and excited about the future of the club."

When a deal between Checketts and prospective owner Matthew Hulsizer did not come to fruition before an NHL-mandated deadline, the Blues were in Stillman's hands and he did not drop them. On May 8, 2012, the Board of Governors approved the sale.

Former Blues captain David Backes expressed the feelings of the club, calling Stillman "a guy who's passionate, from the St. Louis area. He's around the rink as much as the players are, he's on the road trips. What more could you want?"

Blues general manager Doug Armstrong added, "I've had a chance to know him over the last couple of years. The first thing that jumps out is that he's passionate about hockey. He plays in three-on-three tournaments in Minnesota and Wisconsin in the middle of the winter, he skates with the [Blues] alumni, so he loves the game. He's nice to have around because he cares about hockey, cares about hockey players, and he challenges you by asking interesting questions. He's a fun guy to be around."

Stillman is a steward, not an owner, but he never envisioned himself as either, and certainly not a Stanley Cup champion. But when the Blues orchestrated the most historic turnaround in NHL history in 2019, his group accomplished a feat that no other regime could—putting the team's name on the Cup.

"Well, the operative words there are 'the group,'" Stillman said. "This has been very much a team effort by a large group. It starts with the players and coaches who made it happen on the ice, and it extends to everyone else in the organization: the other owners in our group, our alumni, the fans and businesses that have supported us over the years, civic and business leaders… the list goes on and on. We 'got it done' together, and that makes it even better."

75 Where Were the Blues on 9/11?

For the first time in five months, the temperature in Alaska had climbed above 40 degrees when the Blues arrived for their training camp getaway in September 2001. And it wasn't just barely warmer than 40—temperatures actually reached 75 degrees.

"We had one of the greatest days of our lives," former Blues coach Joel Quenneville said. "We went on a fishing trip with all the scouts and coaches down on the Kenai River. We caught more fish, more salmon, and the weather was absolutely beautiful. [It was] a gorgeous day."

But it was about to turn deathly dark.

When they awoke the next morning, the Blues were preparing to begin the long road back from losing to the eventual Stanley Cup champion Colorado Avalanche in the 2001 Western Conference final.

"It was going to be our first day on the ice," Quenneville said. "But right out of a dead sleep, we got the news. Somebody said, 'You've got to turn on the TV.'"

At approximately 5:30 AM in Alaska, the Blues were glued to what the rest of the world was witnessing—broadcast footage of two airplanes flying separately into the World Trade Center towers in New York, a third plane crashing into the Pentagon in Washington, D.C., and yet another flight (perhaps bound for the White House) wrecking in a field in Pennsylvania after terrorists were reportedly overtaken by passengers.

History remembers it painfully as 9/11. But in the moment, few knew what to make of the events of September 11, 2001.

"Everything has changed, as far as the way we are," Blues general manager Larry Pleau said. "We even had a feel of it right here, how things have changed. We're how far away, and we had a little feel of it right here."

Pleau was referring to a Korean Air flight from Asia that failed to divert from its approach into Anchorage International Airport as commanded by the control tower. Contact with the crew had been lost, forcing authorities to evacuate the local federal building, a downtown mall, and the 22-story Anchorage Hilton, where the Blues were staying.

No suspicions were being ignored following the terrorist attacks on U.S. soil. Government officials ordered the shutdown of all domestic airports. The Korean Air flight in question was met by military jets and steered to the nearest Canadian airport, Whitehorse, in the Yukon Territory. Others were escorted there, too.

The Blues' plans of opening training camp later that morning were scrapped.

"We're athletes, but we're also people," former Blue Jamal Mayers said. "Six degrees of separation—we all know somebody or know somebody who knows somebody who was in New York. A lot of our thoughts aren't really here right now."

Bill Laurie, the team's owner at the time, was set to join the club the following day, but his trip never materialized due to the airport closure.

"Your hockey team...could be here awhile," Joette Storm of the Alaskan-area Federal Aviation Administration office said.

The Blues were scheduled to play two exhibition games against the San Jose Sharks later in the week, but those games were put on hold and later canceled because the Sharks were unable to fly in. Likewise, the Blues were stuck, unable to fly out.

"We were trapped [and] couldn't get a plane," Blues traveling executive Mike Caruso said.

Instead of facing San Jose, a matchup that had led to the sale of 5,000 tickets, the Blues conducted a Blue and White intra-squad scrimmage in Anchorage's Sullivan Arena. The scrimmage was at least something for the arena, which underwent $140,000 in renovations for the exhibition games, and the proceeds of the Blues-only game did go to a local charity, but it wasn't the competitive atmosphere many people were anticipating.

"I feel bad for the fans of Anchorage," Pleau said. "We'd like to play [the Sharks]. But I think this is the right thing to do, the right thing for the league to do."

The elimination of the exhibition games made for some disappointment among locals, and it created some difficulty for the Blues' staff, whose goal it was to evaluate the 40 or so players in camp and cut down the team to the desired roster.

"We can see the good things in the game as far as overall hockey sense," Quenneville said. "How [they] play, watching them even in the scrimmages, you can get an opinion."

The Blues had a top line of Keith Tkachuk, Doug Weight, and Scott Young, but also saw good glimpses of Pavol Demitra, Cory Stillman, and Daniel Corso. Because of the glut of defensemen in camp, Chris Pronger took some shifts at left wing, but

Quenneville joked, "[It's] safe to say we like to have him on the blue line."

The intra-squad scrimmage and the daily practices were the only hours in the day the Blues were able to focus on something other than the attacks of 9/11. A few players, such as Pronger, made several fishing trips to let his mind wander.

"We're virtually in the middle of nowhere, so far away from where we want to be," Pronger said. "For the most part, it was as productive as it could be—a good camp under the circumstances."

Looking back, the acts of terrorism were isolated to that one day. But at the time, no one knew if they should expect more tragedy.

Young acknowledged checking the TV news throughout the week to make sure "there was no disaster that day."

As reports surfaced over the next few days, the club learned that former Blues player Ace Bailey, who was the director of scouting for the Los Angeles Kings at the time, was among those killed in one of the flights that crashed into the World Trade Center.

Enough was enough. Finally, after eight full days in Alaska, the Blues were able to return to St. Louis, flying out on Monday, September 17.

"We were only going to be there for four or five days, I don't know how long, but we were there a lot longer than that," Quenneville said. "At least we had our hockey family around us, if not our own families. It was a tough moment. The guys were good, but it was such a different tone to camp."

76 Ulterior Motive

On April 14, 1994, Brendan Shanahan made perhaps as many fans as a player could make in one day.

In an indelible sequence of events, Shanahan was high-sticked by Keith Tkachuk, who was playing for Winnipeg at the time. Shanahan went to the locker room, received 40 stitches, came back to score two goals in the Blues' 3–1 victory, and then wrapped up the day by walloping Tkachuk.

It turns out there was much more to the story. In a widely unknown fact, Shanahan was informed by a club official in the locker room that he was only a few penalty minutes short of becoming just the second player in NHL history to record 50 goals, 100 points, and 200 penalty minutes in a single season.

Shanahan had already reached 50 goals and 100 points prior to the Winnipeg game, but he needed the penalty minutes to join Pittsburgh's Kevin Stevens in the league's 50–100–200 club.

The Blues were hosting Winnipeg in the final game of the regular season, and the result mattered little to the club, which was already in line for the No. 5 seed in the conference.

In a scoreless game, a 22-year-old Tkachuk, playing in his third season in the NHL, caught Shanahan in the face with his stick. The mishap caused a laceration on Shanahan's upper lip, leading Tkachuk to the penalty box with a double-minor.

"Actually, he was just trying to get out of my way," Shanahan said, who went to the training room for repairs.

As Brett Hull was converting the ensuing power play, registering his 57th goal of the season and 700th point his career, at least some people thought that Shanahan might not come back—not because he was badly injured but because the stakes were minimal.

Brendan Shanahan gets off a shot in front of Chicago Blackhawk Bryan Marchment during the second period on Sunday, April 19, 1993, a first-round playoff game in Chicago. Shanahan later tied the game, and the Blues went on to win 4–3. (AP Photo/John Swart)

In the dressing room, Shanahan asked teammate Kelly Chase, who was not playing that day, how he looked. Chase replied, "More chicks for Chaser."

Chase continued to antagonize Shanahan.

"He was taunting me, telling me how well Tkachuk was playing while I was getting stitched up," Shanahan said. "And so the only reason I returned to the game—and this sounds bad coming from the job [I had as the NHL's Vice President of Player Safety]—the only reason I went back on the ice was to get revenge against Tkachuk."

But before Shanahan would have an opportunity to drop the gloves, he had a chance to pick up the Blues.

Alexei Kasatonov intercepted a Winnipeg clearing attempt and passed to Shanahan, who banged in a shot off the Jets' defenders for goal No. 51, point No. 101, and a 2–0 lead. Not long after, the Blues had an odd-man rush and Shanahan converted a pass from Craig Janney for No. 52, No. 102, and a 3–0 advantage.

"Actually, what's funny is, I was sort of disinterested in the puck, but the puck came to me," Shanahan said. "The first one, I shot it and it deflected off a couple of their defensemen and went in. Then maybe my next shift, I was out there trying to find Keith again and I found myself on a three-on-one and got another goal.

"Guys were trying to celebrate with me but I still was not happy because I couldn't find a way to get on the ice at the same time as Tkachuk. The next time I saw him go on, I think Philippe Bozon was about to go on and I just grabbed Philippe by the collar and yanked him back onto the bench and I jumped over."

Finally, Shanahan had his chance.

"I don't even think I took my gloves off," he said. "I just started to pound on [Tkachuk]. It wasn't a courageous or fair fight. He wasn't that interested. I remember everyone jumping into the pile and having arms and elbows rubbing up against my face, which was completely swollen."

Despite Shanahan's intent, Tkachuk indicated that he was caught off guard.

"It was an accident, but I know he was pissed off," Tkachuk said. "I just wish he would have grabbed me first and said something. But I have a lot of respect for him. He's a great player, and he was the kind of guy you modeled your game after. I'm glad that I was the guy he picked to get his penalty minutes."

Shanahan's punishment included a game misconduct, which gave him 211 PIMs on the season and put his name in the NHL record books with Stevens. As Shanahan skated off the ice, the crowd at the Arena roared and, already a popular player in St. Louis, his legacy was cemented.

Ironically, Winnipeg went on a three-minute power play and Tkachuk scored his 41st goal of the season on the man-advantage, breaking up Curtis Joseph's shutout bid.

After the game, Jets coach John Paddock said that Shanahan should be suspended for the first game of the playoffs.

"That's what I really hope," Paddock said. "A superstar can't be hit? It's a joke."

Shanahan was not suspended, but he was forced to walk around with what he called a "duck lip."

"What's funny is, Chaser was friends with [former St. Louis University basketball coach] Charlie Spoonhour, and a few days before the playoffs started, Kelly and Charlie went to some bar in the Central West End," Shanahan remembered. "Spoon was [talking about] the game [against Winnipeg], his first ever, and he just couldn't believe the intensity.

"He was saying to Kelly, 'So, you're telling me when you went down and talked to your friend, his lip was split right open and all he wanted to do was get back on the ice and get into a fight?' Kelly was like, 'Yep.' Spoon said, 'How's he doing now? Is he home resting?' Kelly said, 'He's standing behind you having a beer.'"

Spoonhour turned around and smiled. He and Shahanan also became friends, and the coach later used the story to motivate his basketball players at SLU.

Chase said, "Spoon would tell them, 'This 24-year-old kid is not only out drinking a beer, but he's holding the bottle up to his lip and using it as an ice pack. And you guys are crying about hangnails? I've got to introduce you to some hockey players.'"

77 Staniowski Stands on Head

Goaltender Eddie Johnston collected two Stanley Cups with the Boston Bruins, but by the time he came to St. Louis in the mid-1970s, he was a household name on his way to becoming a backup.

In 1976, after the Blues turned in a sub-par regular season, finishing 29–37–14 for third place in the Smythe Division, they met Buffalo in a preliminary-round, best-of-three playoff series.

The Sabres boasted one of the most famous lines in hockey history, dubbed the French Connection. Left winger Rick Martin, center Gilbert Perreault, and right winger Rene Robert each had French Canadian roots, which was their obvious link, but their fame stemmed from their skill level. After being assembled in 1972, the trio combined for 1,023 regular-season points and 66 playoff points before meeting the Blues.

In the 1976 postseason, the assignment to keep the French Connection quiet belonged not to Johnston but to a 20-year-old, second-round draft pick of the Blues named Ed Staniowski.

And if that was a surprise to everyone, imagine being in Staniowski's skates.

"Leo Boivin was the coach at the time, and I remember Leo coming in the dressing room prior to the game," Staniowski said. "I played about 11 games with the Blues in the run up to the playoffs and had a little bit of success, and the team was playing really good in front of me.

"Leo was a hard-nosed guy, a no-nonsense guy. I remember he came in the dressing room, and I remember those big hands of his, and he poked me in the chest with his finger and said, 'You've got the start kid.... You're going against Buffalo.' I was like, 'Wow!' It was a pretty exciting moment for me."

Staniowski didn't known what exciting was…yet.

Buffalo managed 105 points during the regular season, which was second in the Adams Division, so the Sabres received the home-ice advantage in the series. The Blues would host Game 1 and then go on the road for Games 2 and 3.

"We knew it was going to be a tough series because it was a short series," Staniowski said.

In front of 12,334 at the Arena, Staniowski stopped 37-of-39 Sabres shots, leading the Blues to a 5–2 win in Game 1.

"We managed to pull a win in that first game," Staniowski said. "It was end to end, the French Connection was in their groove. But our guys really stepped up and played well. The crowd got into it. We won and had the momentum."

The series shifted to Buffalo, and as one St. Louis scribe phrased it, Staniowski nearly "disconnected the French Connection."

Martin, Perreault, and Robert generated many of Buffalo's 57 shots in Game 2, while the Blues took aim only 16 times. But the Sabres still needed overtime to win 3–2.

"The thing about the French Connection, they moved the puck so well," Staniowski said. "I mean, when you've got a line that's been together for a number of years and can tic-tac-toe that puck and Martin, who could just crank it—you had to be positioned early."

The series was tied one game apiece and remained in Buffalo for Game 3. In the rubber game, Staniowski stopped 32-of-34 shots, but the Sabres won 2–1, again in overtime.

Buffalo's Don Luce scored the series' clincher on Staniowski, who was referred to as "unconscious" by the Sabres media. Luce was the trailer on a three-on-two odd-man break and beat the Blues goalie on a shot that went off defenseman Ricky Smith.

"I did not see it, and it snuck between my legs and that was it," Staniowski said. "But it was an exciting series, especially for a young first-year goaltender in the league."

Staniowski was 1–2 in the series, but he posted a 2.04 goals-against average, limiting the French Connection to only one goal.

"I can take it easy next year," Johnston said. "We've got a goaltender."

Staniowski blushed.

"Coming from Eddie Johnston, that was pretty special because I think the world of EJ," Staniowski said. "We called him Popsy because he was the father figure for the team and he was a great mentor to me. That meant a lot to me to have EJ make a comment like that. He was just a classy guy all around.

"It was a memory in my life I've really been proud to be part of. It certainly gave me a taste of things to come, of playoff hockey and the NHL. There's the [regular] season, and then there's the playoffs."

Staniowski couldn't replicate that success in the following years, and with Mike Liut entrenching himself in St. Louis, Staniowski was traded to Winnipeg after the 1980–81 season.

"The opportunity presented itself for me to be a starter in Winnipeg," he said. "That's why I moved there. I've always questioned that move because I would have loved, quite frankly, to play my whole career in St. Louis. It was a great town, great memories, great people."

78 Danton's Murder-for-Hire Case

On April 16, 2004, a day after the Blues' season ended with a playoff loss to the San Jose Sharks, FBI agents from San Francisco and local police barged into the hotel room of Mike Danton, but the troubled player was gone.

Apparently tipped off that he was being sought by authorities, Danton attempted to skip the Blues' charter flight home to St. Louis and buy his own ticket out of town. But at the San Jose airport, Danton was arrested and charged with conspiring to commit the murder-for-hire of an "acquaintance," a story that would take many twists and turns before anyone following the case felt like they had a clue about the actual truth.

Some people, including the judge who issued the sentencing, say they still don't know the facts.

"It was crazy, but we knew all about Mike Danton," ex-Blues general manager Larry Pleau said.

The New Jersey Devils selected Danton in the fifth round of the 2000 NHL Draft, but he suited up for only 19 games with the club. He was suspended twice for failing to report to the team's minor-league affiliate in Albany, New York, including sitting out the entire 2001–02 season.

"He won't play for us again," New Jersey president and general manager Lou Lamoriello said.

Despite Danton's troubles with the Devils, the Blues traded for him in 2003 and put the 24-year-old in the lineup as a fourth-line forward. Danton rewarded them with a productive season, scoring seven goals in 68 games with his new team.

"We knew his background. It wasn't the best," Pleau said. "We knew his agent had a lot to do with him, but we felt he was a player who could help our team. I believe in second chances. If you talked to the [players], he was fine with them. I don't know what happened at the end. We were all trying to figure that one out."

While playing for the Blues, Danton hired a hit man, according to authorities, to kill an acquaintance, which they believed was his agent, Larry Frost. Katie Wolfmeyer, a 19-year-old girl whom Danton met at the team's practice facility and dated, was also charged in conspiring to commit the crime. The hit man that

Wolfmeyer allegedly hired, and would be paid $10,000 by Danton, turned out to be a local police dispatcher.

The murder was never committed, but there was enough evidence to eventually convict Danton, who was sentenced to 7½ years in prison in 2004. If it ended there, it would be enough to make an interesting tale of a professional athlete involved in a crime conspiracy. However, that part hardly scratched the surface of a tale that witnessed Danton not only return to his sport but save the life of a teammate using the instructions he learned in prison.

"Mike's entire life has revolved around hockey," Danton's biological father, Stephen Jefferson, once said. "You see Mike and he had a hockey stick in his hand."

But as Danton headed for a career in the NHL, you did not see him with his family. A "buildup of incidents," according to Danton, led him to be estranged from his father, mother, and siblings. In fact, the relationship was fractured enough that he legally changed his last name from Jefferson to Danton, which was the first name of a youth player he had met while assisting at hockey camp.

Meanwhile, Frost had become Danton's agent and basically the player's surrogate father. Frost said Danton was "like a son to me."

But in the court proceedings, it came to light that Frost had threatened to go to Pleau with information that might have "ruined" Danton's career. There was also speculation that Danton owed Frost $25,000 and feared that he needed to kill Frost before Frost killed him.

Danton, however, never acknowledged the identity of the intended target and Frost, despite being the only occupant in Danton's apartment on April 15, when the crime was arranged to take place, denied that it was him.

The Blues were on the road in San Jose, scheduled to play Game 5 of their series against the Sharks. The Blues lost 3–1 and were eliminated from the playoffs. Shortly thereafter, Pleau was notified that authorities were inquiring about Danton's whereabouts.

"The FBI was after him, the police were after him. He wasn't in the room," Pleau said. "There were so many questions. Nobody knew the truth.... Nobody knew."

Taped phone calls with the hit man, along with $3,000 in Danton's unlocked home safe—mentioned on one of the calls as the down payment for the murder-for-hire—were enough evidence to lead to the charges. Danton originally pleaded not guilty but later accepted a plea agreement, and on November 8, 2004, he was sentenced to 7½ years and fined $850.

"The exact reason or reasons why you felt you had to engage in this murder plot remain a mystery to me," U.S. District Judge Williams D. Stiehl said at Danton's sentencing. "In more than 18 years on the bench, I have never been faced with a case as bizarre as this one."

It was about to get even more bizarre.

Danton was freed on parole in 2009 after serving five years. He told the parole board that his biological father, Steve Jefferson, was the intended target of his plot, a claim that still hasn't been proved one way or another.

Out of prison, Danton was accepted into St. Mary's University in Halifax, Nova Scotia, and on January 27, 2010, playing his first hockey game in nearly six years, he scored a goal in a 3–1 loss.

After two seasons at St. Mary's, Danton played in Austria. It was while he was in Austria in 2011 that he played a role in saving the life of a teammate. Marcus Bengtsson hit his head on the ice and started convulsing, leading Danton to put his hand in the player's mouth to assure his air passage was clear.

"I have seen seizures before," Danton said. "In prison, druggies would come in off the streets and have withdrawals. So when [Bengtsson's] convulsions did not [stop] after a couple of minutes, I knew something was wrong."

Some say Danton was a hero. Other say he was a villain.

Wolfmeyer, the 19-year-old girl who was also charged in the murder-for-hire plot, was acquitted after three hours of jury deliberations.

Wolfmeyer's attorney, Arthur Margulis, said that she was "just a young girl taken by an athlete, a hockey star."

79 Business Role Model

Shortly after Bruce Affleck was named the Blues' chief operating officer in 2012, he asked his employees for money.

Affleck requested each of them to stop by his desk and say hello. And if you brought a dollar, you were free to leave for the rest of the day. The money went for office goodies for the employees, but the real purpose was to meet everyone face-to-face.

"The biggest part of the job is people," Affleck said. "You have to understand people."

Affleck knows enough of them around the Blues' organization. A former defenseman who played five seasons with the club during the 1970s, he has held nearly every position possible within the franchise.

"I was a player, then I was added to the broadcast team, VP of sales, marketing, suites, VP of broadcasting, president of the alumni, and then when Tom [Stillman] bought the team, I got into discussions with him [to be COO]," Affleck said.

The discussions were lengthy and detailed, and after Affleck provided Stillman with a business model, Affleck was offered the job. But the approval of the Blues' new owner may have had less to do with Affleck's comprehension of the numbers and more to do with his understanding of the inner-workings of the franchise.

"He's done half the jobs here," Stillman said. "It's beyond having a specific knowledge. I think it was a combination of experience, knowledge of so many areas of the business side, and his skills in working with and managing people."

The first lesson Affleck learned in his new role is that you don't get much for a dollar anymore—literally.

"When we signed Scott Stevens [in 1990], we were paying him $600,000," Affleck remembered. "We raised ticket prices $1 because we had 600,000 people coming through the doors. That paid for Scott Stevens. You can't do that now. If somebody is getting $6 million, you just can't do that. So the business has changed, obviously."

Players are making a lot more now than they were making in Affleck's day. In fact, he remembers when the players themselves didn't know how much each other made.

"I was in the sauna with Barc Plager, it was 1975," Affleck said. "Here I am, a rookie, sitting in the sauna with the captain. He said, 'Do you mind me asking what you make?' Nobody knew what anybody was making, but I told him it was like $85,000 or something. Well, Barc was making $45,000. He thought he was being loyal to the Salomons, which he was, but it was just out of whack. Once players got to see the open books on everybody, it was huge. It's pretty easy to say, 'This guy got 12 goals last year, I got 24, so I should be getting paid more than him.'"

As the salaries increased, so did the need for a larger sales department.

"When I was hired as sales manager, I had a staff of two," Affleck said. "I went to the league [officials] in 1989 and said, 'Do you ever have meetings for all of the sales people?' They said, 'Well, not every team has a [sales] department.' Chicago didn't have a sales department at the time."

But tickets weren't as difficult to sell in St. Louis, Affleck admitted, in the late 1980s and early 1990s.

"Brett Hull made me a pretty good salesperson," he said. "It was a lot easier to sell when he was around."

Affleck recalled one particular off-season when the Blues held their annual open house, during which fans could purchase season tickets and pick their individual seats.

"You're hoping to get 200 season tickets. If you did, you're pretty excited," Affleck said. "Well, this was when Hullie was hot."

There was no ice on the arena floor during the summer, so the sales staff would set up tables inside the rink, and four to five employees would handle the ticket sales.

"By noon, we literally had 10 people on tables and the lines were up into the stands," Affleck said. "Literally, there were 400–500 people in line. The people at the tables were taking the [ticket] forms and just throwing them on the floor behind them, just trying to take care of everybody. We sold more than $1 million—probably 900 season tickets—in a couple hours. It was crazy."

These days, the NHL is facing more entertainment competition, and the pool of sponsors is much more limited.

"When we moved down to this building, we had no football team, no casinos, and we had 11 more corporate headquarters," Affleck said. "How much do the Rams [who arrived in St. Louis in 1995] take out of the business side? Did we get hurt by the casinos? Yeah, we did. All sports did. And 11 corporations have moved out of town. It's tough grinding out there."

Affleck is no longer the Blues' COO, but he continues to grind with the organization.

"He is really working hard," Stillman said. "He's really given his all to the Blues' organization over the years. He is revered around here, and that reflects itself in the way that management and staff pull together as a team."

80 Spanish Conquistador

While playing with the Toronto Toros of the World Hockey Association in the mid-1970s, Gilles Gratton once streaked across the ice in practice, wearing nothing but his goalie mask and a pair of skates.

If someone were to compose a list of the top 10 wackiest things the goaltender did in his career, that would not make the cut.

In what may be the single-most bizarre tenure of a player in Blues' history, Gratton, who was 23 at the time, made three starts and six appearances before the club put him on the "voluntarily retired" list.

"He believed in reincarnation and claimed he had been a Spanish Conquistador in a previous life," said former *St. Louis Post-Dispatch* hockey writer Gary Mueller.

In what was evidently Gratton's second life, he was acquired by the Blues in a trade with Buffalo in July 1975. The club had dealt goaltender John Davidson a month earlier, and they stockpiled the position with Eddie Johnston, Ed Staniowski, Yves Belanger, and Gratton.

"My first meeting with him was at the Queen Elizabeth hotel in Montreal after I was drafted," Staniowski said. "I was flown to Montreal to sign my contract, and I went up to [owner] Sid Salomon III's suite at the top floor. I knocked on the door and the guy who opened the door was flipping a yo-yo. He was in shorts, a T-shirt, and sandals with a yo-yo, and I'm there in my suit and tie. I shook his hand, and he said, 'Hi, I'm Gilles Gratton. I'm one of the goalies.' That was my first meeting with him. I'm thinking, *One of these things is not like the other.*"

Staniowski would soon learn about Gratton's previous life and exactly why he was reincarnated as an NHL goalie. The next time the two met was in training camp, and when the 1975–76 season began, they roomed together.

"I got the inside scoop," Staniowski said. "Gilles believed that he was paying his dues as a goaltender for various duels that he had been involved in back in the 14th century, back in Spain."

Davidson, who would become teammates with Gratton in New York, added, "He used to really get upset with the commoners, and he ended up putting some against the wall and stoning them. And now God got him back in this life because he's a goalie and they shoot pucks at him."

Gratton was nicknamed "Gratoony the Loony," but he was a likable guy.

"Very gifted, very intelligent," Staniowski said. "An outstanding musician. He could play both the guitar and the piano. I love to debate, and we had some interesting discussions on all kinds of issues, from politics to religion to sports. He was into astrology and astronomy, too."

When he had the desire to play, Gratton was a terrific goalie. A fifth-round draft pick of the Sabres in 1972, he played three seasons in the World Hockey Association with Ottawa and Toronto, winning more than 25 games each year.

"He had a lot of talent," Davidson said. "Didn't want to play, though."

Or as Staniowski clarified, "Things had to line up before he was inclined to play."

Literally, things had to "line up."

There was a report that when Gratton played in Toronto, he refused to play one night because the moon was aligned with Jupiter.

"He was a wacko," former Blues teammate Bruce Affleck said. "He was mind-provoking, but he flew at a different level than anybody else I had ever known. He used to have a beer at pregame. I didn't get too close to him, but yeah, he was definitely different."

Once, when the Blues were hosting a banquet, the club asked players for the name of the guest they would be bringing. Gratton wrote down the name of his dog.

"I told him no," Blues public relations director Susie Mathieu said. "He told me if he couldn't bring his dog, he wouldn't attend. I said, 'It doesn't work that way.' We were going to a nice hotel, and the banquet is for humans."

Even if Gratton started a game in net for the Blues, it didn't mean that he finished it.

On November 28, 1975, the Blues were playing on the road against the New York Islanders. After being hit in the arm on a shot by the Islanders' Bob Nystrom, Gratton skated to the club's bench.

"He said that he couldn't continue in goal because his side was hurting from an old injury—a very old injury," Mueller said. "He said he had suffered a fatal injury in the 14th century when he had been stabbed in the side by a lance."

Johnston was forced to come in cold and, in what ended as an 8–2 loss to the Islanders, allowed all the goals against.

The next day, Gratton and Blues coach Garry Young got into a shouting match at practice, the club put Gratton on the voluntarily retired list, and the goalie went missing for days. He eventually returned and apologized, but he was done with the Blues after two wins and a tie.

"I retired undefeated," Gratton quipped.

But it was hardly his choice.

"Gilles Gratton today regretfully submitted his resignation as a member of the St. Louis Blues to [owner] Sid Salomon III," the club announced in a statement.

The Blues initially declined to put Gratton on waivers, preventing him from re-signing with the Toros.

Gratton eventually got his release from the Blues in March 1976 and signed with the New York Rangers, where he played alongside Davidson. Gratton played 41 games and was 11–18–7 with a 4.22 goals-against average.

Following his days with the Rangers, there was speculation that Gratton became a photographer.

"I heard that he bought into a bunch of RadioShacks in Montreal and has done well," Davidson said. "I don't know that for sure, but that's the last I heard."

If you're counting at home, that would be Gratton's third life.

81 MacTavish, the Last Helmetless Player

Craig MacTavish felt blessed when his hockey career wrapped up with the Blues following the 1996–97 season.

The longtime NHL center won a national championship at the University of Lowell. He won four Stanley Cups—three with the Edmonton Oilers and another with the New York Rangers. He took the final faceoff before the horn sounded in the 1994 Cup finals, ending the Rangers' 54-year championship drought.

Yet when MacTavish ended his 17-year career in St. Louis, his success on the ice was only part of his good fortune. He was the last player in NHL history to play without wearing a helmet, a choice that he never regretted after escaping without any serious injuries.

"That's something I'm thankful for, that I've gotten out of the game with my health," MacTavish said.

In 1979–80, the NHL released a mandate that required its players to wear helmets, but players who signed before June 1979 were grandfathered in. A ninth-round draft pick of Boston in 1978, MacTavish wore a lid during his two collegiate seasons at Lowell and in his first two NHL seasons with the Bruins. But he discarded the helmet after a trip to the minors and never went back.

"It was just a comfort thing for me," MacTavish said. "I got used to not wearing it."

"Mac-T," as he is often called, left Boston to sign with Edmonton as a free agent in 1985. He spent nine seasons with the Oilers, winning Stanley Cups in 1987, 1988, and 1990. Mac-T has many great memories from his time there...and only one memory involving a head-related injury.

It came in 1997 after MacTavish was acquired by the Blues in a trade that sent Dale Hawerchuk to the Philadelphia Flyers. At age 38, MacTavish was hip-checked by Detroit's Vladimir Konstantinov. The move flipped him head over heels along the boards.

He landed on his head.

"I don't get caught off guard very often out there, but it was totally unexpected for me," MacTavish said at the time. "We're both going for the puck. I thought we were going to collide and he...whatever. It was dirty. I don't mind playing solid, hard-nosed hockey. But that happens a lot with him."

Other than the 40 stitches he received in his lip, however, MacTavish walked away unscathed.

Former NHL player Bill Masterton was not as lucky.

On January 13, 1968, Masterton was playing in his first NHL season with the Minnesota North Stars when he landed on his head after a hit. He was not wearing a helmet. Two days later, Masterton died from his head injuries, becoming the first player in league history to die as a result of an incident on the ice.

It took more than a decade, however, before the NHL required players to wear helmets. MacTavish put his helmet back on for the 1988–89 season, but the change lasted only one year. In spelling out his rationale, he cited a reason used by others who preferred not to wear helmets.

"I felt infallible when I first put it on," MacTavish said. "They make you play more reckless. I was crashing into the front of the net. I felt like I had a whole suit of armor on."

Coach Jimmy Roberts makes a point to Geoff Courtnall during the first period against the Pittsburgh Penguins on Thursday, December 19, 1996. At right is a helmetless Craig MacTavish. Roberts was named interim coach when Mike Keenan was fired. (AP Photo)

Defenseman Jamie Rivers joined the Blues in the mid-1990s and said that while it wasn't uncommon to face players without helmets in practice, it was unreal how fierce a competitor MacTavish was without one.

"We'd go out there and it was amazing, competing in drills and being totally cognizant of the fact he didn't have a helmet on," Rivers said. "I knew as a guy going into him, I didn't want to push him or get my stick up high. For me as a player, I made sure I had better body control against him. And I just remember watching him kill penalties. He'd go out and block shots, and in some instances, he would raise his hand and cover his head. But for him to be the last guy to be without a helmet, it's really funny because he wasn't a prima donna. He was in every corner, every faceoff. He was in the mix every shift. He was gritty."

MacTavish actually kept a helmet in his locker stall while he was with the Blues. But the green lid with the purple mask on top actually belonged to his son, Nathan.

"I'm sponsored by the Ninja Turtles," MacTavish quipped. "They're paying me multi-hundreds of dollars to wear this."

All kidding aside, the decision to wear a helmet in the NHL was a personal one, and MacTavish understood that what was best for him might not have been the best for others.

"Whether someone else would choose to go without one, I hope not," he said. "I hope not, for their sake."

Mac-T was luck-Y.

82 Liut Worth the Wait

Mike Liut's arrival in St. Louis was a bit delayed but well worth the wait for the Blues.

The team selected Liut in the fourth round in the 1976 NHL Draft, when he was playing hockey at Bowling Green State University in Ohio. Liut remained in school for two more seasons, and former Blues general manager Emile Francis would keep tabs on him when the Falcons came to town to play St. Louis University. When it came time for Liut to sign on the dotted line, however, he joined the World Hockey Association.

"I wanted to play professionally, but I took a hockey scholarship to Bowling Green University because I did not want to miss my chance to get a college education," Liut said. "I was drafted by St. Louis but went with Cincinnati [of the WHA] after graduation because they offered me more money. I believe two years in that league gave me a good hockey education."

After Liut played two seasons with the Cincinnati Stingers, the WHA merged with the NHL. The Blues retained his rights, so the goalie finally came to St. Louis in 1979 at age 23. His goals-against average in his second season with the Stingers was 3.47, so there were some skeptics when he arrived. But the 6'2", 180-lb. net-minder who adopted the butterfly style because he once saw former Blue Glenn Hall utilizing the technique on the back of a Cheerios box, quickly converted those skeptics into believers.

Liut led a revival of sorts with the Blues.

In 1979–80, his first season in the NHL, Liut posted a record of 32–23–9, winning more games than any goalie in the NHL. He played in 64 games, second only to Chicago's Tony Esposito

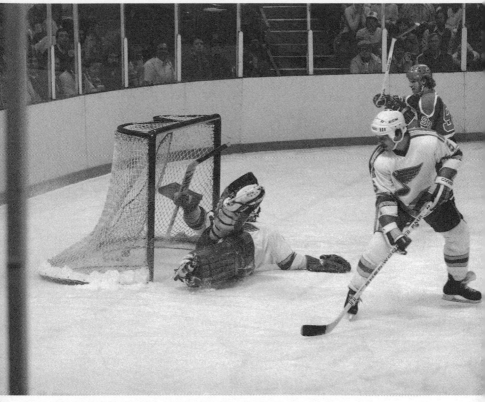

Goalie Mike Liut finds himself on his back after being triple teamed on a scoring drive by Edmonton Oilers Paul Coffey, Wayne Gretzky, and Charlie Huddy who scored the goal in St. Louis on January 11, 1983. Gretzky is pictured in the background after the score. Defenseman Rob Ramage (5) of the Blues is skating away. (AP Photo/Wiley Price)

that season. He set team records in both games played and minutes played (3,661).

"I've established myself by working my butt off every night," Liut said.

In the 1980–81 season, Liut went 33–14–13, finishing second in wins to Los Angeles' Mario Lessard (35). With the help of a 16-game unbeaten streak (10–0–6), Liut became the first goalie since Montreal's Bill Durnan (in 1944 and 1945) to record 30-win seasons his first two years in the league.

"I wanted to become as good as I can be, to be able to play with anybody," Liut said. "I thought I was ready if I got a chance to play. I needed the St. Louis organization to give me the opportunity. Without that, I would still be a relative nonentity."

That season, Liut stopped all 25 shots he faced in the NHL All-Star Game and was named MVP of the Campbell Conference's 4–1 win over Wales.

"Liut did for us what he's been doing all year for St. Louis," Campbell coach Pat Quinn said.

Liut was no longer a nonentity, and neither were the Blues. With a new back-stopper, they made a 59-point jump in the standings over the course of two seasons, climbing to second in the NHL standings with a record of 45–18–17 (107 points) in 1980–81.

"Mike Liut is the best young goalie in the league," former Blues coach Red Berenson said. "We improved more than any other team in the NHL last season, and we had the farthest to come. But Mike had to stand on his head in a lot of games for us to do it. Whatever progress we're going to make will be tied closely to Mike's continued development."

Liut, who was not eligible for the Calder Trophy as the NHL's top Rookie the Year because of his time in the WHA, was named co-Player of the Year with Edmonton's Wayne Gretzky by *The Hockey News*.

Liut was 71–47–25 with a 3.35 GAA when he agreed to a five-year, $1.5 million contract extension in December 1981. Because of owner Harry Ornest's cost-cutting measures, however, Liut would only remain a Blue until February 1985.

After the club acquired Rick Wamsley in June 1984, Liut was sent to Hartford for forward Mark Johnson and goalie Greg Millen.

When Wamsley was originally acquired, Blues GM Ron Caron said that he would not trade Liut.

"I meant it," Caron said. "But it's like being on a ship, and when the ship starts to right the course, you have a right to change your mind. I love Mike Liut as a human being—he's intelligent, good leadership—but my owners pay me to make decisions, and I hope I can make the right ones."

Liut was in the fourth season of his five-year contract, making $400,000. He could see the move coming.

"I knew that as soon as somebody would give them what they wanted in return, they were going to take the trade," Liut said. "I'm sure Harry has been promoting a trade of some sort because of my salary. But it's a business decision."

Liut, who played seven more seasons in the NHL with Hartford and Washington, remains the Blues' franchise leader for goalies in games played (347), wins (151), and minutes played (20,010).

83 The Other Lemieux

When Alain Lemieux signed a free-agent contract with Pittsburgh in 1986, Penguins equipment manager John Doolan jokingly offered the center No. 33.

"I teased him that he was only half as good as his brother," Doolan said.

That would be Mario Lemieux, who would score 1,723 points in 915 NHL games on his way to becoming one of the biggest superstars in the history of the hockey. The younger Lemieux wore No. 66.

But before there was "Super" Mario, there was Alain, who was 4½ years older than his younger phenom brother. In junior hockey, Alain was a bit of a budding star, too, recording 142 points in 72 games with Chicoutimi of the Quebec Major Junior Hockey League (QMJHL).

The Blues made the elder Lemieux the 96th overall pick in the 1980 NHL Draft, to which he responded his following junior season with 166 points in 69 games with Trois-Rivieres of the QMJHL. He was second in scoring behind a youngster named Dale Hawerchuk.

"I learned a lot just by watching him when I was young," Mario Lemieux once said. "I think every kid learns from his older brother. He was a very good hockey player, very skilled. He showed that by what he did in junior [hockey] and making it to the NHL."

Alain Lemieux made his league debut with the Blues on November 24, 1981, but played only three games that season. In 1982–83, his first full season, Alain registered 34 points in 42 games while playing on a line with Wayne Babych and Perry Turnbull.

But Lemieux still couldn't establish himself in the NHL, and he opened the following season in Montana with the Central Hockey League. He was recalled by the Blues, scoring four goals in 17 games, but then he was demoted and continued to bounce around in the minors.

The knock on Lemieux, who was 6' and 185 lbs., was his lack of consistency and his play in the defensive zone. The year that he netted 34 points for the Blues, he finished the season with a minus-10 rating.

"It's always the same thing," Alain said. "I'm going to work hard on my defense. But it's tough because I'm an offensive player. I guess I'll have to change my style a little bit. I'm not a superstar, so they want me to come back and [defend] my man."

The Blues' top three centers in 1983–84 were Bernie Federko, Doug Gilmour, and Doug Wickenheiser. Lemieux was in a battle for the fourth center spot with Dave Barr, who was a better defensive player.

"I've got to make this team," Lemieux said. "It's my last chance."

Blues coach Jacques Demers believed that with Mario now in the NHL, after being selected No. 1 overall by Pittsburgh in 1984, Alain had more motivation.

"I think if I had pride, which I hope he has, I'd want to show my brother that I can play in the NHL, too," Demers said. "[Alain is] not a very open person, but I can sense a little more desire in him this year."

Alain did make the Blues' roster, and with brother Mario being selected first overall by Pittsburgh, the two brothers faced each other for the first time in their careers on November 8, 1984. Alain won family bragging rights with the Blues' 6–2 victory over the Penguins.

But Alain wouldn't suit up again until an injury to Bernie Federko opened up a spot in the lineup on November 24. Alain scored his first goal of the year that night, and three nights later he netted his first-career hat trick in a 6–1 win over Vancouver.

"When you don't play for so long, you start to wonder what's going on," Lemieux said. "It really feels good to help the team."

But by January, Lemieux was demoted again, this time to Peoria, Illinois. He scored one goal in two games with the Rivermen, but in the second game he suffered a shoulder injury. His time in St. Louis was almost done.

Lemieux had asked for a trade and on January 29, 1985, Blues general manager Ron Caron dealt him to Quebec for center Luc Dufour.

"I like this town, and it's a good bunch of guys here," Lemieux said of St. Louis. "But I want to play and I didn't have a chance to prove what I can do, so I had to be traded. Caron was fair to me. He traded me to a good team, so I'm happy."

Demers wished Lemieux good luck.

"It'd be tough to crack our team at center, but I think he can help Quebec," he said.

Quebec gave Lemieux more ice time, including time on the power play, and he did produce. In 30 games, he had 11 goals and 22 points. But in 1985–86, he reportedly showed up overweight, and after seven games without a point, the Nordiques let him go.

Lemieux then played two seasons in the American Hockey League, posting 171 points in 136 games, leading to a tryout with Pittsburgh.

"I think he can still play in this league," said Mario, by then a legend in the making. "I think he could help this team. He's a good player with the puck, and if he can play good defense, I think he's got a good chance."

Alain signed with Pittsburgh, and in February 1987, he played one game in a Penguins' uniform. Unfortunately for the family, it was a game Mario missed because of bronchitis. In the game, Alain wore No. 11, which might have meant he wasn't half as good as his little brother.

84 Goalie Shoots, He Scores

On February 21, 1971, a snowstorm limited attendance to 815 for a Central Hockey League game between the Oklahoma City Blazers and the Kansas City Blues, the minor-league affiliate of the St. Louis Blues.

Those who stuck around to the end of the Sunday game, which ended just before the clock struck midnight, witnessed history.

With less than a minute remaining in regulation at Royal American Arena, the Kansas City Blues' Michel Plasse flipped the puck the length of the ice, and when it went into the empty net, he became the first professional goaltender in the modern era to score a goal.

The historical goal sealed a 3–1 victory for the Kansas City Blues after some tense moments.

"We were ahead 2–1, and we got a penalty," said Plasse, who was 22 years old at the time. "Oklahoma City pulled out its goalie and put on an extra forward [for a six-on-four advantage). They were really putting it to us, believe me."

The Blazers pulled netminder John Adams with 55 seconds to play in regulation and shot the puck into the Blues' zone. The puck went to Plasse with 44 seconds remaining.

"They threw the puck into our end, and when it came right to me, I skated out a bit, maybe 10', and flipped it down the ice," Plasse said. "It went up over the Oklahoma City players and straight into the enemy net. It was a hell of a shot."

Plasse acknowledged thinking that there was a "small chance" he could score, but that wasn't his intent.

"I was just trying to clear the puck out of there," he said.

Plasse, a Montreal native, was drafted No. 1 overall by the Canadiens in the 1968 amateur draft. Without Plasse ever appearing for the Habs, his rights were traded to the St. Louis Blues for cash on December 11, 1970.

Kansas City was St. Louis' CHL affiliate from 1967–73, and Plasse played only one season for the Kansas City Blues in 1970–71. The 5'11", 172-lb. netminder suited up in 16 games and posted a 2.63 goals-against average. But it wasn't the goals scored on Plasse that earned him so much attention. Instead, it was the one he scored.

Scoring Goalies

Billy Smith	November 28, 1979*
Ron Hextall	December 8, 1987
Ron Hextall	April 11, 1989 (shorthanded)
Chris Osgood	March 6, 1996
Martin Brodeur	April 17, 1997
Damian Rhodes	January 2, 1999*
Martin Brodeur	February 15, 2000 (game-winning)
Jose Theodore	January 2, 2001
Evgeni Nabokov	March 10, 2002 (power play)
Mika Noronen	March 10, 2004*
Chris Mason	April 15, 2006*
Cam Ward	December 26, 2011
Martin Brodeur	March 21, 2013
Mike Smith	October 19, 2013

* Last player to touch puck before opposition scored on themselves.

After scoring against Oklahoma City, the stick that Plasse used was sent to the Hockey Hall of Fame. The puck was retrieved and went home with him.

"I'll keep it forever," Plasse said.

Two months later, the former top-overall pick finally made his NHL debut with the Blues, recording a 4–3 victory over Los Angeles on March 30, 1971. But it would be the only game he would play for the Blues, who traded his rights back to Montreal for cash on August 23, 1971.

Plasse played for six NHL clubs before retiring with Quebec after the 1981–82 season. He finished with a career record of 92–136–54 with a 3.79 GAA.

It wasn't until eight years after Plasse's goal that the first goalie netted one in an NHL game.

The New York Islanders' Billy Smith was credited with a goal on November 28, 1979, when Colorado rookie Rob Ramage, who later played for the Blues, made a blind pass and scored into his own net. Smith was the last Islander to touch the puck.

Eleven goalies have scored a combined 14 goals in NHL history, including three by New Jersey's Martin Brodeur.

On February 21, 2001, the 30-year anniversary of Plasse's milestone achievement, he said the novelty had worn off a bit.

"It seems such a long time ago," said Plasse. "So many goalies score now. But at least I can always say I was the first one."

Four years later, on December 30, 2006, Plasse died of a heart attack at age 56.

85 Harvey Finishes Hall of Fame Career with Blues

Three players in the history of the NHL have won the Norris Trophy as the league's best defenseman at least seven times, and one finished his career with the Blues.

Boston's Bobby Orr claimed the award eight times, while Detroit's Nicklas Lidstrom and Montreal's Doug Harvey were each honored seven times.

After a distinguished career, during which he went to 11 consecutive NHL All-Star Games and won six Stanley Cups, Harvey wound up with the Blues from 1967–69. He was given the triple title of general manager, coach, and player with the club's minor-league affiliate, but it turned into a stint with the Blues when the defenseman, at age 44, volunteered his services.

"Doug Harvey is a fine student of the game, an outstanding teacher, and he will be a great asset to our organization," said Blues general manager Lynn Patrick, announcing the hiring of Harvey on January 29, 1967. "He should be especially helpful in the development and growth of our young hockey players. We are fortunate to be able to get a man with Doug's background and ability."

Harvey, who had played in 1,043 NHL games prior to his arrival, not to mention a couple hundred games in the AHL, was given the freedom to suit up with the Kansas City club. When asked about the arrangement, he said he'd continue playing "as long as my legs hold up."

During the 1967–68 season with the Kansas City Blues, who played in the Central Hockey League, Harvey played 59 games, posting four goals and 20 points. He had six assists in seven playoff games before the club was eliminated.

The night that Kansas City was ousted from the postseason, the St. Louis Blues had dropped Game 6 of their first-round playoff series 2–1 against Philadelphia in double overtime.

"Al Arbour was our captain and our best defenseman. He got injured and couldn't play in the overtime," former Blues coach Scotty Bowman said. "He had a pulled groin, and we need some help for the seventh game a couple of days away.

"We got fortunate. In those days, you couldn't bring up players from your farm team if they were still playing. But they got knocked out, so I had Doug on the phone right after the game. I said, 'We've got the seventh game in Philadelphia, and we're going to need some help.

"He said, 'I've got three players ready to help.' I said, 'Who are they?' He said, 'Our best forward is Gary Veneruzzo, and we've got a big winger named Craig Cameron...and myself.' And I said, 'In that case, come on.' He got in his car the next morning, picked up Veneruzzo and Cameron, and they drove to St. Louis."

Harvey played about 40 minutes and was the Blues' No. 1 star in a 3–1 win over the Flyers, clinching the series. Harvey had four assists in eight playoff games.

"He played very well," Arbour said.

Harvey made such an impression that, even at age 44, he was asked to return for the 1968–69 season, also receiving the title of assistant coach. The defenseman played all 70 games for the Blues that season, registering two goals and 20 assists.

"We had such a good ending with him, Harvey went to training camp," Bowman said. "For that whole year, he was outstanding."

Legendary Canadiens coach Toe Blake took note. "Who'd have ever thought, seven or eight years ago, when he left Montreal, he'd still be playing today? But, when he played against Montreal the other night, I'll tell you, he wasn't the worst player on the ice."

Harvey had aspirations of returning to the Blues for the 1969–70 season.

"I take 'em a game at a time, a year at a time now," he said. "I enjoy it. I never expected to bounce back up to the bigs at my age. You never know what's ahead of you. As long as they feel I'm doing the job, I'll guess I'll hang around."

But Harvey, who had widely known alcohol issues, was not brought back. There was a report about a barroom brawl that he was involved in, which might have played a role in his departure. The laid-back Harvey said of the incident, "It was nothing— nothing at all."

He was inducted into the Hockey Hall of Fame in 1973, had his No. 2 retired by Montreal in 1985, and was ranked as No. 6 on *The Hockey News*' list of 100 greatest hockey players in 1998.

"He was a very good player, but he had his problems," Arbour said. "He drank a lot. But he was a good player."

86 Hull Scores 86

Brett Hull scored 86 goals during the 1990–91 season, but more than two decades later, the right winger wonders what might have been.

The NHL record for most goals in a single season was 92, established by arguably the greatest player to ever play the game, Wayne Gretzky, who accomplished the feat with the Edmonton Oilers in 1981–82.

Well, with 25 games left in the Blues' 90–91 season, Hull said, "You could see there was a chance for something special, possibly breaking Wayne's record."

Hull had a hulluva start with 19 goals in the Blues' first 19 games that season, including back-to-back hat tricks against the Toronto Maple Leafs on October 24–25. The right winger had eight hat tricks that season but never lit the lamp more than three times in one game.

"He wouldn't score more than three goals in a game because he said he didn't want to have somebody shadowing him," former teammate Kelly Chase said. "He said, 'I don't want them shadowing me like they used to shadow my old man.'"

Hull had followed in the footsteps of his father, the "Golden Jet," Bobby Hull, who netted 913 goals in 1,474 games in a career that combined time in the NHL and World Hockey Association with the Winnipeg Jets and the Chicago Blackhawks.

"I had a game plan that I wanted to be invisible," Hull said. "I wanted to change [lines] right after I scored. I never wanted to celebrate. I just wanted to be out of everyone's mind."

That plan became increasingly difficult for Hull, who buried 72 goals the previous season and was developing quite a reputation playing alongside center Adam Oates.

But the challenge didn't hold Hull back. He scored at least one goal in 13 consecutive games—22 goals in all—from January 22 to February 3, 1991.

As Chase remembers, "[Paul MacLean] used to say, 'Okay boys, let's go out there and win 1–0. As long as Hullie scores, everyone will be happy.'"

During the entire season, Hull's longest stretch without a goal was three games, which happened twice.

"There were hat-trick nights and those were big nights, but he just seemed to score almost every game, one or two," former teammate Garth Butcher said. "He was a guy who would walk off the ice after scoring two goals and just hand his stick to a fan. If I had two goals with a stick, I'd be hanging on to it for dear life. But he was onto the next [goal]."

Hull always had an answer, regardless of who stood in his way.

"I remember in Boston, he already had a goal or two, and he undressed Ray Bourque at the blue line and went in and scored," ex-Blue Gino Cavallini said. "Bourque pushed the net off and shattered his stick into 1,000 pieces. The look on Brett's face—I mean, he almost felt bad."

In what turned into a pursuit of 50 goals in 50 games, Hull had 46 going into Game No. 48 of the Blues' season. As if to alleviate the suspense, he pumped in four goals in his next two games, giving him 50 goals in 49 games.

"Once he got around 50," Cavallini said, "every time the puck went in the net, you were just shaking your head."

And somehow, Hull remained invisible.

"I remember going, 'Okay, this guy is up to 80 goals and he's still open," Butcher said. "It's not like people were saying, 'Who's this guy wearing No. 16?' They were well aware of him, but he just found a way to get that open shot."

Home, road, wherever. Almost incomprehensible, Hull registered 47 of his goals away from the friendly confines of St. Louis.

"He had that personality that really nothing got underneath his skin, except for maybe the coaching," Cavallini said.

The Blues' coach at the time was Brian Sutter. While Hull credited Sutter for making him into a better player, Hull was mystified about his absence on the penalty-killing unit and in empty-net situations.

"I got so frustrated and so mad that I finally just said '[Screw] this, I'm not going to score an empty-net goal if he starts putting me out there,'" Hull said. "I ended up being six goals short of one of the great records ever. Maybe I could have gotten a few empty-netters and a couple of shorties, then I could have gotten 93."

The breakdown that season included 57 even-strength goals and 29 power-play goals. None of Hull's goals came with an empty-net, while 11 of Gretzky's 92 goals were empty-netters.

"Hullie always says, 'Gretz, you know how many goals I would've had if I would've been out there at the end of games?'" Chase said. "Gretz laughs and says, 'Don't blame me. I didn't coach you.'"

But even Gretzky, the "Great One," marvels at the achievement.

"Eight-six goals, no empty-netters, very special," said Gretzky, who also had the second-most goals in a single season with 87 in 1983–84.

In the final game of the Blues' season, Hull did pass Pittsburgh's Mario Lemieux for the third-highest total in NHL history. Lemieux posted 85 for the Penguins in 1988–89.

Hull surpassed Lemieux on a pass from teammate Paul Cavallini, Gino's brother. Blues broadcaster John Kelly had the call on TV: "Here's Paul Cavallini, ahead to Hull, he's in alone...a shot...he scoooooores! Brett Hull, No. 86."

On the 20th anniversary of Hull's remarkable season, in 2011, Gino asked Paul about the memorable moment.

"I said, 'Do you remember the goal?'" Gino recalled. "And he said, 'It was 20 years ago. How could I remember the goal? It wasn't like he wasn't going to score anymore.'"

"You never think he's going to stop at 86," Paul added. "He's going to stop at the last second of the last game. That's when it was over."

87 Blues Get Bold

If not for a bold move by the Blues' Emile Francis in 1982, his successor Ron Caron wouldn't have had one of the pieces necessary to complete the famous trade for Brett Hull.

A few hours before the 1982 NHL Draft, Francis dealt the Blues' first-round picks in both 1982 and 1983 to the New Jersey Devils in exchange for defenseman Rob Ramage, the NHL's No. 1 overall pick 1979.

"In all the years I've been in the league, I've never traded a first-round draft choice," Francis said. "But then, I've never had the opportunity to obtain a premier player like Ramage."

The trade marked one of the first transactions in New Jersey's history after relocating from Colorado. The Devils received the Blues' No. 8 overall pick in 1982 (Rocky Trottier) and No. 6 overall choice in 1983 (John MacLean).

But as Francis boasted, "We got the man we wanted."

Ramage, who played as an underage junior in the World Hockey Association the year before the draft, was a prized pick in

Rob Ramage (5) takes control of the puck in front of the Hartford Whalers' Stewart Gavin (7) and the Blues' Jim Pavese (35) during the first period of a game in St. Louis on January 8, 1987. (AP Photo/Oscar Waters)

1979. He went to Colorado at No. 1, followed by the Blues' selection of left winger Perry Turnbull at No. 2.

Ramage scored 20 goals and posted 62 points in his second NHL season and went to his first All-Star Game, but he didn't reach the expectations of the top pick. The defenseman was inconsistent and he wasn't the heavy hitter that some expected, so the pressure began to mount.

At 23, Ramage stepped down as Colorado's captain, a honor which he received after Lanny McDonald was traded to Calgary. He also requested that the Rockies, who were on the verge of leaving Denver, trade him.

"I was a little too critical and took the bad things to heart too much," Ramage said. "It definitely had an effect on my mind."

While the Rockies went to New Jersey and became the Devils, Ramage went to St. Louis and became a Blue on June 9, 1982. He welcomed the move, saying, "When I joined the Blues, I knew it wasn't up to me by myself.... One player doesn't make the difference of whether a team has a good year or a bad year."

The 6'2", 210-lb. Ramage added depth to a Blues' defensive group that included Jack Brownschidle, Gerry Hart, Ed Kea, Tim Bothwell, Guy Lapointe, and Rick Lapointe. After a slow start, he finished with 51 points in his first year, and with 60 points in his second season, he was back in the NHL All-Star Game.

Ramage credited assistant coach Barclay Plager with his turnaround.

"Barc has helped me with my defense, and I think my offense has improved some," Ramage said. "I guess my consistency is the big thing that's better."

In six seasons with the Blues, Ramage became more than a dependable defenseman. Eventually named as an assistant captain, he ascended to No. 9 on the club's all-time scoring list and he was the team's highest-scoring defenseman.

But in 1988, the Blues had their eye on Hull, and Calgary wanted Ramage and goalie Rick Wamsley. Ramage had been dealing with patella tendinitis—chronic pain around his kneecaps—and was a minus-20 when the trade was finalized on March 7, 1988.

"When you pick up the sports page, it's going to be under transactions," said Ramage, who was 29 at the time. "And that's about as black and white as you can put it. All the emotions that may run rampant following the trade really won't mean too much in another week or so."

After another bold move, Hull would go on to rewrite both the record books for both the Blues and the NHL. For Ramage, he went on to win a Stanley Cup with Calgary in 1989 and another with Montreal in 1993. He also spent time as the captain in Toronto, where he wore Barclay Plager's No. 8.

Unfortunately for Ramage, his post-hockey career has also made headlines.

In 2008, Ramage was sentenced to four years in prison in Canada after being charged with impaired driving. In 2003, he was the driver in a head-on car accident, in which his passenger, former Chicago Blackhawk Keith Magnuson, was killed and the driver of the other car was seriously injured. Ramage's blood-alcohol content was twice the legal limit, according to court reports. An appeal in 2010 was denied, but in 2012 he was granted full parole.

88 Towel Man Tradition

If Blues' season-ticket holder Ron Baechle is in the restroom when the team scores, he has to hurry out quickly. Few fans want to miss a goal, but Baechle has a job to do.

Since the 1989–90 NHL season, Baechle has been tossing a towel into the crowd after every Blues' goal and leading the crowd in a count of the team's tallies…1–2–3 and so on. The arena's audio system dings in unison and the crowd roars as Baechle, also known as the Towel Guy, is shown on the Jumbotron.

"It's been amazing because I never dreamed it would turn into this," said Baechle, who over the years has worn a white tuxedo adorned with airbrushed Blues logos. "My intention was not this. It was just to be a fan and support my team."

Baechle, a self-employed businessman who works in signs, lettering, and logos, didn't originate the idea. In the late 1980s, Baechle and a friend traveled to Peoria, Illinois, for a minor-league game, during which a Rivermen fan named Paul Martin was launching linen into the crowd.

"I think they called it the Towel Brigade," Baechle said. "After about the fourth goal, it was kind of neat. The gentleman that I was with, he said, 'Well, there's something you can bring back to St. Louis.' I didn't think much of it."

But when Baechle returned to his seats in Section 206 at the old Arena, he started bringing more than popcorn. After kicking around the idea for a while, Baechle carried a few balled-up towels into the rink one day.

"I took time to tell everybody that we had seen them do this in Peoria and we were going to try to start it here," Baechle said. "It was trial and error because I was bringing towels too big and I was hitting people in the head. I got called every name in the book."

On February 23, 1991, Baechle got an unexpected boost. The Blues ran up the score in a 9–2 victory over the Boston Bruins, a night when Baechle's arm probably felt like it was going to fall off.

"That's the most they ever scored here," said Baechle, who now has Nos. 1–9 sewn into his jacket. "We were cheering, 'We want 10! We want 10!' The big thing is you want to cheer your team on, but you want to kind of rub it in on the opposition and say, 'Hey, we just scored on you.'"

In the mid-1990s, when the Blues moved into Kiel Center from the Arena and Baechle moved to Section 314, his schtick grew even more. The club started displaying him on the Jumbotron at the new facility, and the more fans who were aware of the Towel Man, the more popular he became. There were commercials with McDonald's and local banks, which began to sponsor Baechle and put their logo on his towels.

"We started throwing a towel after every goal," he said. "It just got to a point where the money would help buy the tickets, the towels, and kind of support my habit. One misconception is that people think the Blues give me my seats. There have been times that I'll request a certain game, and they've been good, but I pay for my tickets.

"I always tell everybody I don't take myself seriously, but I take what I do seriously because people think that I'm representing the team. So I make sure that I don't do anything that would be disrespectful."

In 2012, *Sports Illustrated* named Baechle one of the year's Noteworthy Sports Superfans. He is now in his 29th season of counting Blues' goals.

"I think traditions just happen," he said. "I don't think you can say, 'I'm going to do this, and it's going to become a tradition.' This is my 23rd season and the Blues have been in existence for 46 years, so I've been here for half their existence…. People tell me they love it, so I keep doing it. I just told myself, as long as I'm having fun doing it, I'm going to keep on doing it."

Even if Baechle has to race back to his seat from the restroom.

"It works out good that I have a towel," he said, "because I don't have to stop and wait to dry my hands."

89 Attend Blues Alumni Fantasy Camp

Longtime Blues fan Rick Ackerman absorbed a hip check from Bob Plager and took a cross-check from Keith Tkachuk, but the retired school teacher loved being on the receiving end of the two heavy-duty hits.

In fact, Ackerman paid for the experience.

If you're a Blues fan who wants to lace up your skates with players of the past and present, the Blues Alumni Fantasy Camp is the sheet of ice for you. Fans 21 years and older, male and female, pay hundreds of dollars apiece to play with the pros and afterward listen to stories not fit for print.

"That's what this camp is all about," Ackerman said. "It's a celebration of St. Louis Blues' hockey. It's just a wonderful opportunity to find out that these guys are just like us. They put their pants on just like we do. They just have a little more talent when it comes to their profession, that's all."

Ackerman had a heart attack approximately two decades ago and also suffered from back pain, forcing him to stop playing hockey. But after moving back to St. Louis from Ohio, Ackerman saw a brochure for the camp and thought, *I've got to do this.*

There was one problem—his doctors told him no.

"I told them, 'You know what? If I die, I'll go out the happiest man on the planet, doing what I love to do more than anything else,'" Ackerman said. "What better death could you have?"

Ackerman arrived for his first camp without any equipment. The Blues told him to go in a back room and grab whatever he could find.

"There was a pair of gloves with 'B. Hull,' written on them," said Ackerman, who tried on the mits worn by the Blues' all-time leading goal scorer, Brett Hull, and said they fit, well, like a glove. "So I snatched those up."

Tkachuk, who retired after the 2009–10 season with 538 goals in 1,201 career games, likes to see the excitement and the smiles on the faces of the attendees.

"You have to make it fun so everybody enjoys themselves," Tkachuk said. "To be able to be on the same ice as the guys you watched in the NHL I think goes a long way. The fun really starts when we get on the ice."

Allegedly, the Blues Alumni Camp is no-contact. Try telling that to Ackerman.

"I'm in front, and I had talked some trash with Plager before the game, telling him, 'Keep your head up, Bob,'" Ackerman said. "So at one point I'm in front of the net for either a pass or deflection. The next thing I know, I'm on my butt. He hip-checked me. [He] got me good, and we just laughed and laughed. When he skated by he said, 'You've got to keep your head up, kid.'"

Ackerman said when push comes to shove, the campers relish being knocked around by the former NHLers.

"They know what we want," he said. "In my game against [Tkachuk], I don't know if he was covering me, which would be just stupid. But I'm doing whatever I can, and the next thing I know I've got somebody's stick in my back, crunching me down, and there's Keith Tkachuk. I have the picture to prove it."

But no picture was as perfect as Ackerman's goal, which he scored while wearing Hull's gloves. It came while he was playing on a line with Blues owner Tom Stillman and franchise points-leader Bernie Federko.

"Stillman set me up in front of the net, and I popped it in top shelf," Ackerman said. "To this day, I will swear a little of Brett Hull's DNA must have stuck in those gloves and worn through my fingers. I'm just not very good. I'm not, and it was the prettiest goal you'd ever want to see."

Ackerman saw Hull later and gave him credit for the goal.

"He said, 'No, you did it,' and I said, 'No, it was you,'" Ackerman said.

That year, the camp named Ackerman the MVP, giving him a memory of a lifetime. But perhaps the story paled in comparison to the tales the ex-Blues told the participants after dinner.

"[The attendees] love the whole atmosphere, the stories, just to get a chance to talk to former players," Tkachuk said. "The bottom line is when you get there, it's all about the fun. I think everybody enjoys the activities that they put on—the band, the round table discussions, and some of the guests they bring in. You need about a two-week vacation after it, but otherwise it's good."

The camp is no vacation. It's as close to playing in the NHL as many will ever come.

"I'll never be one of the guys," Ackerman said. "But this is the next best thing."

90 Go Ask Susie

The Blues' Susie Mathieu never thought of herself as a pioneer, but the first female vice president and public-relations director in NHL history paved many roads for women in the sport.

Mathieu had worked as a PR assistant for the Blues and the Minnesota North Stars in the 1970s when she had a chance encounter with Blues general manager Emile Francis at an airport. She told Francis that she was returning home from Minnesota so that her husband, once an assistant trainer with the Blues, could take classes for his master's degree at St. Louis University.

"Emile said, 'Great, come to work as soon as you can,'" Mathieu remembered. "I had no clue what the job was…. I never asked him. We got back to St. Louis and I called him. He said, 'I want you to become the PR director with the Blues.' I said, 'Yeah, I can do it.'"

In 1977, Francis made Mathieu the league's first female PR director, and the first press release that she was asked to send out was the announcement of her new position.

"I thought nothing of it," Mathieu said. "I already knew everybody in the St. Louis media. Well, lo and behold, I kind of forgot that I was female and there hadn't been a female PR director in the NHL up to this point."

Mathieu's appointment set off shock waves outside of St. Louis.

"The Canadian media was questioning, 'How will you deal with the dressing room?'" she said. "My response was, 'Well, the PR director's job is not done in the dressing room. It's done in my office."

People asked about a female being involved in a violent sport.

"I don't play," Mathieu quipped.

The Blues' new hire didn't play hockey, but suddenly she was doing everything else for the club, including marketing, promotions, and more.

"For some of those years, the most creative thing that we could come up with was the Garry Unger Ironman award because the team's performance was not great," Mathieu said.

In 1983, however, the Blues' future in St. Louis was uncertain as Ralston Purina sought to sell the team, which was eventually taken over by the NHL. As a longtime admirer and friend of Bing Devine, who was president of the NFL's St. Louis Cardinals, Mathieu was asked to step in as PR director of the football team that year.

"He said, 'Bill Bidwell [the team's owner] wants to hire you, and he's already cleared it with the commissioner [Pete Rozelle]," Mathieu recalled. "I thought it was flattering, but why would you have to clear it with the commissioner? I already went through that saga with being the first woman, and Bing said, 'Well, you are the first woman [in the NFL].'"

Mathieu took the job, but as she traveled to London with the Cardinals for a preseason game, new Blues owner Harry Ornest called and offered her a job. She didn't accept right away, but after returning from London, she met with Bidwell.

"He said, 'I know what you're about to say,'" Mathieu said. "He said, 'Follow your heart.' I said, 'Seriously, you're going to say that after you took a risk hiring a woman?' He said, 'Absolutely. If you can't be happy in what you're doing, you need to do something else.'"

Mathieu followed her heart back to the Blues. In 1986, her diligence and dedication led to a promotion, making Mathieu the first female vice president in club history. It didn't come with a raise, but it did come with more responsibility, of course.

"I got into [player] contracts," Mathieu said. "The general manager's secretary usually did that, but the GM never seemed

Do You Bleed Blue?

The Blues have had a handful of creative marketing slogans over the years, but nothing compares to the "Bleed Blue" campaign in the early 2000s.

It was the creation of former team executive Jim Woodcock and his partner, Mark Schupp, of the Schupp Company.

"We were in my office for essentially a brainstorming session," Woodcock said. "It was clear five minutes into the moment that we felt there was promise with Bleed Blue, that we had it."

Woodcock admitted that bleeding a specific team's color wasn't a ground-breaking theme in sports. After all, longtime Los Angeles baseball manager Tommy Lasorada had coined the phrase, "I bleed Dodger blue," many years before.

"I'll never claim it was the most original concept because you could have, 'Do you bleed green for Michigan State?' or 'Do you bleed purple for the Collinsville Kahoks?'" Woodcock said. "But the key for us was how can we activate it and how can we apply the concept of 'Bleed Blue' in a way that was unique to St. Louis and, more specifically, the St. Louis Blues? That was the challenge and the opportunity."

The campaign was launched with billboards and pocket schedules that included pictures of a kid's scraped knee, drawing blue blood of course, and vampire fangs dripping the same color.

"While somewhat of a simple 'call to action,' it really made an impact on the audience," Woodcock said. "They could relate and see themselves in our creative execution of the campaign."

Crowds started showing up at Blues' games with blue paint on their arms and faces with Band-Aids covering up the "blood."

"We would get emails from fans and they would preface the beginning of the email with, 'I want to tell you first off that I 'Bleed Blue,'" Woodcock said. "That's when you know a campaign has made an impact, when your consumers adopt the theme as their own. We had hoped for that, we had somewhat anticipated that, but I think we all have to admit that it really snowballed in a manner that we didn't totally anticipate.

"It provided so many different opportunities for our fans to personally, and imaginatively, express their enthusiasm and passion for the Blues. Our marketing partners got on board, as well. Everyone seemed to relate to 'Bleed Blue.'"

The NHL could relate.

In the inaugural year of the award, "Bleed Blue" took home the honors for the league's best-marketing campaign, topping finalists from Toronto, Atlanta, Edmonton, and Minnesota.

"We want to make it as lasting as 'Hockeytown' is for Detroit," Woodcock said. "We hope 'Bleed Blue' will always be the foundation for our promotion."

The campaign ended in 2004, however, around the time that Woodcock left the Blues and the NHL entered a lockout that canceled the season.

Here are some of the Blues' other advertising slogans and the years in which they were used:

Rebirth of Blues (1977–78)
Check Back in Checkerdome (1978–79)
Blues Power (1986–87)
Put Your Nights on Ice (1988–89)
Join our Next Generation (1989–90)
25 Years of Fun and Games (1991–92)
New Ice, New Sweater, New Coach, Same Great Fans (1994–95)
Put in Some Ice Time This Winter (1995–96)
30 Years of Memories (1996–97)
You Wanna Go (1997–2000)
Bleed Blue (2000–04)
Back in Blue (2005–06)
Blue Revolution (2006–07)
Whatever It Takes (2007–08)
The Last Piece of the Puzzle is You (2009–10)
Every Game Counts (2010–11)
Don't Stop Believing (2011–12)
Long Live the Note (2012–13)
We All Bleed Blue (2013–14)
Our Town. Our Team (2014–16)
All Together Now (2017–19)

to have one. Whenever Ron Caron would go out of town, Harry Ornest would fire his secretary to save money."

It was becoming obvious that Mathieu put the Blue Note above all else, so her favorite Blue at the time perhaps surprised no one.

"The person she idolized was Barclay Plager," said Mathieu's husband, Allen. "Barclay bled blue. She bleeds blue."

In February 1988, when Plager died of cancer at age 46, it was Mathieu who helped with the arrangements.

"Susie went with me to the funeral home," said Bobby Plager, Barclay's brother. "We picked out the gravesite together. She was there every day with me. I couldn't do it alone. It was tough on me. It was tough on her, too, but she was there."

A month later, in March 1988, it was Mathieu who went to the airport to pick up Brett Hull after the Blues acquired him in a trade with Calgary.

"I drove Brett to the old Hampton Inn," she said. "Can you believe we took players to the Hampton Inn?"

Mathieu and Hull became attached at the hip, a personal assistant in every sense of the word for No. 16.

"Susie is there 24 hours a day for you," Hull said. "She's second to none. Without her, this organization would just crumble."

In 1990, when Hull was negotiating a contract with the Blues, Mathieu was in the middle of it—well, sort of.

"Every time they would break because they were at an impasse, Brett and his agent, Bob Goodenow, would come to my office," Mathieu said. "I remember Bob would say, 'Susie, get me the first flight to Chicago.' I was getting phone calls from my son [Joseph], who was five or six at the time. He said, 'Mom, if you don't sign Brett Hull, don't bother to come home."

Under owner Mike Shanahan, Mathieu made it her responsibility to get players into the community, setting up player appearances at local stores and things like that.

"We were probably the first team that got them around to the different signings," Shanahan said. "The first one was with Curtis Joseph and Brett Hull. She got them out there, got them set up. It was really neat. There was no job that was too small for her to do.

"I don't know that anybody ever worked as hard as she did. I don't know anybody who loved her job as much as she did. You didn't look at it as male-female. She was just really, really good."

Mathieu admitted there was pressure being a woman.

"I felt if I failed, I'm not failing just myself—I'm failing for any woman who wants a job like this," she said. "I tried to be better than anybody. I developed an attitude that there was no job that couldn't be done. That's probably why they said, 'Go ask Susie.'"

In 1995, after other women had followed in Mathieu's groundbreaking footsteps in the NHL, she resigned from the Blues. She admits that a strenuous relationship with former general manager and head coach Mike Keenan and little desire to add arena football to her job description played a role in her decision.

"It was a compilation of factors," Mathieu said. "When I'm questioning the GM and coach, I had reached my uselessness with the Blues. It was a good time for me to leave."

Mathieu's reputation later earned her work in hockey with the World Cup and the Olympics, and her top-notch performance certainly opened the door for more women in her industry.

"People say, 'You're a pioneer,'" Mathieu said. "Well, I didn't think I was a pioneer. You didn't think along those lines. You're thinking, *I can do the job*. I was thinking, *Why are there even gender issues?* I'm glad it has changed."

91 "We Had the Cup"

If the Hartford Whalers had been interested in what Blues general manager Ron Caron was offering, one of the most regrettable trades in franchise history might have never materialized.

The Blues were in first place in the NHL standings with a month to play in the 1990–91 regular season, but Caron was itching to make a trade. He'd had conversations with Hartford GM Eddie Johnston as well as Vancouver GM Pat Quinn.

"The Professor," as Caron was affectionately called, was eyeing Hartford defenseman Ulf Samuelsson among others on the Whalers' roster. Simultaneously, Caron was feeling out Quinn about defensemen Garth Butcher and Doug Lidster.

One day before the NHL's trade deadline, Caron finally reached Johnston late in the evening.

"EJ gave me the bad news," he said. "They had traded three-for-three with Pittsburgh, and Samuelsson was in there. I said, 'Uh-oh, I'm down to one [trading partner].'"

In a trade Hartford perhaps quickly wished it had back, Johnston packaged Samuelsson, Ron Francis, and Grant Jennings to Pittsburgh for John Cullen, Jeff Parker, and Zarley Zalapski.

Quinn told Caron not to "hold hope" that his club would part with either of their defensemen. But when the Whalers moved on, Caron turned up the heat on the Canucks.

Seeking the franchise's first Stanley Cup, the Blues possessed offensive stars in Brett Hull and Adam Oates. They had scoring depth in Geoff Courtnall, Cliff Ronning, and Sergio Momesso, who combined for 51 goals that season.

The club had an offensive-minded defensemen in Jeff Brown and Paul Cavallini and a sturdy blue-liner in Scott Stevens. But

Caron was looking to add more grit on the backend, and he reportedly offered Courtnall, Ronning, forward Gino Cavallini, and defenseman Robert Dirk to the Canucks for Butcher and forward Dan Quinn.

"Pat said, 'I'll sleep on it,'" Caron said at the time. "I said, 'I may go and sleep there!'"

When the Blues and Canucks touched base at 7:00 AM the morning of the trade deadline, Caron continued to be more eager than Quinn to pull the trigger. Did they finally have an agreement on the personnel they had been discussing? No deal, Quinn said.

"I said, 'Uh-oh,' and I lost my pants," Caron said. "I put my pants back on. I went on the attack. I went into a very long explanation, proving to him that he has a better chance to win with the guys I'm giving him."

The deal wasn't dead.

Quinn told Caron that if he would change out two players—Vancouver wanted Momesso instead of Gino Cavallini—they might have a deal.

"I said, 'Okay, I even have the prepaid tickets and the flight numbers for all six players," Caron said.

Both sides finally agreed, and despite the fact that the Blues were 39–18–9 (87 points) and in first place, Caron followed through with a four-for-two deadline deal on March 5, 1991, sending Courtnall, Ronning, Momesso, and Dirk to Vancouver in exchange for Butcher and Quinn.

The reaction was widespread, ranging from the Blues' locker-room to the bench of the rival Chicago Blackhawks.

"The staff thinks it will help the club, and they're in charge," Blues star Brett Hull said. "I have nothing but faith in them, but they got me."

Blackhawks head coach Mike Keenan said, "Changing that many players at this point is going to be an interesting situation to watch. Obviously they felt it was important. Only time will tell what changing that many people on the roster will do."

In the immediate aftermath of the move, the Blues remained defiant.

"He who fears is already defeated," Caron said, standing firm. "I don't know what else I could have done to make our team better."

The Blues basically gave up their second line. Courtnall was on his way to a fourth-straight 30-goal year. And Momesso, although he had taken a dip in the 1990–91 season, netted a career-best 24 goals the year before while playing with Hull.

"I didn't want to part with Courtnall, but getting Dan Quinn will offset the production we're going to miss," Caron said. "If you want an important piece of the chemistry, you have to be willing to yield."

Former Blues coach Brian Sutter seemed to give the outgoing players less credit.

"We gave up a lot of bodies," Sutter said. "The guys we gave up have been important parts of our team, but we felt we had to upgrade ourselves in certain areas. We have. Serge is a third- or fourth-line guy. Cliffie is a fourth-line guy who plays the power play. Dirkie is our sixth defenseman. It's really hard to trade those guys. They've come so far, but we had a chance to upgrade our club."

Following the trade, the Blues went 1–4–2 in their next seven games but they put together a 7–0 run before meeting Detroit in the first round of the playoffs. After falling down three games to one in the series, the Blues rallied for three straight victories to advance past the opening round.

"We may not have won the Detroit series without Butcher," Caron boasted.

The Blues met Minnesota in the second round. The North Stars finished the regular season with a mark of 27–39–14 but were

The Trade in Detail

To the Blues:
Garth Butcher, D
Dan Quinn, C

To Vancouver:
Geoff Courtnall, LW
Sergio Momesso, LW
Cliff Ronning, C
Robert Dirk, D
Fifth-round pick in 1992 (Brian Loney)

dangerous with Dave Gagner, Brian Bellows, Brian Propp, Mike Modano, and Ulf Dahlen.

Again, the Blues fell behind 3–1 but this time couldn't recover. The power play was at the center of the failure, converting just 10 of 80 opportunities in the two rounds.

Ronning, who had six goals and nine points in six playoff games for Vancouver, might have come in handy for the Blues' man-advantage. Quinn, meanwhile, had four goals and 11 points in 13 playoff games for the Blues.

"If we had kept Ronning for power-play purposes, he could have provided stimulation and improvement," Caron said. "But Quinn did not play bad for the amount of ice time he got. In my opinion, we would not have done better. Minnesota didn't allow the individual game. There was no open ice there, and the players we let go need open ice."

Courtnall went on to post three goals and eight points in six playoff games for Vancouver. Momesso contributed three assists in his half-dozen games. Dirk was a minus-4 for the Canucks, who fell four games to two to Los Angeles in the first round.

"We were [back] in St Louis at the end of the season, after [the Blues] lost to Minnesota, and they were still trying to justify the trade," Dirk said. "It hurt when they said that even though they lost out, they still had a better team than before. I don't know how they can say that. We were the best team in the NHL before the trade.

"We had the Cup. It was right there. Our chemistry was perfect. Brett Hull and Adam Oates got the goals, and everybody supported them. Hull and Oates and Scott Stevens got the headlines, but that was fine with the other guys. Everybody was working for the Cup, but then they made the trade…. I know trades are part of the game, but to me, it just didn't make any sense."

Caron concluded, "The game of sports is a game of second-guessing. The same people who pat you on the back are the first to complain. If you win, it's nice. If you don't win, it's not nice. I cannot be pressured by that."

92 Visit the Hockey Hall of Fame

If you're standing at the intersection of Yonge and Front streets in Toronto and feel you're at the wrong place, you're not alone.

The entrance to the Hockey Hall of Fame has thrown off many a visitor over the years. The Hall is housed in a former Bank of Montreal building, which was constructed in 1885. It certainly has eye-catching architecture, but the main doors to the Hall offer no public access, so visitors are asked to enter through the Brookfield Place shopping level and walk past a food court before reaching hockey's Holy Grail.

However, the trip is worth the extra navigation and, judging by the turnstiles, hockey enthusiasts are finding their way into the Hall of Fame with ease. Open 362 days a year—the doors are only closed on induction day in November, Christmas Day, and New Year's Day—the Hall welcomes an estimated annual 300,000 visitors looking for a glimpse of its ancient artifacts.

"If you're a hockey fan, you have to go to the Hall of Fame," said Ken Davies, the manager of Kirkwood Ice Rink near St. Louis. "It was a neat experience. I was surprised at how extensive it was [with] really cool stuff. It's something every hockey fan should do, for sure."

The Hall of Fame officially opened in Toronto on August 26, 1961, at the Canadian National Exhibition, west of downtown. But by the mid-1980s, high operation costs and attendance concerns led to the renovation of the bank building, where former NHL president John Ziegler envisioned a state-of-the-art experience.

"We agreed that if we were going to plan on a new leading-edge facility, it would have to serve not only as a museum but also as a place where fans could have fun and interact with the exhibits," Ziegler said.

The $27 million project was christened in 1993, welcoming 500,000 visitors in its first year. Through another $12 million enhancement between 2000–06, the Hall continues to change and keep the 57,000-sq.-ft. facility a fresh experience.

There are 16 sections on the unique exhibit tour, and regardless of whether you're a hardcore fan or a casual observer, you don't want to skate past any of them. Grab a stick and take aim at current NHL goalies in a virtual interactive game, test your broadcasting skills, try your hand at trivia, touch the Stanley Cup, or simply take in the world's largest hockey memorabilia collection.

"They had some pretty cool interactive stuff where the kids could shoot pucks," Davies said. "I was really fascinated by a lot of the older stuff, [such as] some of the older sweaters from the original teams in the NHL. But the first thing we did, we were looking for any local connection, and being a Kirkwood kid, we found the exhibit for [Kirkwood native] Pat LaFontaine."

Blues Hall of Famers

Players		Builders	
Doug Harvey	1973	Emile Francis	1982
Dickie Moore	1974	Scotty Bowman	1991
Glenn Hall	1975	Al Arbour	1996
Jacques Plante	1978	Roger Neilson	2002
Lynn Patrick	1980	Cliff Fletcher	2004
Guy Lapointe	1993		
Peter Stastny	1998	**Media**	
Wayne Gretzky	1999	Dan Kelly	1989
Joe Mullen	2000	John Davidson	2009
Dale Hawerchuk	2001		
Bernie Federko	2002		
Grant Fuhr	2003		
Scott Stevens	2007		
Al MacInnis	2007		
Glenn Anderson	2008		
Brett Hull	2009		
Doug Gilmour	2011		
Adam Oates	2012		
Brendan Shanahan	2013		
Phil Housley,			
Chris Pronger	2015		
Paul Kariya	2017		
Martin Brodeur	2018		

A visit is certainly not complete without a walk through the Esso Great Hall, which houses the portraits and biographical sketches of each of the 405 honored members of the Hockey Hall of Fame. Among the likenesses of the 280 players enshrined are Terry Sawchuk, Jean Beliveau, Gordie Howe, Bobby Hull, Bobby Orr, Mario Lemieux, and Wayne Gretzky.

In 2002, former Blues center Bernie Federko was inducted into the Hall. He became the first Blue who played the bulk of his career with the franchise to be enshrined.

348

"The humbling part about it is I never looked at myself as one of those guys," said Federko, who played 13 seasons with the Blues and finished with a franchise-best 927 games and 1,073 points. "You never expect greatness out of yourself. You never judge yourself. People have to judge you. I grew up watching and adoring Jean Beliveau, Gordie Howe, Bobby Hull. For someone to put you as their equal is humbling.

"I still have to pinch myself every time I walk in there, or even go to one of the ceremonies, because it is one of the coolest things to wear that [Hall of Fame] coat. I mean, the ring means an awful lot, but you put that coat on with the crest on it, to know that there are only 259 players that can wear that, that is surreal."

In 2019, the Blues donated one of their Stanley Cup rings, which is also on display.

93 The Record Shop

Many hockey players spend their careers toiling in the minor leagues, trying to reach the NHL. In 1991, after a second-round playoff loss to Minnesota ended the Blues' season, three players couldn't wait to go back to the minor leagues with the Peoria Rivermen.

"We're going down to win a Cup," former Blue Kelly Chase said as he departed St. Louis along with teammates Dave Thomlinson and Pat Jablonski.

Peoria played in the International Hockey League at the time, and after a 58-win regular season, one that witnessed a record-breaking run, the team trailed Phoenix two games to none in its second-round series of the Turner Cup playoffs.

Though they were down, the Rivermen were excited about the culture they had finally created in the organization. The team endured four consecutive losing seasons but had built up the crowds at Carver Arena with a roster that featured Tony Twist, Tom Tilley, Steve Tuttle, Guy Hebert, David Bruce, and a rookie named Nelson Emerson.

The players got heavily involved in the community and hosted team parties every Monday—also known as the Rock-n-Roll BBQ Show—during which a few of them would demonstrate their instrumental abilities.

"They were emotionally invested in Peoria," said Dave Eminian, the Hall of Fame beat writer who has covered the Rivermen for the *Peoria Journal-Star* for three decades. "Some of them had been here a long time. Those guys were part of teams that lost 50 games year after year after year. All of the sudden, it all came together in that 1990–91 season."

Peoria, under 48-year-old "rookie" head coach Bob Plager, lost its first game of the season. No problem—the Rivermen then rattled off 18 consecutive victories, setting a professional hockey league record that lasted 21 years before the Norfolk Admirals of the American Hockey League broke it in 2012.

Plager kept the Peoria players loose, and that was a key to their success. In the 17th game of that streak, the Rivermen were trailing Kalamazoo 2–1 after the first period and the locker room was silent during the intermission.

"Plager walked into the center of the room, stared at us, and we thought he was going to peel a layer off of us," Thomlinson remembered. "Then he shrugged and said, 'C'mon guys, let's really try to win this one.' And he walked out."

Peoria won the game 7–2.

"Bobby was great," Tilley said. "He knew we had the talent. He just let us play."

The Rivermen proved they could win even when they were shorthanded.

In February, the Blues had called up six players from Peoria and the Rivermen lost another to food poisoning prior to a game in Milwaukee, leaving them with just 10 skaters.

"The Admirals were laughing at us during the pregame warmups, asking us where the other half of the team was," Thomlinson said.

The puck dropped and Plager created even more of a shorthanded situation for Peoria, benching forward Tony Hejna when his play wasn't up to par.

"I'm on the bench saying, 'Please Bobby, can Tony play now?'" Thomlinson said. "He just shook his head no again and again."

But the Rivermen won again, walloping Milwaukee 11–6. Bruce netted five goals and four assists. Chase had a hat trick, and Emerson added a goal and three assists in the team's league-leading 40th victory of the season.

Chase, Thomlinson, and Jablonski were back with the Blues late in the regular season, but after the parent team fell 3–2 to the North Stars in Game 6, the three chose to jump into the playoffs with Peoria.

"I asked if I could go back down because I knew it was a special team," Chase said. "[Blues coach] Brian Sutter was so mad at me because I had asked to go to the minors. His point was, 'You finally made it here, where you can stay, and now you want to go back down there and play?'"

After Peoria had dropped the first two games at home, Game 3 was in Phoenix.

"I can remember seeing their cab pull up in the hotel parking lot," Eminian said. "Half the team was waiting for them in the lobby. It was just an emotional scene."

Peoria bounced back in the series but trailed three games to two heading into Game 6. In that contest, Chase scored two goals

Minor League Affiliates

Here is a list of the St. Louis Blues' current minor-league affiliates:

American Hockey League
San Antonio Rampage
City: San Antonio, Texas
Home: AT&T Center
Founded: 1971
Affiliation with Blues began: 2018

ECHL
Tulsa Oilers
City: Tulsa, Oklahoma
Home: BOK Center
Founded: 1992
Affiliation with Blues began: 2017

and assisted on Kevin Miehl's game-winner in overtime for a 4–3 win, forcing a Game 7. In the winner-take-all matchup, Michel Mongeau netted two goals and the Rivermen won by the same score, 4–3, and moved on to the final.

In the Turner Cup, Peoria held a three-games-to-none lead, but Fort Wayne won back-to-back games. On two goals from Thomlinson, the Rivermen won 4–2 in Game 6 to beat the Komets and clinch the Cup.

"That parade we had, I can still hear those thousands of Peoria fans screaming downtown as we assembled," Thomlinson said. "As we closed in on the championship, you could feel the city getting ready to explode. We deserved a storybook ending for ourselves and the fans, and that's what we got."

Peoria set 41 team, league, or pro hockey records that season, leading defenseman Dominic Lavoie to dub Carver Arena the "Record Shop."

Bruce scored 64 goals and was named by *The Hockey News* as the minor-league Player of the Year. Thomlinson netted 53 goals, including 27 on the power play.

"Steve Tuttle scored 24 goals that season as a third-line checker," Eminian said. "That was Bob Plager's checking line.

"A lot of the NHL scouts back in that day rated that team as the equivalent to what an NHL expansion team would be. It was considered at the time as the best team in minor-league history."

Plager was named the IHL's Coach of the Year.

"Bobby Plager was loose, funny, the perfect coach for that team," Thomlinson said. "We don't win 18 straight or win a championship without him."

Plager began the next season coaching the Blues but abruptly resigned a month into the season. Fourteen players from Peoria's Cup team were also in the NHL the following year.

With their hockey careers wrapped up, the 1990–91 Rivermen players have returned home on a few occasions to celebrate the club's achievement.

"It's a special group of guys," Chase said. "When we get back, the stories are bigger and better."

When they met for a banquet in 2012, it happened to fall on the same evening that Norfolk broke Peoria's consecutive-win record. The Admirals picked up No. 19 in a 2–1 win over Albany that night en route to 28 straight, setting the new record.

"Is that amazing or what, that it happens on a night when we're all here together?" Thomlinson said. "That's going to be hard to accept. It's part of our identity, a part of who were are, and always will be."

Once again, Plager put the Rivermen back in line.

"You can lose a record, but you can't take that history, those championship moments away," he said. "That will always belong to the Peoria Rivermen."

94 Hull & Oates

There was Wayne Gretzky and Jari Kurri in Edmonton, Mario Lemieux and Jaromir Jagr in Pittsburgh, and Stan Mikita and Bobby Hull in Chicago.

One of those players, though, claims that the NHL's most magical duo resided in St. Louis.

"Brett Hull and Adam Oates were the greatest 1-2 scoring punch in the history of hockey," said Bobby Hull, Brett's father. "Stupidly, some hockey people didn't think they were good enough to play together, and they broke it up."

It only lasted 33 months, but in that span Hull had the three highest-scoring years of his Hall of Fame career, and Oates, with back-to-back 100-point seasons, set the tone for his Hall of Fame campaign, as well.

No one ever thought the Blues' tandem wasn't good enough together—quite the opposite. "They were the black and white keys on the piano," former teammate Brendan Shanahan said. "They made great music together."

But when Oates wanted to renegotiate a contract he had signed only a few months earlier, it was just a matter of time before one-half of the popular "Hull & Oates" hit would be moving on.

That day came faster than it took the two to connect on a goal, ending one of the most memorable times in team history and giving Blues' fans only a glimpse of what No. 16 and No. 12 could have accomplished in unison.

"I think clearly if we played a lot longer, we would have had some incredible numbers," Oates said. "Who knows where we would have gone?"

The Blues acquired Oates on June 15, 1989, in a trade that was certainly more notable for the player leaving. Franchise scoring leader Bernie Federko, along with Tony McKegney, were packaged to the Red Wings for Oates and Paul MacLean.

"They weren't going to trade Steve Yzerman," Oates said. "I was the other offensive center."

Oates was instant offense. As soon as he made a pass to Hull, the relationship took off.

"The minute he got there and we started playing together," Hull said. "We kind of had the same—I don't know what you want to call it—mind-set."

Term it whatever you will, it existed.

"No question we both felt that feeling right away," Oates said. "The trust factor between the two of us was incredible. It was almost a 'he knew that I knew that he knew' thing. I made plays where I thought Brett would be. So we started asking Brian [Sutter] to play us together more. And the 'Hull & Oates' thing had a good ring to it, so that didn't hurt."

The season before Oates arrived, Hull scored 41 goals with the Blues, and Oates had 62 assists with the Red Wings. So, in essence, it was like the Blues were throwing a lit match on a puddle of gasoline.

"I think we were both ready to go to the next level," Oates said.

In their first season together, Hull struck for 72 goals and Oates ignited for 79 assists. By the second year, they were deathly, with Hull reaching a career-high 86 goals and Oates exploding for 90 assists. Forty-one of Hull's goals were set up by his Oates.

"The chemistry Adam and I had was…it was just ridiculous," Hull said. "It just felt like every time we were on the ice, we had a serious chance of scoring."

Hull could score from anywhere, but as former Blues defenseman Jeff Brown said, "As good as Hullie was at shooting the puck off his front foot, it seems like Oatsie was always sliding it in his wheelhouse."

They began to drive their opponents nuts.

"You kept looking at the scoring summaries and they said, 'Oates 2 assists, Hull 2 goals,'" Detroit general manager Ken Holland said. "It went on for weeks and months and years."

Brett Hull hugs former teammate Adam Oates during the ceremony to retire Hull's No. 16 on Tuesday, December 5, 2006, in St. Louis. (AP Photo/ Tom Gannam)

Hull was getting much of the credit because he was the goal-scorer. That didn't bother Oates at all.

"I would rather pass and watch you score than score myself," Oates told Hull.

Hull responded, "It was just the dead opposite for me. There's nothing better, I felt, than hammering a shot and beating the goalie. We were almost a perfect pair."

Oates said for every one kid asking him for an autograph, Hull had 10.

"Some guys are destined to be presidents and some vice presidents," Oates said. "He was a goal-scorer, a superstar. There are very few superstars in life."

But Oates wanted to be paid like a superstar.

After the pair's breakout season, the Blues restructured Oates' contract to reflect his performance. Instead of a deal that would have paid him $800,000 over the next three years, Oates traded it in for a four-year, $3.04 million extension. He would make $320,000 in 1991–92, $330,000 in 1992–93, and $945,000 in both 1993–94 and 1994–95, along with a $500,000 signing bonus.

"I was really pumped up about it," Oates said in July 1991. "It's great to get recognized that way. [Jack] Quinn and [Ron] Caron were great to me. They didn't have to do it."

But by the end of the calendar year, Oates wanted to renegotiate. He ranked fifth in salary among Blues' players, following Hull, Shanahan, Garth Butcher, and Dave Christian.

At one point, Oates' camp and the NHL Players Association doubted the validity of the contract, but Quinn countered, "I have the signature. He's committed as a Blue through the 1994–95 season."

Exasperated, the Blues traded Oates to Boston on February 7, 1992, for center Craig Janney and defenseman Stephane Quintal.

"That's part of sports and part of the game, but it really [stunk]," Hull said. "We could have been a foundation for a number of years. Adding pieces to the pie to strive for that Stanley Cup in St. Louis would have been really something special. It was unfortunate."

There was no denying it.

"We had a connection," Oates said. "He made me a better player. I hope I made him a better player, too."

Both players went on to enjoy both team and individual success with other organizations, but when Oates returned to St. Louis for the retirement of Hull's No. 16 jersey, he said, "Brett, nothing compares to the three years I got to play with you."

95 Blues Light Lamp 11 Times

In the aftermath of a 6–0 loss to Quebec late in the 1994 NHL season, former head coach Bob Berry did not treat the Blues kindly.

"We got spanked a little in practice," forward Brendan Shanahan said.

The next opponent on the Blues' schedule was the Ottawa Senators, who were in just their second season in the league at the time. Undoubtedly, the Senators were having their struggles, going a stretch of 12 games without a victory, but they had just snapped that drought against San Jose in the game prior to meeting the Blues at the Civic Center in Ottawa.

Berry's wake-up call worked, however, as the Blues turned around and spanked the Senators 11–1 on February 26, setting a franchise record for goals in a single game. The club's 11 goals eclipsed the old mark of 10 goals in a game, which had been done on three previous occasions. The outburst also gave the Blues the largest margin of victory (10 goals) in team history.

"If you're going to do something, you might as well do it all the way," said Shanahan, who led the way with his third hat trick of the season and five points in all.

"It's nice to be part of that. I was part of it the other way when Detroit scored 11 goals against us last year," Shanahan said, remembering an 11–6 loss to the Red Wings on November 25, 1992.

The Blues' win over Ottawa was so lopsided that Senators starter Craig Billington was replaced at the start of the second period by rookie Darrin Madeley, but Billington quickly returned after Madeley gave up three goals on five shots in less than eight minutes.

The Blues netted four goals in each of the first two periods, building an 8–1 lead. What was left in the crowd of 10,575, some of whom began looking for the exits in the middle period, began cheering when the visitors scored. The Blues added three more in the final frame.

"It was nice to be able to smile in the third period," Shanahan said.

Fourteen of the Blues' 20 skaters picked up at least a point. In addition to Shanahan, the Blues received significant production from their Russian trio. Vitali Prokhorov netted two goals and an assist, Vitali Karamnov had a goal and two assists and, after finishing as a minus-5 in the loss to Quebec two nights earlier, Igor Korolev had two assists and was a plus-2 against Ottawa.

"Hey Igor, you were a plus tonight," Shanahan said.

The other goals came from Jeff Brown, Kevin Miller, Tony Hrkac, Jim Montgomery, and Philippe Bozon.

It's hard to imagine, but in the highest-scoring game in the Blues' existence, all-time leading scorer Brett Hull was kept out of the net himself, held to two assists.

"We had a very tough, hard practice in Quebec, and we responded to that," Berry said. "I'm very pleased with the way we

Who Scored?

The Blues set a franchise record in goals with an 11–1 win over Ottawa on February 26, 1994. Fourteen Blues players combined for 27 points in the game. Here's the breakdown:

Player	Goals	Assists
Brendan Shanahan	3 goals	2 assists
Vitali Prokhorov	2 goals	1 assist
Vitali Karamnov	1 goal	2 assists
Jeff Brown	1 goal	1 assist
Kevin Miller	1 goal	1 assist
Jim Montgomery	1 goal	0 assists
Philippe Bozon	1 goal	0 assists
Tony Hrkac	1 goal	0 assists
Brett Hull	0 goals	2 assists
Igor Korolev	0 goals	2 assists
David Mackey	0 goals	2 assists
Steve Duchesne	0 goals	1 assist
Bret Hedican	0 goals	1 assist
Rick Zombo	0 goals	1 assist

played. We played hard all night. Ottawa made us play hard. As lopsided as the score was, they were still taking runs at us at the end. It was tough to relax.

"We weren't trying to rub their noses in it; I don't want anybody to do that to me, and I didn't do that to anybody tonight," added Berry, whose club improved to 32–22–8 (72 points). "We just tried to play for 60 minutes. We've been talking about that all year."

The Senators, whose goal was scored by Evgeny Davydov, fell to 10–45–8 for 28 points.

"It's been a struggle for us," head coach Rick Bowness said. "After our 5–8–2 start, we might have led people to believe we're a lot better than we are."

With their 11-goal night, the Blues might have led fans to believe they were better than they really were, too. In their next eight games after manhandling the Senators, the team went 1–6–1, finishing fourth in the Central Division with a record of 40–33–11 (91 points).

The Blues were swept by Dallas in the first round of the playoffs that season. How many goals did the club total in its four-game conference quarterfinal series? Answer: 10. One short of that memorable night in Ottawa.

96 Yzerman Turns Out the Lights

As the Blues' plane returned home in the wee hours of May 17, 1996, and players were greeted by a throng of fans at Lambert International Airport, goaltender Jon Casey appeared especially devastated, his face flushed the color of Detroit's red uniforms.

The difference in the Red Wings' 1–0 double-overtime win in Game 7 of the Western Conference semifinals was what one person in the Blues' organization labeled a "1 in 100" shot by captain Steve Yzerman from the blue line.

But Casey had played splendidly after replacing Grant Fuhr in the first round, when Toronto's Nick Kypreos "fell" on Fuhr and injured the goalie's knee. And the Blues' backup was hardly to blame in the series loss.

"He's the reason we're still here," Blues winger Brett Hull said. "There's nothing you can do about a goal like that. Jon was screened, and he just never really picked it up."

The Blues managed only 80 points in the Western Conference during the 1995–96 regular season, well behind top-seeded Detroit (131). In fact, the 51-point differential would have put the Blues in the NHL record book had they been able to hold on to the series against the Red Wings.

The club overcame a two-game hole in the second-round series and led Detroit three games to two. Igor Kravchuk netted the game-winner in a 5–4 OT victory in Game 3, Casey blanked the Red Wings 1–0 in Game 4, and Wayne Gretzky bounced back with a goal to help the Blues win 3–2 in Game 5.

"We're up 2-0. The next thing you know it's 3–2, and we're going into St. Louis for Game 6," Detroit general manager Ken Holland said.

"Things can turn around in a hurry," Blues coach and general manager Mike Keenan said.

Things did turn around.

Early in Game 6, the Blues took two penalties and had a couple of turnovers, leading to a 2-0 advantage for visiting Detroit. Late in the first period, the Red Wings' Darren McCarty ran over Casey, who gave up two goals in the last nine minutes of a 4–2 loss. The series was even again at three games apiece.

Keenan announced that Casey was questionable for Game 7 with a stiff neck, although some questioned whether the injury was legitimate or a ploy by Keenan. As it turned out, Casey returned to the Blues' crease for the deciding game in Detroit.

And it was a classic.

Casey and Detroit netminder Chris Osgood traded terrific saves throughout regulation. In the first period, Casey used a right leg to deny Igor Larionov, then he used his right arm to halt Yzerman's rebound attempt. In the second frame, Osgood turned away Brian Noonan with a blocker then gloved a puck headed for the net after a Peter Zezel slap shot.

Although there were a combined 67 shots between the Blues and Red Wings, the game was still scoreless heading into the second overtime.

When asked after the series which was the biggest save, Osgood replied, "Honestly I can't remember. The game was so long, so emotional."

The emotion was about to reach a crescendo. Just 1 minute, 15 seconds into the second OT, Gretzky lost the puck in the neutral zone and Yzerman gathered it.

"There was a turnover in the neutral zone. I was at the blue line, and I didn't think I had anybody coming with me on a two-on-two," Yzerman said. "I was just trying to get the puck past the defenseman's leg."

At the blue line, Yzerman fired a shot that looked like it was running up a ramp.

"It was kind of a rising shot, and it went in under the crossbar," Yzerman said. "I don't score very often from the blue line. I was definitely surprised it went in."

On the Blues' bench, center Adam Creighton had as good a view as anybody.

"I can still see the puck going in the net," Creighton said more than 15 years later. "They always show that shot that Stevie Yzerman took, and I could just see it. When I see the highlight of it, I still always think, 'Geez, I was sitting right behind that puck and saw it go into the net.'"

Even though they were underdogs in the series, the Blues were devastated.

"You're just kind of numb," said Hull, who had six goals in 13 postseason games that season. "You sit in the room and you're on the bench and on the ice, and nothing but positive thoughts go through your head. You picture yourself scoring."

Casey declined a postgame interview request, but the saddened look on his face when he arrived with his teammates at the St. Louis airport spoke to his disappointment. He was not alone, however.

"There's never any satisfaction," Blues defenseman Al MacInnis said. "You started out with 26 teams, and with a break or a bounce, we could have been in the Final Four. It's tough to swallow."

In the Western Conference finals, Detroit was looking for its first Stanley Cup since 1955. But they lost four games to two in a memorable series against the Colorado, the team that went on to win the Stanley Cup. The Avalanche might have been the team to knock off the Red Wings, but it was that memorable series against the Blues that did in Detroit.

"That series took a lot out of us," Holland admitted. "We had run away and hid in the regular season [to win] the Presidents' Trophy. But we used up a lot of energy, a lot of emotion to win that series and didn't have anything left the next series. I've been fortunate to watch a lot of series, and I think that series was one of the great series that I ever got to witness."

97 Sacharuk Joins Exclusive Club

With the effect that Boston Bruins defenseman Bobby Orr was having on the game offensively in the late 1960s, NHL clubs were in search of blue-liners who could shoot the puck. The New York Rangers had two, and that worked to the benefit of the Blues.

New York boasted Brad Park, who netted 25 goals and 82 points in 1973–74. The Rangers also had Larry Sacharuk, who scored 50 goals in one season of junior hockey in 1971–72 and then posted 41 goals and 111 points in 106 games in the American Hockey League.

"[The Rangers] didn't need me," Sacharuk said. "They had Brad Park doing that kind of job."

The Blues did need Sacharuk, and on August 29, 1974, they acquired the offensive-minded defenseman from New York in exchange for left wing Greg Polis. (The Blues also received a first-round pick in the deal, but returned it to the Rangers for Derek Sanderson.)

"We fully expect Polis to score 40 goals," said Blues president Sid Salomon III. "We realized that when we traded him. But we needed someone on right defense and on the point on our power play. We think Sacharuk is just the man we needed."

Sacharuk's career with the Blues lasted only from 1974 to 1975, but it was one for the NHL record books.

On April 6, 1975, Sacharuk scored his 20th goal of the season, a plateau only three defensemen in the history of the league had accomplished prior to the start of that year: Park, Bobby Orr, and Flash Hollett. Sacharuk was one of four defensemen who netted 20 goals in 1974–75, a list that included Guy Lapointe, Serge Savard, and Denis Potvin.

"To compare it, back then it was like a forward getting 50 goals or probably 60," said Blues defenseman Bruce Affleck, Sacharuk's teammate. "The NHL had a number of 50-goal scorers by then but only three 20-goal scorers on defense. It was a big deal. And he was a right-handed shot, and there weren't very many righthanded shots back then."

After arriving in the trade, Sacharuk complained of back pain on the first day of training camp. Surgery was considered, but after sitting out all of camp while rehabbing, Sacharuk returned for the season opener. In the Blues' first two games, he had four goals and one assist, including a hat trick against Vancouver in Game 2.

"I am happy with the way things have turned out," Sacharuk said of his new home in St. Louis. "I wanted to stay in the NHL, and I have been able to do that with the Blues."

Part of New York's reasoning in trading Sacharuk, despite his offensive upside, was that he was a liability defensively.

Twenty or More

Here is a list of Blues defenseman who have scored 20 goals or more:

Name	Goals	Season
1. Jeff Brown	25	1992-93
2. Al MacInnis	20	1998–99
3. Jeff Brown	20	1991–92
4. Larry Sacharuk	20	1974–75

Here is a list of the most goals scored in a single season by NHL defenseman:

Name	Goals	Season	Team
1. Paul Coffey	48	1985–86	Edmonton
2. Bobby Orr	46	1974–75	Boston
3. Paul Coffey	40	1983–84	Edmonton
4. Doug Wilson	39	1981–82	Chicago
5. Paul Coffey	37	1984–85	Edmonton

"I've always had that reputation, but I think it's wrong," he said. "Because I carry the puck a lot, people say I'm weak defensively. But when I'm skating, I can make things happen, and that is what the game is all about."

Fans marveled at Sacharuk's goals, and during one game in Washington, he did, too.

"Washington was the first NHL rink with a replay scoreboard," Affleck said. "So [Larry Sacharuk] scores a goal. I was playing with him, and we line up for the faceoff. Washington wins the faceoff, and their guy skates around Larry as he's watching the replay."

Sacharuk broke the Blues' defensive scoring record when he surpassed Jimmy Roberts, who set the mark of 14 goals in 1967–68 and 1968–69. Sacharuk had that record in the bag by March 1, but he didn't score No. 20 until the season finale at Kansas City.

"I was honored to get it," said Sacharuk, who had 11 of his 20 on the power play. "It put me up there with some respected names, and I'm happy to be among them. It was a plateau I wanted to reach."

After one season, however, the Blues traded Sacharuk back to New York for center Bob MacMillan. Sacharuk played only 44 more games in the NHL before bouncing around the WHA, AHL, CHL, and Europe and retiring in 1983.

On March 11, 1993, Blues defenseman Jeff Brown scored two goals in a 5–2 win over San Jose, picking up Nos. 20–21 to break Sacharuk's franchise record. Brown finished with 25 goals that season, which remains the club record.

98 Hrkac Circus

The day that he set the Blues' franchise record for most goals in a playoff game, Tony Hrkac didn't even know he would be in the lineup. Or at least we hope not, considering his drink of choice that afternoon.

As an NHL rookie in 1987–88, Hrkac scored 11 goals in 67 regular-season games prior to the Blues meeting the Chicago Blackhawks in the first round of the playoffs. The Blues were leading the best-of-seven series two games to one heading into Game 4 on April 10, 1988. And based on teammate Greg Paslawski's memory, Hrkac must have been fairly confident that he wasn't playing.

"I had surgery that year on my back, and I was just [traveling] with the team," Blues forward Greg Paslawski said. "'Hrk' comes in my room that afternoon and had a couple of cocktails. Next thing you know, he's getting on the bus and he finds out that he's playing."

In a game that epitomized his nickname, "The Hrkac Circus" put on a show, scoring four goals in a 6–5 victory over the 'Hawks in front of 15,207 at Chicago Stadium. Hrkac netted the game-winner while the Blues were shorthanded with 4 minutes, 45 seconds remaining in regulation.

"You dream about having games like this," Hrkac said after the game. "But you never know if they will happen."

The Blues' Frank St. Marseille had two playoff hat tricks in the late 1960s and early 1970s, but no one before Hrkac or after him has ever duplicated the four-goal performance he delivered in the 1988 postseason.

"That's quite an accomplishment," former Blues coach Jacques Martin said at the time. "Before you go into a series, a playoff, you look for certain players to step to the forefront. This was a big game by Tony."

The Blues had several injuries, which is in part why Hrkac was inserted into the lineup. In addition to Paslawski, Mark Hunter and Steve Bozek were both dinged up as the club got set to face Chicago. Jocelyn Lemieux and Doug Evans received their first career playoff starts.

In Game 3, the Blues had fallen 6–3 to the Blackhawks and were never able to catch up after falling behind 3–0. But on Hrkac's first career playoff goal, the Blues held a 1–0 advantage just three minutes into Game 4.

The goaltender for the 'Hawks that day was Darren Pang, who is now the television color analyst for the Blues. Pang knocked down a slap shot from Blues defenseman Gordie Roberts, but Hrkac, flying down the right side, put the rebound in the back of the net.

There were a combined 14 power plays that day, with the Blues converting two of their nine chances and Chicago capitalizing on three of its five chances.

The Blackhawks netted two man-advantage markers and added another at even strength to open a 3–1 lead on the Blues. Rick Vaive stood in front of Blues goalie Greg Millen, and a shot by Trent Yawney went in off Vaive for the two-goal cushion.

But the Blues clawed back into the game on goals by Doug Gilmour and Brett Hull, with Gilmour's goal on the power play tying the score 3–3. Then, in a game in which Chicago would hold three leads, the Blackhawks went up 4–3 on their power-play goal.

"There were quite a few penalties back and forth," Hrkac said. "That gave me a lot of chances to play. I just went out and tried to make the most of them."

That's when the second, third, and fourth acts of the Hrkac Circus got underway.

He pulled the Blues back to a temporary 4–4 deadlock with five seconds left in the second period with a power-play goal. Gilmour, who finished with three assists, unleashed a shot from the right point that Hrkac turned into his second goal of the game on a deflection.

Pang continued to receive offensive support, however, as Vaive answered with his second goal of the game for a 5–4 lead in the third period. But again, Hrkac responded by redirecting a shot by Paul Cavallini for a 5–5 score.

Two deflections, two more goals, and Hrkac had a hat trick.

"I just put my stick down and they hit it," Hrkac said, speaking of his second and third goals. "You just want to create your own openings out there. Paul and Dougie found me. They just hit my stick."

In the pressbox watching the game, Paslawski, Hunter, and Ron Flockhart were looking on in amazement as the Blues had rallied for a third-straight time.

"I remember the three of us, we were betting on who would score the winning goal," Paslawski said. "One of us, it wasn't me, picked Hrk to score."

The Blues went on the penalty kill, but on cue Gilmour sprung free Hrkac up the right side and Hrkac beat Pang with a shot from the circle with less than five minutes left in regulation.

"I think the goaltender in that situation was looking for a pass," Martin said. "[Hrkac] realized it quick. He was very deceptive with his shot."

Hrkac played 41 games in the playoffs throughout his career and finished with seven goals. So he accumulated more than half of his postseason output in one day, a day that he didn't even plan on lacing up his skates.

"It was unbelievable," Paslawski said. "What a game. It was like 'Hrk, Hrk, Hrk, Hrk…four goals! He was in the right place at the right time."

99 Wayne's World

The definition of the word *enterprise* is a "project to be undertaken, especially one that is important or difficult, or requires boldness or energy."

So it makes perfect sense that the Blues' decision to trade for Wayne Gretzky came down to a meeting at Enterprise Leasing in St. Louis.

"It was a secret meeting," says Bruce Affleck, a longtime employee of the Blues. "There were 14 corporations here that owned the Blues at the time, all bright guys. We wanted to make sure that we could sign Gretzky to a long-term contract before the deal was done. Could we afford to do it? Are we going to have to bump up ticket [prices]?

"We had been talking about it for weeks, how it would be unbelievable. Part of it, we were already selling out the new building [for the most part]. But he would help sell all of the single seats. Then they made the agreement that they could sign him."

Wayne Gretzky celebrates his first goal as a member of the St. Louis Blues against the Vancouver Canucks in Vancouver on Thursday February 29, 1996. (AP Photo/Chuck Stoody)

The big news wasn't out yet in St. Louis, but in a small city, it doesn't take long for word to get around. And what was supposed to be a private meeting wasn't very private at all. The room where talks to acquire Gretzky were taking place had glass walls, and the meeting, held on a weekday, went past 5:00.

"Here it is closing time, and people are walking out of their offices," Affleck said. "The board room is right by the main entrance. There's [Blues coach Mike] Keenan and all these corporate leaders. I mean, the press was on it right away."

Gretzky, 35, was in the final year of his contract with the Los Angeles Kings, and speculation was increasing that he was unhappy in L.A. and the club might trade him. The Kings started the 1995–96 season with a record of 10–5–5, but they went 8–25–10 in their next 43 games.

Word that the Blues were interested moved as swiftly as a No. 99 pass. When they hosted the Kings at the Kiel Center on February 24, 1996, fans wanted Gretzky to switch allegiances on the spot. "Give him a Blues jersey," one fan yelled.

After the Blues and L.A. skated to a 2–2 tie, Gretzky was put on the defensive when asked if he would like to play in St. Louis alongside good friend Brett Hull.

"It's just better for me not to comment on that," Gretzky said. "I read the rumors and hear the gossip you guys do. I really don't know what's going on."

Three days later, Gretzky was a Blue.

On February 27, the club traded a package of Patrice Tardif, Roman Vopat, Craig Johnson, a fifth-round draft pick in 1996, and a first-round pick in 1997 to the Kings in exchange for the "Great One."

Gretzky had left St. Louis with the Kings, but once the trade was complete, he met the Blues in Vancouver for their next game on February 29. Upon his arrival at the Westin Bayshore hotel, Gretzky went up to Keenan's suite.

"He talked to Mike, and he was pumped. He was excited," said Mike Caruso, a longtime Blues' employee and current vice president. "The next day, we were at Eight Rinks [practice facility], and it was like he was a Beatle trying to get off the bus. They had the picture in the *Vancouver Sun* the next day of him getting off the bus. It was a mob scene."

It was no different inside the rink.

"The people were hanging off the rafters," former Blues center Adam Creighton remembered. "They must have had about 4,000 for practice. And that was in Vancouver, not in St. Louis. You think about how popular he was then.... I think they had to turn people away for practice."

It seemed no one was turned away when the Blues returned home on March 5, 1996. The largest crowd in Blues' history (20,725) squeezed into the Kiel Center, and when Gretzky skated onto the ice at 7:35 PM local time, he received a two-minute ovation. One fan held a sign that read, "Wayne's World Comes to Hullywood."

Gretzky didn't show up on the scoreboard that night, but the Blues won 2–0 on a shutout by his ex-Edmonton teammate Grant Fuhr.

A couple weeks later, Gretzky returned to Hollywood, playing his first game back in L.A. He netted a goal and assisted on the game-winner as the Blues topped the Kings 3–1. His former city booed when he touched the puck, but they cheered his goal.

"There has been a lot of attention on me," Gretzky said. "I told Brett Hull sitting in the locker room before the game that I really, honestly, truly, can't wait to get to Dallas and have a normal hockey game where there's not so much on me and we can start focusing on the whole team."

On the ice, Gretzky lived up to expectations, posting eight goals and 21 points in 18 regular-season games with the Blues. And at the box office, Gretzky was the hit the Blues brass expected,

Making the Trade

Here are the components of the Wayne Gretzky trade:

The Blues got:
Wayne Gretzky
Los Angeles got:
Craig Johnson
Roman Vopat
Patrice Tardif
Fifth-round pick in 1996 (Peter Hogan)
First-round pick in 1997 (Matt Zultek)

After-Trade Performance (including regular season and playoffs):
Gretzky, C, with the Blues:
Games: 31
Goals: 10
Assists: 27
Points: 37
Post-Blues: Signed with New York Rangers as a free agent on July 21, 1996.

Johnson and Co., with the Kings:
Johnson, LW/C
Games: 429
Goals: 62
Assists: 141
Points: 203
Post-Kings: Signed with Anaheim Ducks as a free agent on September 9, 2003.

Roman Vopat, LW
Games: 57
Goals: 4
Assists: 8
Points: 12
Post-Kings: Traded to Colorado along with a sixth-round pick in exchange for Eric Lacroix on October 29, 1998.

Patrice Tardif, C
Games: 15
Goals: 1
Assists: 1
Points: 2
Post-Kings: Signed with Buffalo Sabres as a free agent on September 9, 1997.

Peter Hogan
Never played in the NHL.

Matt Zultek
Never played in the NHL

selling out its last nine regular-season home games. The *Post-Dispatch* estimated a revenue increase of $1.2 million, doubling the $600,000 the team owed Gretzky on the remainder of his contract.

After the Blues' victory in L.A., however, the club went 1–7–4 in its final 12 regular-season games, finishing fourth in the Central Division with 80 points. They entered the Western Conference quarterfinals against Toronto on a five-game winless skid but won four games to two over the Maple Leafs.

In the conference semifinals against Detroit, the Blues lost Games 1 and 2, and in the second game Gretzky was a minus-4 with no points. Keenan publicly ripped Gretzky, wondering whether "something was bothering him."

At the time, the Blues reportedly had a three-year, $23 million contract extension on the table for Gretzky.

"During Round 2, I got a call from [Blues President] Jack Quinn saying, 'What's wrong with your guy? I'm getting major heat from people above me on the offer,'" Mike Barnett, Gretzky's agent, told the *Post-Dispatch*. "He said he told a lot of people that he took the offer off the table."

The Blues then won Games 3, 4, and 5, taking a three-games-to-two edge in the series. Gretzky was a catalyst, registering two goals and two assists.

"When they won three, they said, 'We'll get it done,'" Barnett said.

Following the Sunday afternoon game, the Blues returned from Detroit and Keenan paid a visit to Gretzky.

"[Keenan] came up and tried to make up with [Gretzky]," Affleck said. "[Keenan] goes up to [Gretzky's] room in the Ritz [Carlton] and knocks on the door. Mike had a six-pack of beer on him, and the story goes that Wayne had one and Mike had the others. Wayne didn't say anything to Mike, but I think at that point, he'd had enough."

The Blues lost the series, falling in Games 6 and 7, with Steve Yzerman's shot in double overtime beating them in the deciding game. On the flight home, Affleck said, "Hull and Gretzky are sitting together at the back of the plane, and I came back. They pulled me in and Gretzky said, 'There's no way I can play for this guy.'"

The team insisted that Gretzky rejected their contract offer, but Barnett denied that claim. Quinn countered that Gretzky essentially rejected it by "not signing it."

By June, with the Great One set to become a free agent and fans growing impatient, the Blues made a new two-year, $12 million offer and finally a three-year, $15 million proposal. The money for Gretzky's signing bonus was to be deferred, but there was a disagreement on whether he was owed interest on the deferment. According to reports, Gretzky told the Blues that he would enter free agency and they responded by pulling their offers completely.

On July 22, 1996, Gretzky left St. Louis behind, signing a two-year contract with the New York Rangers totaling less than $6 million per year.

"My instincts were that maybe money wasn't all that important," Gretzky said. "Don't get me wrong, I'm still being paid very nicely. But my gut feeling was that I wanted to come here. I was always intrigued by New York. I always thought it was a great place to play. What tipped the scales was to play with Mark [Messier] and with a team focused on winning a championship. I wanted to come here, and I'm thrilled they wanted me."

In the end, Gretzky's departure was about respect.

"If people at that level are questioning his contribution and ability to be a benefit to the organization in the future, when for all purposes they were still not done [in the playoffs], as evidenced by the next three games, that might be an insight into what might happen in the future," Barnett said. "Wayne chose not to put himself into a position to have that second-guess take place based on the quality of his last shift or his last game."

100 Play "Gloria"!

Music producers and promoters spend years trying to come up with a catchy tune that the public will latch on to and turn into a No. 1 hit and many times the note and the effort falls flat.

And then there's Laura Branigan's single "Gloria" which reached record-setting status not once but twice, and the second time not because of any calculated marketing scheme.

The Blues adopted the song as their anthem midway through the 2018–19 season and it became the soundtrack of their Stanley Cup success.

If the Blues won, which they did 16 times en route to the first championship in their 52-year history, "Gloria" was played at

Enterprise Center—not to mention homes, schools, supermarkets, parks, and anywhere else that had speakers. In other words, you couldn't go anywhere in St. Louis without hearing it, and if so, you were probably humming it in your head.

So how did a song that was released by Branigan in 1981 find new life with the Blues 38 years later? Well, the answer is organically, after five of the club's players visited a bar in South Philadelphia in January.

With the Blues hovering near the bottom of the NHL standings, the team traveled to face the Flyers on January 7. The day before, a group that consisted of Joel Edmundson, Alexander Steen, Jaden Schwartz, Robby Fabbri, and Robert Bortuzzo went to The Jacks NYB to watch the Eagles-Bears NFC wild-card game with some friends.

"We have a buddy, he's a Philly boy, and he texted us, 'Hey, come over to my place and we'll watch the game,'" Edmundson said. "We thought we were going over to his apartment, so when we pull up to this corner place, we texted him, 'We don't think we're here.' But he comes out, and he's like, 'Guys, don't be scared—it will be a good time.' So we go in there, and there's like 30 guys straight out of Philly, some of them might have been in the mob, I don't know, but when we walked in, they give us a standing ovation.

"We watched the game with them, and every commercial break a DJ would play music, and he played 'Gloria' a couple of times. This one guy who had a few too many drinks just kept yelling, 'Play "Gloria"!' They kept playing it and everyone would get up and start dancing and they just kept saying, 'Play "Gloria"! Play "Gloria"!' Steener just thought, 'Hey, we've got to take this song for us.' Then [Jordan Binnington] gets a shutout the next day, we played 'Gloria.'"

Fans eventually found out, and as the victories piled up, the popularity of "Gloria" grew to the point where many wondered if Branigan might come to St. Louis perform the hit. What some didn't know, though, was that in 2004, Branigan had passed away from a brain aneurysm at age 52. So when people were reaching out to her active social media accounts, they were actually messaging her former manager, Kathy Golik, who made it her own personal mission in life to keep her friend's presence alive.

"I became aware of it back in February when I saw it on Twitter," Golik said. "Somebody said, 'They're using "Gloria"' and at first I didn't really delve into it. I thought, 'Well, maybe just that night they played it.' Then, as the Blues were progressing, some people were putting up their fan-made videos at the arena and I was starting to see a little more buzz on Twitter. It was like a little snowball rolling down a hill, and it got really big."

It turned into an avalanche as the Blues beat the Colorado Avalanche in the final week of the regular season and wrapped up third place in the Central Division. Their season could have ended and the song fallen off the charts several times during the playoffs, but the club kept persevering and the people kept screaming "Play 'Gloria'!"

There were T-shirts and other Blues' paraphernalia produced bearing those words and sold in the team's gift store, continuing what had become a cult phenomenon.

"It's cool how that brings people together and makes the fans feel like they're in this room," Blues center Ryan O'Reilly said during the season. "It kind of brings us all together and gives us that connection with the fans. It's pretty special."

Golik said that Branigan, who was named best pop female vocalist in 1982 after "Gloria" spent 36 weeks on the U.S. Billboard Hot 100, would have been honored.

"The wonderful thing about when you're a singer is, you know, that music lives on," Golik said. "Your work remains and people can hear it. I don't think it should be, 'Okay, she's gone; let's put her in a box and put her up on a shelf and that's it.' We're not to let her be forgotten, let her music be forgotten. To her, it wasn't about the awards, the glamour, and all of that. She wanted to touch people's lives with her artistry, and when I see things like [the Blues' use of 'Gloria'], I know she's accomplished that.

"She would be absolutely elated about all of this, and she would also be humbled at the same time. That's kind of the really bittersweet part of it. There's so many things that occur; I'm happy about them, but I wish I could just pick up the phone and tell her about them. She's not here personally to see it, but I believe that she's here in spirit. I've been having a fabulous time representing her, just interacting with the team, the fans. I think I have the joy that I know she would have."

And perhaps the best part about the story is that it was unforced and unrehearsed.

"It's just one of those things where it kind of took off," Blues forward Brayden Schenn said. "It's just those boys in South Philly there… that was their tune. They played it, and it just kind of caught on from there. The whole city got behind just one song."

"This is so neat from my perspective because it's like, I didn't do anything," Golik added. "It just evolved from that story in the bar, and then the fans picking up on it. To me, that's the beauty of it. It just happened and everyone is just riding the wave now."

Acknowledgments

From my earliest memory, I wanted to be a sportswriter for the *St. Louis Post-Dispatch*, and I was blessed to be able to accomplish that.

Never did I dream of writing anything longer than a 20-inch newspaper story until one afternoon in 2012 when I was sitting at my computer and in popped an email from Don Gulbrandsen at Triumph Books. The subject line read: "Book opportunity."

I assumed it was spam.

As it turned out, Don was truly inquiring about my interest in writing *100 Things Blues Fans Should Know & Do Before They Die*.

I nearly died.

My position as the Blues' beatwriter for the *Post-Dispatch* at the time required me to be around the team every day. But as a lifelong St. Louisan, I had followed the organization much longer and also had a good grasp on what the Blues meant to the city since their inception in 1967.

I couldn't think of a more exciting assignment than to research the tales of the team, many of them untold, and put them in the hands of the Blues' beloved fans.

I am proud of the final product and have many people to thank, beginning with the fine folks at Triumph Books, including Don Gulbrandsen, Adam Motin, and Karen O'Brien. Thanks for your belief in me, your patience, and especially the "Book opportunity."

A special thanks to the Blues and everyone in the organization who made time in their days to relive the memorable moments. I conducted more than 40 new interviews with past and present personnel, including Bob Plager, Scotty Bowman, Al Arbour, Glenn Hall, Bernie Federko, Garry Unger, John Davidson, Brett

Hull, Kelly Chase, Brendan Shanahan, Geoff Courtnall, Keith Tkachuk, Larry Pleau, Michael Shanahan Sr., Tom Stillman, Bruce Affleck, Mike Caruso, John Kelly, Chris Kerber, Ken Wilson, Susie Mathieu, and Jim Woodcock.

I also want to express my sincere gratitude to a great bunch of *Post-Dispatch* beatwriters who have done a marvelous job covering the Blues since the first puck dropped. I would not have been able to provide nearly as many adjectives without the accounts of Wally Cross, Gary Mueller, Ron Cobb, Bob Broeg, Dave Luecking, Tom Wheatley, Jeff Gordon, Bernie Miklasz, Dan O'Neill, Derrick Goold, and Tom Timmermann. I'd also like to thank editors Roger Hensley, Don Reed, and Mike Smith for being a big influence on me and allowing time for this project.

Other contributors whose efforts made this book possible include the late former *Sporting News* writer Larry Wigge, whose work over the years has been the model for all hockey scribes; Tim Beever, whose wealth of archived Blues articles gave me access to decades-old news; Chris Pinkert, the Blues' director of digital media, who provided a big assist on the Brett Hull foreword; and of course No. 16 himself, who in his playing days was so good at giving the Blues the "lead" and did it again with his opening remarks in this book.

Finally, a few words for my family. My grandparents, Claude and Jean Sizemore, made my sportswriting dream possible by purchasing my first laptop at a time when laptops cost as much as a new car. My mother, Terry, who passed away in 2003 of ovarian cancer, was my driving force, preaching to me that "life is what you make it." And my father, Wally, was my support team, calling countless times with positive words of encouragement.

One memory that I'll always carry from this time of my life was sitting in a hospital room with my wife, Sarah, our four-year-old daughter, Georgia, and our newborn son, Eli. We were watching the Blues' game on Fox Sports Midwest when broadcaster John Kelly, a good friend, congratulated us on our new addition. Everybody in the room, including a few visitors, beamed like the red light when a goal is scored.

After leaving the hospital, there were many challenges trying to finish a 100-chapter book. It simply would not have been possible without Sarah, Georgia, and Eli cheering me on from the front row. I love you guys!

Sources

Books

Halligan, John and John Kreiser. *Game of My Life: New York Rangers.* Champaign, IL: Sports Publishing, 2006.

Jackson, Patti Smith. *The St. Louis Arena Memories.* St. Louis: GHB Publishers, 2000.

Pepple, R. Ted. *The Last Face Off: The Doug Wickenheiser Story.* Printed by author, 2000.

Plager, Bob and Tom Wheatley. *Tales from the Blues Bench.* New York: Sports Publishing, 2003.

Starkey, Joe. *Tales from the Pittsburgh Penguins.* New York: Sports Publishing, 2006.

Woodcock, Jim. *Note by Note*: *St. Louis Blues Hockey Club.* St. Louis: Pinnacle Press, 2002.

Newspapers

St. Louis Post-Dispatch
St. Louis Globe-Democrat
The Kansas City Star
New York Times

Magazines

The Sporting News
The Hockey News
Sports Illustrated

Websites

stltoday.com

sportsillustrated.cnn.com

NHL.com

LetsgoSabres.outlastmedia.net

Yahoo.com

GreatestHockeyLegends.com

Hockeyfights.com

HabsWorld.net

Goaltendinglegends.blogspot.com

KCstar.com

Hockeydb.com

Hockeyreference.com

NewYorkTimes.com

Hockeydraftcentral.com

HHOF.com

pjstar.com

stlouisgametime.com

TheAthletic.com